The Girl from
Station X

The Girl from Station X

My Mother's Unknown Life

Elisa Segrave

Union
Books

First published in Great Britain in 2013 by
Union Books
an imprint of Aurum Press Limited
74–77 White Lion Street
London
N1 9PF
union-books.co.uk

A catalogue record for this book is
available from the British Library.

ISBN 978-1-90-852612-0

1 3 5 7 9 10 8 6 4 2

2013 2015 2017 2018 2016 2014

Typeset by SX Composing DTP, Rayleigh, Essex

Printed and bound by
CPI Group (UK) Ltd, Croydon, CR0 4YY

To my mother's four grandchildren

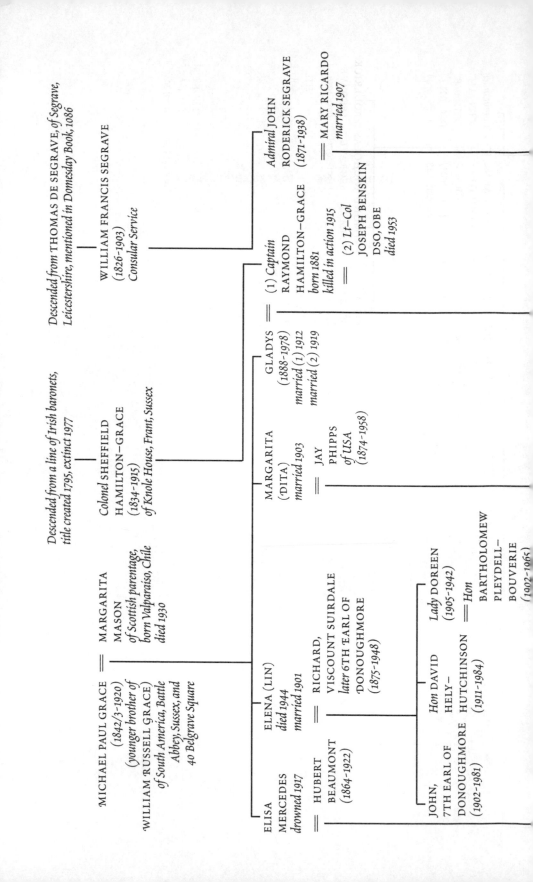

Descended from THOMAS DE SEGRAVE, of Segrave, Leicestershire, mentioned in Domesday Book, 1086

WILLIAM FRANCIS SEGRAVE
(1826-1903)
Consular Service

Admiral JOHN
RODERICK SEGRAVE
(1871-1938)
= MARY RICARDO
married 1907

Descended from a line of Irish baronets, title created 1795, extinct 1977

Colonel SHEFFIELD
HAMILTON–GRACE
(1834-1915)
of Knole House, Frant, Sussex

(1) *Captain*
RAYMOND
HAMILTON–GRACE
born 1881
killed in action 1915
= (2) *Lt-Col*
JOSEPH BENSKIN
DSO, OBE
died 1953

GLADYS
(1888-1978)
married (1) 1912
married (2) 1919

MARGARITA
('DITA')
married 1903
= JAY
PHIPPS
of USA
(1874-1958)

MICHAEL PAUL GRACE
(1842/3-1920)
(younger brother of
'WILLIAM 'RUSSELL GRACE
of South America, Battle
Abbey, Sussex, and
40 Belgrave Square
= MARGARITA
MASON
of Scottish parentage,
born Valparaiso, Chile
died 1930

ELISA
MERCEDES
drowned 1917
=

ELENA (LIN)
died 1944
married 1901
= RICHARD,
VISCOUNT SUIRDALE
later 6TH EARL OF
DONOUGHMORE
(1875-1948)

HUBERT
BEAUMONT
(1864-1922)

Lady DOREEN
(1905-1942)
= *Hon*
BARTHOLOMEW
PLEYDELL–
BOUVERIE
(1902-1965)

Hon DAVID
HELY–
HUTCHINSON
(1911-1984)

JOHN,
7TH EARL OF
DONOUGHMORE
(1902-1981)

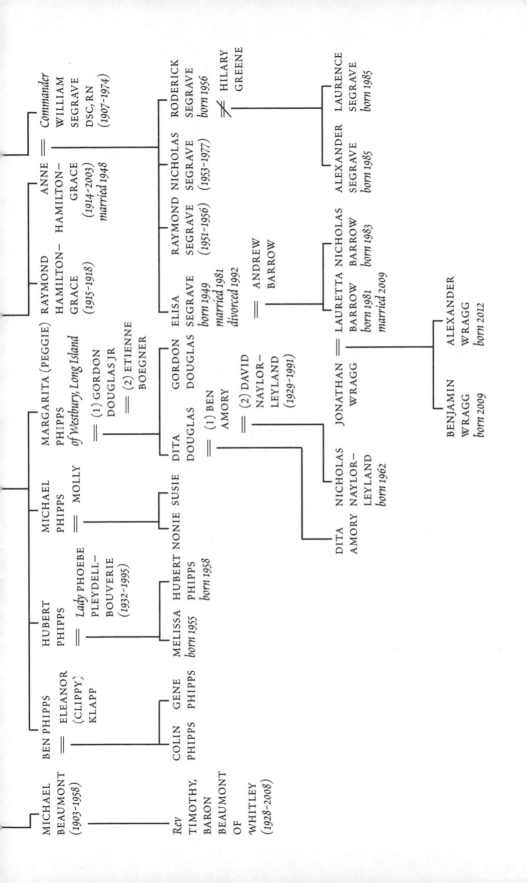

Contents

Preface

In the early 1990s, my mother, Anne, began to show the symptoms of Alzheimer's, painful for any family. There were other problems. Despite her background of social and financial privilege, my mother had led a life marked by loss, including the premature death of her father and little brother, and the early deaths of two of her four children. She had also been widowed at sixty. For a long time, she had been dependent on alcohol – so much so that it was not always easy to differentiate between the deterioration caused by her Alzheimer's and the accidents and confusion caused by her drinking. She had also, for many years, been dependent on others and her lack of resilience was a cause of emotional distance between us – this came to a head in 1991 when, with two small children and just separated from my husband, I was diagnosed with breast cancer.

Even before she started losing her mind, I was used to seeing my mother as vulnerable and needy – and, indeed, had lost sight of her having been any other way. Sometimes I felt I hated her for the disruption she caused. But I also knew her story was not as simple; she had not always been like this.

In the mid-1990s, there was an unexpected development. Her house in Sussex, where I mainly grew up, was sold and she was moved to somewhere smaller. She was a hoarder and it took ages to sort out her belongings. But in her attic – in what subsequently felt like a miracle to me – a whole box of her diaries was discovered. They began in the 1930s when she was fifteen and continued into the early 1950s. I became gripped by these closely filled-in exercise books, with details of her upbringing, her family, the upheavals and adventures of the Second World War, her romances, the early part of her life as a wife and mother and her enthusiastic travels. But most of all, they told me about my mother's feelings – the part of her that had, for so long, remained obscure to me.

I too am a committed diarist, and I felt that she was reaching out to me through her diaries. As I read on, and thought about her writing more and more deeply – including attending sessions with a therapist who, when I read out to her passages from the diaries, sensitively cast light on some of my mother's behaviour – I began to build up a different picture of her. I talked to my mother's oldest and most loyal friends, and tried to get their slants on her; and discussed her with my children, who each saw her in a different way from me, and from each other.

Many facts about her life, of course, I already knew. She was born on 1 July 1914, the daughter of a cavalry officer of Irish origin and of an heiress whose Irish father had made a fortune in South America through guano and shipping; and the early diaries show the world of an upper-class young woman with all its pleasures and luxuries, from finishing schools to tennis parties and balls. I knew also that she had worked in intelligence during the war, having enlisted early in the Women's Auxiliary Air Force. But I had no idea of the roles that she had played during her various posts, which included spells at Bletchley Park, Bomber Command and in post-war Germany, nor of the ability and commitment that she displayed throughout much of the war. Nor was I prepared to read in such depth about the intense emotional attachments that she formed – unsurprisingly, of course, given the upheavals of the times.

I decided to write about my mother – at first, as an attempt to understand her further. This book is based around extracts from her diaries that, I hope, capture both her and a profoundly unsettled period in British history when a country at war also underwent rapid social change. But I have also tried to convey the singular and often moving experience of gradually uncovering a woman whom I never expected to know so well.

I have changed a very few names for reasons of privacy. My brother Roddy is hardly mentioned, as he has his own story to tell. He was given the opportunity to see the advance text of the book. However, its story and its perspective are mine.

Part 1

The Merry Meadow

I am very reserved and <u>never</u> show my feelings so that <u>very</u> few people know what I am like inside . . . I <u>long</u> for romance, I should like to be truly in love with a man and have one in love with me, the real true love, nothing else would do. I'm afraid I shall never have the pleasure of marrying anyone as I don't like men.

Diary of Anne aged sixteen, 16 October 1930, Rome.

Chapter 1

In my mother's garden is a mulberry tree. My mother walks towards me, her hands, drenched with mulberry juice, reaching at my throat. She's going to strangle me . . . 'Elisa, I'm *getting up* at you!'

My mother shows me a newspaper. A girl called Elisa, nine like me, was murdered. Her body was found in a cornfield. There was blood on her sock.

My mother sits on my bed at night and talks in an odd, slurry way. I call it 'preaching' – she isn't really talking *to* me but *at* me. She calls me 'lovey', but although I often long for her to hug me, this way of talking makes me want to hide under the bedclothes. She sits very close and turns her right hand awkwardly this way and that, a habit that my father imitates when she gets like this, as he does when she declares: 'I'm Irish!' Her fingertips are orange, from cigarettes, and a sour smell comes off her.

Often she does not come to say good night to me, so I go up to bed alone to my room at the top of the house. Later I creep down both staircases to listen for my parents; I hear my father's voice telling her: '*Go to bed! For God's sake, go to bed!*'

I feel the whole house rocking beneath me.

I imagine that I see my mother mounting the last few steps to my landing in her white dressing gown, her eyes screwed up with rage – or is it madness?

I remember a beach in Spain, I must be two or three. My mother wades into the sea, leaving me alone on the sand. I cannot see her out there in the waves. Will she ever come back to me?

Spain is where I sometimes have my mother to myself. She is taking me to a children's party. It starts at my usual bedtime; the family is not English like we are. I go alone with my mother, clinging to her skirts as I remember so often doing then. The party is in a flat and we have to go up in a lift. Getting out, I trip, and start bawling. Inside, the other children are dancing in a circle. I am the youngest. Some of them come towards me and stretch out their hands, inviting me to dance. But I refuse to leave my mother and she is happy to have me with her. Later there is a film show. I am induced to sit on a little chair in a row with the other children. As soon as the lights go out, I yell. Very quickly, I am reunited with my mother. I spend the rest of the evening holding on to her.

I am the firstborn, I am my parents' darling. My father calls me Button Nose. He holds me high on his shoulders and pushes me very fast in my pram up and down Madrid's wide avenue, the Castellana. My father, who works in the Embassy, is proud of me and of my first sentences: 'Button Nose has buns for tea' and '*I can do it!*'

In the summer, my mother takes me and my younger brother Raymond – born in May 1951 – to the seaside in the north of Spain. At the entrance to the beach sits a poor woman, selling apples. My mother buys her apples each day. Her children – ten or more of them – have no toys. Sometimes they steal our buckets and spades and the little boats we bring to the beach.

My mother takes snaps of me and Raymond. Here we are, at Comillas, just the two us, in our sun hats, digging in the sand with our spades.

How sweet my mother is then. She calls me, her eldest, 'my old love' and Raymond, born in Spain, 'my Spanish love'. I want to be with my mother all the time.

My mother is always happy and smiling. When she narrows her blue eyes against the sun I try to copy her. When we are in an aeroplane flying back to England to visit our grandmother, it is I who sit with my mother, and Raymond who's with our young nanny, Doreen. I announce very loudly: 'I've got fleas!' I don't understand why all the adults around us laugh.

When we leave Spain for good, my mother hoards many objects from there: in our house in Sussex are black and white mantillas, castanets, green and yellow cups and saucers with little deer running round them, fans like lace, a big orange bull and, on either side of the dining-room fireplace, two pictures of Spanish gypsies, a man and his wife, their skin the colour of purple grapes. At Christmas, she puts out a Spanish crib. The Moor – one of the Three Wise Men – rides a camel and wears a turban.

When I was seven, my mother took me back to Spain, to a village near Seville, on holiday. She dragged me through streets full of naked children to a shop where she had ordered a donkey harness. I stood outside, staring at a pale canary in a tiny cage. Later, as we walked back, I became worried by the thin mules and dogs, the naked hungry children and the imprisoned canary, and remarked how poor the village was.

'Why can't you notice the *nice* things?' she said.

My mother showed the first signs of Alzheimer's in 1991, when she was seventy-seven, the year I was diagnosed with breast cancer. Perhaps the shock of that finally did for her – the possibility that yet another of her four children might predecease her.

Over the next few years friends, usually hers, would often ask: 'How's your mother?'

I would reply, with apparent nonchalance: 'Oh, she's completely crackers.'

She had planned to take me and my children to the Russian Circus one afternoon in that August of 1991. But we had to go without her. Instead, she was being operated on – again. She had fallen, drunk, the night before. I never actively fought with my mother, but after she broke her leg or hip, for the second or even third time, I began to get anxiety pains in my chest.

Six weeks later, I was in hospital myself. Soon after my mother's fall, I had a lump removed from my breast. Ten days later my lymph glands were taken out, to see if the cancer had spread; it had. In hospital, I was getting persistent calls about my mother's drinking. One of my friends insisted that I must not see her during my impending eight months of radiotherapy and chemotherapy; I should concentrate on my two children and on getting well.

I stuck to this arrangement for a while but I did see my mother that Christmas – she stayed with me, my ex-husband and our two children at our house in Sussex near hers. She brought me a present of a silver ship which she had just taken out of storage – I wonder now if it had belonged to her maternal grandmother, born in Chile. I saw my mother on other occasions during that period, out of duty. I rang her once after chemotherapy, thinking that she might drive over and see me – a fifteen-minute car journey. But she did not, and she did not come to the telephone either. I was told by the person who'd answered her phone that she'd said she was too tired.

When I had come out of hospital the previous autumn my Aunt Rosemary, my father's sister, in her eighties and nervous of travelling alone, had come on a coach to see me from her home over two hours away.

I did not really expect emotional support from my mother during my breast cancer treatment. Nevertheless, I remember complaining to a close friend who'd visited me in hospital just before my second operation that my mother was never there when I needed her. It was *her* mother that I longed for, and that night, after my friend left, I dreamed that my grandmother, now dead, was waiting for me outside her house, Knowle.

My mother had a better relationship with my daughter than she did with me. My daughter was not angry with her as I was, and, indeed, did not have so much reason to be. My mother, though not in England for her birth, subsequently seemed genuinely delighted by the baby. I have a photograph of her standing in her garden looking down shyly at the child in her arms, as though she can hardly believe her luck. And whenever I later criticised my mother, my daughter would defend her, saying: 'She never did anything nasty to me!' At seven, after her first night alone with her grandmother, she declared: 'I love Granny, I really love her!'

My mother on that occasion taught my daughter Snakes and Ladders. When I went to collect her, we all three played Cluedo and my mother, who loved board games, surprisingly didn't remember that she was Miss Scarlett. It was 1989. Later I interpreted this as a sign of her encroaching Alzheimer's. I also remember her bobbing up and down in front of her drinks tray that day, as though doing knee exercises, talking incomprehensibly about 'The Blue Lady'. After several minutes, during which I speculated that the Blue Lady might even be a ghost, I realised that she was imitating the audience in the Albert Hall at the Last Night of the Proms, which had just been on TV. The soprano had worn a bright blue dress.

Despite these flashes of empathy – no one else understood what she had meant by the Blue Lady – my anger against her had increased, as a result of her many drunken falls. After my separation from my husband, a friend had sent me to a therapist who by chance specialised in alcoholism, and, over the next few years, I was encouraged to acknowledge for the first time that my childlike parent had frequently been the centre of attention when I desperately needed help myself. My marriage was over and my son, Nicholas, at six, had had to go to a special needs school. The day that my mother imitated the Blue Lady he had waved a carving knife at me and threatened to jump out of our kitchen window in front of a car.

Although slipping further into madness, my mother still sometimes made sensible remarks. During all those years, as she grew worse, I visited her regularly. My diary of April 1994 describes her being brought downstairs, a bright blue cardigan over her nightdress, dark green trousers underneath. Every so often, she tried to go back up. She asked me about her American cousin Peggie, and whether I thought that Peggie still wanted her to come and stay in America, where she used to go often. I rang America, but unfortunately Peggie was out.

I asked Mr Mainwaring, who worked for my mother, to ring Peggie again after we'd gone, but he said that my mother might be too tired by then.

Mr Mainwaring was kind, but uncouth compared to my grandmother's butler at Knowle, Mr Tash, whom I had loved as a child. He would let me help make an Old-fashioned for my grandmother, placing in it a cherry on a stick. Then he would give me my own cherry to eat from their jar full of syrup. Mr Tash would wear a butler's black cutaway jacket with a starched white shirt and would call my grandmother 'Madam', in his soft, gentlemanly voice. Mr Mainwaring, in an anorak, hung around in the room with us, even lighting a cigarette for my mother from his own mouth. My mother seemed to like him being there and once she took his arm and coyly teased him about a group holiday they had been on.

That day, as I rose to leave, my mother plucked at my sleeve and begged me: 'Don't leave me too much alone!'

When I look back at her remark now – she must have realised that she was slowly losing her mind – I feel sad, even a little guilty. While I was embarking on a new life – having just divorced and having, I hoped, got over cancer – my mother, for one of the few times I can remember, had spoken to me directly. Also, she had conveyed what I had so often longed to hear, that I, her only daughter, meant more to her than those who looked after her daily with such devotion.

But although I wrote down her plea in my diary, I didn't take it in. I couldn't afford to. I was still terrified that I would never be rid of her; that she would always cripple me. Indeed, I see with a shock that a few days after that I wrote in my diary: *I wish with all my heart my mother would die.*

I had just received a letter from my literary agent saying that my first book, a black comic diary about the time I had cancer, would be published the following year. At last, my life might belong to me.

In autumn 1992, my mother decided to go to Madrid. She was hoping to see some of the friends that she and my father made there when I was a baby. ('Prehistoric peeps!' he had pronounced disparagingly, when she had first suggested a visit. Now, nearly twenty years after he'd died, she was attempting, without him, to fulfil her wish.) But most of those friends were dead.

Some were from old Spanish families, and had appealed to my mother's romantic side. There were Marquesas, Duques, Condesas. There was Margarita Taylor, a lady of Irish origin who ran the tea room by the British Embassy. During the war, it had been a conduit for getting refugees from the Nazis, mainly Jews, British officers and Poles, across the Pyrenees and out of Spain through Gibraltar and Galicia. Margarita Taylor had dressed the refugees as British customers while they waited to be told their escape plans. I even remembered being taken there by my mother as a little girl to eat cakes. Then there was Russian Natasha, who, my father said, had once resembled a gazelle but by middle age had turned into 'a hideous old buffalo' (she had offended him by complaining that his dog Raven murmured in his sleep, demanding: 'Stop him groaning!'). Natasha's maiden name, Bagration, was an aristocratic Georgian name, like that of General Bagration in *War and Peace*. My father teased my mother, referring to Natasha as 'Buggeration', but remained fond of her English husband Charlie, who, years after he retired from the Foreign Office, did a superb translation into English verse of Pushkin's long poem *Eugene Onegin*.

Another friend from 'the old days' in Madrid – my mother's pet phrase – was the Marques de Santo Domingo, or Paco. Paco's life had been saved during the Spanish Civil War by his English governess, Miss Ettie, who had hung a Union Jack out of the window, declaring to 'the Reds' that only British lived there. My mother loved that story.

On a holiday to Spain when I was seven, my mother had taken me to stay with Paco and Miss Ettie near the old walled town of Avila. I had been unable to chat to the friendly local children, who kept asking in Spanish: 'Have you made your first Communion?' Instead, I wandered in Paco's garden, floating the heads of huge overblown red roses in his fishpond. Paco and I named the stately blooms 'The Princesses'.

My mother took me to the market below the walls and told me of Santa Teresa, so badly treated by the people of her town that she left Avila forever, shaking its dust from her shoes.

On that visit of autumn 1992, my mother had chosen the Ritz, because it was where she and my father and their friends of forty years ago would congregate for their midday drink. She seemed pleased to be back there and said that she recognised the manager, a tall dark man who looked aristocratic.

Her first wish was to glimpse our old house, and we took a taxi there. Doreen, who had looked after me and Raymond as children in Spain, and Nicholas, now eight, were with us. On the way, my mother told me that there was an apricot tree in our garden, where I used to run about. But, today, although we searched the street, there was no sign of our old home, and my mother, back in the town after so many years away, seemed deflated. She decided to return to the hotel with Doreen, and I began walking with my son in the place where I spent the first years of my life.

I half-remembered our house and I certainly remembered our young Spanish maid Julia – 'Hoolia' – with her quick movements and long thick black hair down her back, and Nanny Benny, the Scottish nanny who came before Doreen. I recalled my mother, on one of Nanny's days off, trying to button my light blue 'cherry dress', fumbling with its red cherry buttons and laughing happily at her incompetence.

I remembered our drives to the mountains outside Madrid on Sundays and how the car invariably broke down, leaving us waiting in the parched landscape. My visiting grandmother was furious when I refused to walk on 'the prickies' – my word for the coarse Spanish grass. 'What a town-bred child!' she'd declared.

Then a village *fiesta* – how happy my mother looked! Older Spanish girls in scarlet skirts invited me to ride with them in a donkey cart, but I was too shy. Doreen came out from England after my brother Raymond was born and fed him out of a silver porringer, his christening present. I remember the smell of blackberries cooking in a house by the sea.

Now my grandmother, my father and Raymond were dead. Doreen was seventy-four and my mother seventy-eight. Doreen appeared to be in good health but my mother had become vague. Sometimes I wondered if she was pretending to be more confused than she was, to avoid responsibility. She had always been an escapist, and now surely this new forgetfulness was the perfect excuse.

That evening, we met in the Ritz drawing room, which had a ceiling as tall as a church's, high-backed chairs covered in pink and huge vases of flowers placed near oval mirrors, so there seemed to be double the number of blossoms in the room. Molly, who did part-time secretarial work for my mother in Sussex, was also with us. It was she who had helped organise the trip. I did not expect attention to be given to me or to my son; all, I knew, would be given to my mother.

My mother's younger English friend Maria, who lived part of the year in Spain, had left a plant for her, with a note saying that she would return tomorrow. My mother kept referring to Maria as 'Carmen' – Carmen was Maria's Spanish mother-in-law and a friend of my parents from 'the old days'. She kept repeating: 'Carmen's coming tomorrow.'

But Carmen, like Paco and Miss Ettie, was dead.

My mother was wearing a smart black-and-white suit, half-hidden by a navy-blue jacket. On leaving Sussex that morning she had put on an old brown anorak covered with cigarette burns and dogs' hairs, but was persuaded to take it off. Her hair had been washed, but her teeth needed attention and often she had a distracted air, as though her mind really was wandering.

In 'the old days' in Madrid, she was glamorous. For as long as I can remember, I have owned a silver-framed photograph of her and my father at Raymond's christening there in 1951. My father, in his white naval attaché's uniform, cradles his baby son and my mother, in a spotted dress and white hat, stands beside her husband. She looks animated and pretty; more than pretty – radiant.

Now, if she wasn't careful, she could appear just as an old bag lady.

When Maria came the next morning, she offered to drive my mother to the Escorial – the royal palace that was the historical residence of the kings of Spain. Doreen whispered to me that there was only room in Maria's car for four and we were five. Why didn't we let Molly go, as she had never seen the Escorial, and Doreen would stay with me and my son and go to the Thyssen collection?

My mother just sat there looking vague. Why on earth couldn't she ask me and my son to go with her? I'd never seen the Escorial either and Maria was the mother of one of my oldest school friends. But I said nothing. I was used to my mother having an entourage who indulged her every whim. I could not imagine my aunt, who was close to *her* only daughter, being in this situation. But there were always others between me and my mother, and she allowed it.

After four days in Madrid, Molly and Nicholas and I left for home. My mother and Doreen were staying on. Our taxi driver, who beside his driving mirror had a picture of Jesus and his Sacred Heart, took us to the airport on a route that went past our old house. This time we did see it. It *was* on the corner after all, as Doreen and my mother had thought, but it was no longer 117 – the street numbers had changed. I even thought I recognised it. The apricot tree could still be there, inside its walls.

Chapter 2

North Heath House, Chieveley, Berkshire, England, 1955. I proudly take my parents Alka-Seltzer every morning. I drop the white tablets into the water, which I have fetched from the bathroom in two glasses. Then I watch the water fizz. I pretend that my mother is a little girl of my own age, five; her portrait, as that little girl, hangs in my parents' bedroom. How sweet she is, with her light brown hair, curled at the ends, and her blue eyes. What fun it would be to have her as a companion. How I wish that the little girl in the portrait would come and play with me!

I long for my mother to pick me up, so that I can feel her soft skin. But it is always my father who has me on his lap. My mother holds Raymond, and after tea we play the gramophone, on its lid the picture of the dog, his ears cocked, listening to His Master's Voice; I am worried that the dog's master may have left him and this makes me feel sad. We play 'Bonny Dundee', 'The Teddy Bears' Picnic', 'Speed Bonny Boat', 'Hush Hush Hush, Here Comes the Bogey Man'. Raymond and I dance. My parents seem to love being with us. Our father drives us to nursery school – even once retying my hair ribbon, skew-whiff, so it comes undone and my teacher Miss Booth has to do it again – and on the way he teaches me and Raymond capital cities and the counties of England: the southern, *Kent Sussex Hampshire Dorset Devon Cornwall*, like a horse trotting, he explains, and the northern, *Northumberland Durham and York. Lancashire Stafford North Wales*, like a horse cantering. My father sings us his favourite songs: 'Who were you with last night? Out in the pale moonlight' and

'Hello, hello, who's your lady friend? Who's the little girlie by your side?' In the nursery after tea he plays a game where he sits one of us on his lap then asks: 'Do you feel safe? Are you *sure* you feel quite safe? Are you *sure*?', before his knees give way.

But it is Doreen, whom Raymond and I call 'Deeny', who does the daily grind with us small children – my brother Nicky was born in 1953. Doreen, with the help of Margaret, the nursery maid Raymond and I call 'M'Paul', gives us porridge with brown sugar every morning while we listen to the shipping forecast, Doreen gets our clothes ready for us each day, Doreen takes us on long walks along the road and over the common. It is Doreen, not my mother, who disciplines us, bathes us and puts us to bed.

My mother sometimes walks with us on the common – in May and June there is frothy Queen Anne's Lace, in July poppies and sky-blue cornflowers, but not as blue as my mother's eyes, which are almost turquoise. My mother, with her home movie camera, films me and Raymond jumping up and down in the corn, poppies waving all around us.

My mother always comes to say good night to me.

My mother knows I'm scared of the dark. She wants me to have a night-light and a potty under my bed. But Deeny doesn't approve of night-lights and doesn't want me to spend a penny in the middle of the night. I wake up and creep to the lavatory, and when I come out, Deeny is standing outside her own bedroom in her pink nightdress, her face white with fury.

Doreen is strict but my mother is sweet, fun, magical. She enjoys my imaginary characters – The Grey Lady, three girls called Snippy, Dotty and Gaga, and the Jaily Black Men, huge men on black horses who gallop in at night from behind the pear trees outside my window. When I am ill with a high temperature, my mother takes me to sleep with her in the bedroom she shares with my father. She wakes me during the night to give me brown medicine in a spoon, then describes the fairies she can see out of the window, like little balls of coloured light. I believe her, though I'd imagined fairies as little people. To test whether they exist, when I'm better, I leave a tiny blue flower in a special place on the lawn. Next morning, it has gone. The fairies took it. They do exist. My mother was right.

My mother and I – all of us – are happy at North Heath. Before I go to sleep, she reads to me from a book called *The Merry Meadow*, about a grasshopper, a rabbit and a harvest mouse who live in a meadow full of flowers, where there is always sunshine.

We are moving soon, to live near our grandmother.

'Does our new house have a merry meadow?' I ask my mother.

'Yes, it does,' she replies, with certainty.

How I love my mother then! I associate her with the sea, because of her vivid blue eyes, her star sign, Cancer the Crab (the astrological sign associated with motherhood), and because one of the places where she is happiest is Hope Cove, a fishing village in Devon where we now go most summers.

In Hope Cove's village is a little square with white thatched cottages, framed with hydrangeas, white, pink and blue. Across the road, below our house, is the beach, sandy and safe at low tide, then at high tide the sea splashing up and licking at the sea wall. The rocks under that wall form 'my house' – the smooth pink one the bathroom, the dark grey jagged one the dining room, the light grey smooth one the bedroom. Raymond and I play with our buckets and spades on the sand and in the rock pools. Raymond's bathing pants are white with red crabs on them. My mother insists that we wear sun hats. Raymond points at me: 'You look like a baby in that hat!'

At Hope Cove, my mother is often in a white cotton skirt and top with a pattern of little figures dancing; I remember her in that outfit in Spain. On the beach, she wears a blue bathing suit with a skirt. She puts on a cap covered with yellow daisies and swims far out, to the rock that only appears at low tide, where you sometimes see a puffin. How brave my mother is! As a child, she boasts, she could climb the rocks with bare feet, outdoing the fishermen's sons. She wants us to be as courageous as she was and I want to please her.

My mother knows about the tides and how they affect her prawning.

She wades out to the rocks at the far side of the beach carrying her heavy fishing net and waits patiently for the low tide to turn. Later she returns to the house with a pale cotton bag slung round her neck, full of live prawns; she doesn't think this cruel. One summer, like a boy, she throws a bucket of water at a cat that has got into the garden at Hope, and when we're back home at North Heath, she encourages Raymond to laugh with her at the newsreader on our new television. They close the TV shutters while he's still speaking, my mother saying to Raymond: 'Isn't he hideous?' I know that the man on the television can't see us, but her nastiness – and that business with the cat – cut me to the quick.

From when I was a very small child, I loved my grandmother's house, Knowle. I loved the round dark pink soaps in my grandmother's bathrooms, smelling of carnation. I loved her terrapin, Okie, named after Lake Okeechobee in Florida, where he came from – my mother and grandmother brought him over on a ship, where, with two baby alligators, he travelled in a bath. I loved my grandmother's white Chinese pheasant, which followed me up and down inside his huge cage while I ran to and fro outside. I loved her garden with its row of white rose trees she called 'The Bridesmaids', her big greenhouse with its rich scents and damp heat in winter, her banana tree that she wrapped up in straw when it grew cold. I loved my grandmother's green wooden swing by the monkey puzzle tree, on which a couple of adults could sit facing each other, her sloping lawn with its low box hedges leading to the swimming pool and her old magnolia tree which bloomed there in spring, its petals like huge blobs of cream.

I specially loved the woods where my grandmother and I walked. In spring they were full of primroses, bluebells, azaleas and rhododendrons. I made Gran play a game called 'The Trehernes', about a married couple I had invented who lived in Cornwall, had eight children and ran a riding school. My grandmother was Mrs Treherne on a grey mare, except of course we were on foot. As Mrs Treherne, my grandmother made occasional remarks, while I took charge of the story. I was Jane, the Trehernes' third daughter. I had a bay pony, Tinker, and a seven-year-old twin, Jack. My grandmother was always in a good temper, always relaxed.

By the stream in the heart of the woods was a shed with a pump inside that beat like a tom-tom. When I heard it, I changed our game to 'Deerfoot in the Forest', based on a book about Red Indians that my mother had had as a child in America. My grandmother and I slipped and slithered in the mud down to the stream where the wild garlic grew. Her West Highland dog Kenny went off hunting rabbits. His white coat became filthy. Back at Knowle, he was dried with an old towel on the veranda. Just inside the veranda door was a bowl made of thick china – cream, blue and brown – with words going round it in capitals: *LOVE ME LOVE MY DOG*.

How I adored being with my grandmother! I loved the way she would stand still in the middle of a room, or in a field, or in a bit of her garden, humming, as though there was never any hurry. I loved her smell of sweet talcum powder, the same carnation smell as her little soaps. But later I overheard my father telling a friend: 'Anne doesn't like her mother's house because of what happened there.'

Sometimes I felt guilty that I loved Knowle, and my grandmother, so much.

On the afternoon of my seventh birthday, 24 November 1956, my three brothers and I are at Knowle while our parents are still a few hours away, packing – we have left North Heath forever and will stay with my grandmother till our new house, nearer hers in Sussex, is ready. Deeny has hurt her back, and we have a temporary nanny.

Leaving my two little brothers – the new one is a baby of six months – in the care of Nanny B, whom we like, and who has looked after us before, my grandmother takes Raymond and me for a walk to see her pigs. She knows that Raymond is able to climb the low fence she's had put round the swimming pool to protect our two-year-old brother Nicky, because Raymond, who's five, boasts about it.

'You're too big to fall into swimming pools,' I hear her reply.

We see the baby pigs, protected from their mother – who otherwise might lie on them and kill them – by a manger with a warm, rosy light, then set off back through the wood, and across the big field home. After our walk, my grandmother helps me take off my wellingtons, then I join my brother Nicky in the schoolroom, where my mother as a girl had had lessons with a governess. I make him play horses, using a piece of string I found by the pigs, and we gallop up and down the corridor, each time passing two pictures of a child being stolen by gypsies. The second shows it being reunited with its family, but I don't believe it. The first picture, of the stolen child in white garments, surrounded by gypsies with cruel faces, two pulling at its clothes, sticks in my mind.

Where is Raymond? It's so dark outside. I open the door to my grandmother's dining room, just across from the schoolroom. There is my birthday tea; my cake with white icing, a pink sugar rose and seven candles. But there is no one to eat it. A row of portraits, of women with waxy yellow faces, stare down at me. All the adults, except Nanny B, who is a long way upstairs, bathing my baby brother, are looking for Raymond.

I send Nicky along the corridor to find out what's going on. I don't want to go myself, I am scared, but when Nicky doesn't return, I go anyway, to fetch him. I hear a man's voice – perhaps Mr Tash's – say: 'Raymond's in the pool!' He must mean the fishpond by the veranda. Nicky and I are sent back down the corridor.

That evening my father comes into the schoolroom. He tells me: 'Raymond's gone to Jesus.'

My father only ever uses the word 'Jesus' when swearing. I sense that he is performing a duty that he loathes. I say nothing. I tie Nicky to the piano with the piece of string I used earlier to play horses. I intend to look after him, always.

That night I go to bed in the narrow brown room that I've been put in at my grandmother's. On the wall beside my bed, very close, are pictures of wild boars fighting. They look very cruel. Someone has given me a rubber for my birthday and put one in for Raymond as well. Now it is *my* rubber. My mother does not come to say good night to me.

My grandmother told me years later that it was Katherine, who had come to work at Knowle on my mother's eleventh birthday and who remained at Knowle for fifty years, who eventually found Raymond in the dark. 'Poor Katie, with her stick-thin legs; she couldn't swim!' said my grandmother. My grandmother threw off her winter coat and dived in to save her grandson, but it was too late.

My aunt and her husband drove straight to Knowle from their Dorset home while my father drove through the dark from North Heath with my mother. He had sent his sister a telegram: RAYMOND ACCIDENTALLY DROWNED – as though he might have drowned on purpose! said my aunt, telling me the story years later. She added that, while my mother had sat, completely frozen, unable to cry, my father drank a whole bottle of whisky and shouted at the vicar: 'I don't want my son in heaven, I want him down here!'

The vicar's wife, Veronica, came with her husband from the village for several evenings after that, and up to my bedroom to kiss me good night. I relished her soft skin and her embraces. She was much younger than my mother. I don't remember seeing my mother for days, maybe weeks, after Raymond's accident.

At last, Nicky and I were allowed to see her, and our baby brother was carried in. My mother was in bed, in the room which had been hers as a child. There were pink rosebuds on the wallpaper and in the summer real roses pushed their way through the open windows. As I walked in I thought: 'At least she's got us.'

One morning on the staircase at Knowle, my father pointed to his dark tie. 'I'm wearing this for Raymond's funeral.'

I had not been invited. Raymond now belonged with the adults. He was more important to them than I was.

Each day now at Knowle, I played with Nicky in my mother's old schoolroom. I played with Nicky in our grandmother's garden, and in the rhododendron bushes at the corner of her wood, the place I called

'Our Village'. I busied myself with my infant brother, pretending that I was his guardian, the only person left in the world to look after him. Sometimes I romped with my father's black dog Raven, half retriever and half Chesapeake Bay, the latter breed accounting for his slightly curly coat. Raven was dignified, old beyond his years, and I loved it when I managed to get him to run up and down with me. He would often smile at me, crinkling up his mouth.

We were sent to Ireland that Christmas to stay with Michael, the son of my grandmother's sister Elisa, who had drowned in the sea in Italy; Michael, then an infant, and his father were saved. Michael, a big bearded man, owned Raven's brother, Drake, who was more lively than Raven. I played with him and he chewed a button off my duffel coat.

I don't remember missing Raymond. I do remember wishing powerfully that he was alive again, because then everything could be back to normal and we – and most of all my mother – could be happy.

Chapter 3

Sussex, 1957. It should be wonderful in our new home. We have a large garden, a farm, a playroom as well as a nursery, even a donkey. But now, because of what happened to Raymond, my mother cannot attend to me and my younger brothers. In our new garden, I play with Nicky. Below our big lawn are dark rhododendron bushes, less welcoming than the ones at Knowle in Our Village. Nevertheless, I take my little brother into their shelter and pretend as before that his parents are dead, and I am the only person left to look after him. Nearer the house, the two fishponds have been covered with wire netting.

Doreen's back is still bad, so she is not allowed to work with children ever again. We have a new nanny, who wears an odd stiff white turban, who loves my baby brother. For the first time in my life, I'm left to do what I like. Without Doreen in charge, I can wear trousers every day. I spend most of my time outside. Nicky, just three, is not allowed with me beyond the garden. On my own, I run up to our farm and play in the hay bales. I roam the fields, as far down as the river, where brown water pours very fast over the weir. I pick primroses, I smell the earth around them, I put my face to their delicate pale yellow faces and breathe in their scent. I make a small bunch for Nah, my mother's old nanny, who lives with us, and I put more primroses, with a few mauve windflowers, protected by the primroses' soft green leaves, in a small vase in my own bedroom. I am outside nearly all day. In the fields, where the celandines glitter yellow, I am almost happy.

Out of my bedroom window I can glimpse the Sussex downs; beyond them is the sea. I can see the village church, St Margaret's, across two fields. A long time ago a boy was taking bells there on St Margaret's Day, in a cart pulled by two white oxen. The fields by the church flooded, the river went on rising and the boy and the oxen were swept into the river and drowned. My mother told me the story.

There is a curse on our family, to do with drowning, and on other families who lived at Battle Abbey, the property that my great-grandfather Michael rented after making money in South America.

During the Dissolution of the Monasteries – we learn about this at school – the monks were turned out of the abbey, and King Henry VIII gave it to a Sir Anthony Browne. Sir Anthony, I read in an old book, levelled the abbey's church, and gave a banquet to celebrate. A dispossessed monk appeared and addressed the guests: 'Mark ye, my masters, ye that take God's holy land and use it for your own purpose, God's curse shall be upon ye and your name shall be wiped out of the land by fire and by water.'

Two hundred and fifty years later, the book continues, the house of Sir Anthony's descendants, by then called Montagu, and living at Cowdray, burned to the ground, and other dramatic deaths of Montagus followed; two young men perished in the Rhine, and two adults and three children drowned at Bognor Regis. A Sir Thomas Webster acquired Battle Abbey in 1719; in 1917, Lady Webster and a governess drowned in the lake there. My grandmother's oldest sister, Elisa, who, with her sisters, had lived at Battle Abbey when her father rented it from the Webster family, was drowned in Italy. Aunt Dita's granddaughter died in her parents' swimming pool in America. And now there was Raymond.

At night I'm alone in my room. I line up six soft toy animals in my bed, three each side of me. I burrow down and pull the sheets right over my head, something I did not do at North Heath. Our new Irish nanny is a long way downstairs, dealing with the baby. Nicky sleeps down there with them. The new nanny seems to prefer the baby.

In my child's bedroom I have a shiny Dutch wooden clog, a miniature bookcase painted pink containing the works of Beatrix Potter, a wardrobe made of plywood (flimsy, as I discover while sleepwalking – I nearly pull it over on top of me), a picture of *All Things Bright and Beautiful* and a cabinet full of small china horses of different colours. I have a bookcase full of books, my favourite being *Black Beauty*, which, by the age of six, I had read seven times – my father is proud of this. I know by heart the ending where Black Beauty, now an old horse, after many tribulations, reminisces: 'Often before I am quite awake, I fancy I am still in the orchard at Birtwick, standing with my old friends under the apple trees.'

My mother, like Black Beauty, has her memories, but doesn't share them with me in the way my grandmother does hers. My mother tells her memories in the grand way that she announces her likes and dislikes: 'I hate the white of egg!' I'm not required to answer. I have heard her tell more than once of how, when she was a little girl, she received the news that her grandfather Michael had died. 'I was singing a little song,' she will say. 'So I promised myself I would never sing that song again!' When she talks like this it makes me squirm.

I go to a new school up the road, where most of the other girls are boarders. On my first day an older girl comes up close to me and says menacingly: 'We all know about your brother. The head told the school on Friday.' I don't answer.

My mother buys me a dressing gown with flowers on it. My best school friend says it's posh. When I invite her for the day, I ask my parents if we can have a picnic in the field by the river, so she won't see that my family has a cook. I also invite a girl from the class below us. I tell my mother that she reminds me of Raymond – she has a few freckles on the bridge of her nose, like Raymond did. I want to please my mother. But after the girl has left, my mother says that she doesn't look like Raymond.

I have been to the dentist. The whole inside of my mouth is numb from the injection. I bite into it and chew it – hard. My mother is asleep on the sofa.

23

'My mouth's bleeding!'

'Of course the fish's mouth bleeds when the bait's in it,' my mother mutters.

I stand hesitantly beside her.

She wakes up and starts moaning: 'I want Raymond, I want my Raymond!'

Nah, who looked after my mother as a little girl and cares for her now, comes in and soothes her. I creep away.

I'm sitting on the staircase outside Nah's room. My mother, Nah and Mrs C from the village, whose little girl died, are in there. I hear one of them saying: 'He wasn't like the others.'

I begin to hate Raymond.

At North Heath, my mother had often played with me, joining in my imaginary world. She and I had danced together in the garden by the big copper beech tree, chanting, about one of my invented characters: 'Grey Lady dancing! Boop boop-a-doop!'

There is no merry meadow at our new home. My mother no longer plays with me. It is Raymond's fault.

My mother's mental decline from Alzheimer's in the 1990s, although certainly distressing for her and for those around her, was at first, for me, in some ways a relief. It meant that she could be contained and looked after, by kind Mr Mainwaring, by Mrs Anderson, her devoted housekeeper, and by temporary carers from an agency, all supervised by Molly. There would be no more drunken falls, because she could not go out and buy alcohol. Friends, hers and mine, would express sympathy and Doreen, who, after she left us, had married a gardener like her father, and been happy with him, wrote: *How can you bear to see her like this?* – but the brutal fact was that I preferred to have my mother senile and under control than wild, unpredictable and drunk.

My mother's drunkenness had been going on for years.

One night, she collected me from a teenage party in Sussex. As we set off along the dark lanes towards home she could hardly drive. She went forward in fits and starts, braking jerkily and talking to herself in that slurred voice. Even then I didn't consciously realise that she was drunk (a few weeks earlier, with me in the front seat, she had driven straight into the back of a car at red lights on Clapham Common); or maybe she was drunk so often that I had got used to it.

One winter, when I was ten or eleven, as she was driving me from London to Sussex, she took a short cut. It had been snowing and, as we started down a steep hill, the car stalled. Leaning on the steering wheel, then shaking her head slowly from side to side, as she often did while inebriated, my mother declared: 'I can't struggle any more!'

'You must!' I said grimly. I knew I had to be the sensible one, the one in control. That feeling of having to be in charge went on. I see from a letter I wrote to a friend in 1971, as though I was my brother's parent, that, the day that Nicky passed some important exams, I took him to a night of Roman Polanski films as a treat. By the time I was twenty-one, both my younger brothers had been asked to leave their schools. My grandmother reported that my mother asked her: 'Why can't Elisa look after the boys?' I wonder now whether my grandmother pointed out to her daughter that it was her job, not mine, to look after her own sons.

My mother's drinking did not make her happy, as it seemed to do some drunks – at least in the short term. It made her maudlin. One evening, in my twenties, I came in and found her crawling upstairs. I went on past her. My mother later accused me of heartlessness. Another evening an American friend and I found her on her sofa, shaking her head from side to side like a mad woman. When I thought about these incidents many years later, I felt a cold rage – and powerlessness. I felt rage towards my mother, but also towards those contemporaries of hers who didn't help. After my father died, a woman whom my mother had met on one of her many trips abroad summoned me and told me about my mother's drinking, as though I didn't know already. Another woman spoke to me about it at a book launch. If they were so concerned, why didn't they encourage her to go to an Alcoholics Anonymous meeting, or a clinic? Couldn't they see that her children had had enough?

I met my future husband Andrew, a writer, in autumn 1978 – after more members of my immediate family, including my grandmother, had died. In April 1979, Andrew invited me to a party at his artist brother's studio on a Sunday night.

When I lived as a child in the country, April was my favourite month. Primroses and celandines opened, there was Easter with its chocolate eggs, the first warm sun and the promise of the long light evenings. However, this April weekend, aged twenty-nine, I set off reluctantly to visit my mother in Sussex. My godmother Meg, who had just been to see her, had urged me to go; she was concerned that my widowed mother, who had broken her hip that summer, might be lame for life.

When I got to Sussex I was appalled by the state of my former home. There were dog puddles in passages; elsewhere, antique rugs had been ruined by dogs' messes and stains. My mother was still in her dressing gown although it was the late afternoon. There seemed to be no discipline in her life; everything was done according to whim.

I had a dreadful cold and my mother was very attentive, offering me sweets. On Saturday afternoon we watched the Grand National on TV, and in the evening a programme about women in the armed forces about which my mother made intelligent remarks. On Sunday afternoon, I drove back to London, in time for the party. But I was overcome with depression, a dead weight I couldn't lift off. At the party, I chatted to a former school mate. She had married a close friend of Andrew's who'd done well in the City. Her new baby was having fits and she'd employed an old-fashioned nanny to help. She was pleased about this, remarking: 'It's like having your mother waiting up for you after a party.'

I realised what different experiences we'd had in regard to our mothers. I would have dreaded my mother waiting up, as she would almost certainly have been plastered.

Even now, while trying to enjoy myself, I was half-waiting for another accident to happen. Sure enough, the next day I heard that my mother had fallen, a few hours after I left her, and fractured her leg. This was her second, or even third, break since my father died in 1974; I had lost count. She was in hospital and had already undergone another operation. Her drinking had at last been brought into the open and the doctors had advised her to get dried out. However, she had refused to go to the place they suggested – very near Knowle – as my brother Nicky had been in a psychiatric unit there.

I went by train to visit my mother in the hospital. She looked better than I expected; her hair was tidy and she did not seem as unhinged as she sometimes did. When I entered her room she gave me a defiant look as if to say: 'Don't you dare tell me *why* I fell . . .!' When a nurse brought her lunch, she said she'd been told to offer my mother whisky with it – presumably because without it she would suffer from withdrawal symptoms. My mother said grandly: 'No thank you, I don't drink spirits. They don't agree with me.' When the nurse had gone, my mother did mention her drinking to me, but in a veiled way, saying that one of the young hospital doctors belonged to Alcoholics Anonymous. She told me she'd been suffering from hallucinations and wondered if this was what having DTs was like. She thought a young black doctor had visited her in the night and asked: 'Are you afraid of me?' She imagined that she heard another doctor tell her: 'You are going to be committed to a mental hospital as you tried to commit suicide twice.'

Perhaps I should have taken the opportunity then to discuss her drinking, since she had given me that opening. But I had been schooled for years not to mention it and the whole subject of my mother's drunkenness filled me with fear and shame.

Sitting beside her, I watched different patients go past her door. Each one called out to her. My mother, so charming to strangers, had already made friends. Two were in wheelchairs. One was an old man who loved gardening; another was an old lady from Yorkshire who told us that most of her life she had lived in a house with 'a tortuous staircase'; then, when she finally moved south to a bungalow in Seaford, she fell and broke her leg.

Friends had sent my mother flowers. I was wary; I couldn't allow myself to feel sympathetic. I was constantly wondering what further disaster would occur.

In January 1981, Andrew and I married. My mother seemed pleased but, particularly when my children were little, I would have liked to have had a mother who helped me. When my Aunt Rosemary visited me in London, she did ordinary things, like going with me when I collected my children from school. She came to my son's swimming gala. My mother never did anything like this. Even my friend J's mother, who, like mine, was well off, had come from her home abroad when he and his wife had their first baby. I had just had my daughter and my mother was still on holiday in Majorca – J was shocked by this – and when the baby was four days old it was Molly who came to the West London Hospital and then escorted us and our new baby to our house in Sussex, as my husband had not yet learned to drive.

J's mother, I saw, had even made apple sauce. My own mother couldn't cook. She had once attended a Women's Institute cookery class, but when the instructor began with 'I'm sure you all know how to make a white sauce . . .' she was so terrified that she never went again.

Most women of her generation, even those brought up to be waited on, learned to cook during or after the war. Why was my mother treated like a queen?

The day after her eightieth birthday, 1 July 1994, Nicholas and I went to see her. My son had made her a pavlova, as a birthday cake. She complimented me, all of a sudden, for being 'straightforward and honest'. Mr Mainwaring said: 'You're pleased to see Elisa, aren't you?'

Nicholas went to the kitchen with a very nice Greek girl to put candles on his pavlova. My mother wanted to walk with me up and down the hall, into the kitchen, upstairs to her bedroom, then down again. When Nicholas brought in the pavlova with its candles, she seemed genuinely delighted. Nicholas kept feeding his grandmother strawberries and bits of meringue from his pavlova. This seemed to be the right instinct, because her mouth kept opening obediently, and she would eat each morsel.

Nicholas and I then went with her into her garden where, earlier, she hadn't wanted to go. We went past the fishponds, whose netting had been removed years ago, then by her border full of pink and blue flowers, and urns full of lavender.

I thought that it would seem to most people a beautiful English garden. Was I ever happy there as a child? There was always that undercurrent of fear, of something bad waiting for us, and this must have emanated from my mother. I thought of her poorer friends, such as Russian Olga, who used to visit us from London, often in summer, with their young children; to them, our home must have seemed like paradise.

My mother kept hitching up her trousers, saying that the waist was too loose, and Mr Mainwaring told me that she didn't like to eat. Once, she clasped my own hand, then put it to her breast, which seemed to have shrunk, and I noticed that she no longer wore a bra. We passed the little tower; she had once sunbathed on its roof with her friend Audrey, and I recalled how my father had informed me, aged nine, that the two women were naked. I thought to myself now that there was something humiliating in being married to a woman who preferred her own sex.

Chapter 4

My first book was published in April 1995 and was received favourably. But concern about my mother marred the pleasure I should have felt and a few weeks after publication, despite it being summer, I developed bronchitis verging on pneumonia, and was ill for six weeks.

My immune system had been weakened by chemotherapy, but my illness may have been exacerbated by anxiety about my mother. At first I had been relieved that her Alzheimer's meant that she could no longer get alcohol, but now her condition gave rise to other worries: should she be moved to an old people's home and, if so, what should happen to her house and her possessions? Was she on the right medication, and should I try to get Power of Attorney? Indeed, it seemed to me that I would always be eaten up with worry about her – unless I went first, of a recurrence of breast cancer! I asked advice and sought medical opinion, and, just before falling ill, I visited with a kind friend an old people's home in Sussex, run by nuns especially for those with Alzheimer's. It had been recommended by various friends who had had, or still had, close relatives in there.

The 'home' was actually two sister homes. In the first one, near a road, we waited in the hall. Coming downstairs was a woman who looked distressed. She had a red mark on the bridge of her nose. We said hello and she glanced nervously at us. She started to speak hesitantly, murmuring about it being 'embarrassing' not being in her own house. The nun who then appeared did not seem particularly sympathetic to her plight, and when I asked her how she could be prevented from walking out on to the road and being hit by a car, she looked troubled and did not answer. I asked how long that woman had been there and the nun said two months. Normally, she explained, it took a few weeks for a new patient to settle down.

We chatted to the nun on our tour of the building. She showed us the residents' rooms – dormitories, doubles and singles. We followed her into sitting rooms, common rooms and bathrooms. All was impeccably clean and tidy and there was an atmosphere of peace.

In one common room I found Peggy Langley, who as a young woman, as Peggy van Lier, was a member of the Second World War's most famous escape route, the 'Comet line', which had rescued Allied servicemen from occupied Belgium, Peggy's country. I was friends with her daughter at boarding school, and used to stay in their house in Suffolk. Peggy became a good friend of my mother, who admired her bravery – she had been awarded the Belgian Croix de Guerre, an MBE and the Resistance Cross. My mother also liked the romance of Peggy having met her husband – a British Guards officer who had lost his arm at Dunkirk and then become an important member of MI19 – during that time.

I remembered Peggy as just a wife and mother, limping round her Suffolk kitchen – I suppose she had rheumatism – cooking for her husband and four sons. Only her daughter was expected to help. I remembered how Peggy loved music, and that she had seemed not to fit in among her English menfolk, who liked shooting, and I remembered also how sweet she was. Now, I saw that she was almost bald, a tiny frail woman with a plaintive, slightly hurt expression. I bent down and introduced myself, using just my Christian name, and I reminded her that I was a friend of her daughter. Recognition, sadness, then a flicker of hope crossed her face. Perhaps it was fanciful, but at that moment I felt that her soul was going out to me. Then, a few moments later, she realised that I was leaving and her face closed off. I, like her daughter, was not staying with her and she would be alone again with all the other women who had lost their minds.

I did not like to think of my mother, who might not have recognised Peggy now, coming down the staircase here, bewildered like that woman we had seen earlier, wishing to be back in her own house.

Nearby was the sister home, which was more secure. The patients could not walk out of the building. At first it seemed grander and there was more Catholic paraphernalia – statues of the Virgin Mary and Jesus with his Sacred Heart exposed. (I was used to this from my own upbringing, instigated by my Catholic father, but my mother, after collecting me from a catechism class he had arranged in our local Sussex town, told me that she was revolted by the picture in the hall of Jesus with his exposed bleeding Sacred Heart – 'like something at the butcher's'.)

Out of the window was a formal garden with wallflowers and great sweeping lawns. A busy little red-haired Irish nun with alert grey-green eyes, whom I liked at once – she told us merrily that she was born in the Chinese Year of the Rat, and she did seem busy and alert like a rat – came to meet us. She led us upstairs and introduced us to another, older, nun in charge of the unit.

I couldn't help noticing a patient walking up the corridor very fast, her whole body tilting sideways. With a shock I recognised her – it was Veronica, the wife of the former vicar of the village near Knowle. Although I had seen Veronica many times since – her husband was vicar there for over fifteen years – and I recalled my father's irritation at her skittishness, my very first memory of her came back to me, the evening after Raymond was drowned, when she came to my bedroom at Knowle to kiss me good night. I felt grateful to her now, for having realised that I, a small child, needed comfort.

I could see that Veronica was in a similar state of anxiety to my mother, who often walked up and down repeating: 'I want to go home!', although my mother was still in her own house. The nun in charge said that Veronica walked so much that she feared for her heart. I approached her, saying my grandmother's name, then my own. She did not seem to understand, though she was very polite.

The nun informed me that Veronica's only child was a deaconess.

She suggested that Veronica take me into her room and show me a photograph of her daughter, who as I recalled was the same age as my brother Nicky. In her bedroom, Veronica handed me a framed photograph from her dressing table of a young woman getting married.

I exclaimed: 'She looks just like you!'

I then realised that she had shown me her own wedding photograph.

Shortly after that, I took our cousin Dita, American Peggie's daughter, to see my mother. My mother did not recognise Dita, whom she had known since she was a child, and raised her walking stick as though to attack her. Dita looked shocked. My mother then tried to hand her a pink teddy bear, to apologise. Dita said later that she had not known how bad my mother had got. She added that she felt very sorry for both of us.

Just as Dita and I were leaving, my mother, who did not know that I had visited the homes, suddenly remarked: 'I hate nuns!' I found this disconcerting, all the more so considering her unhinged mental state.

This was not the only time I experienced telepathy with my mother, which generally occurred without my wanting it to.

My mother did not go into the home in 1995. I was made to feel by Molly that it would be cruel. Indeed, taking on more responsibilities than just secretarial work, Molly, who was usually so helpful, completely opposed it, despite putting her own mother-in-law into a home. My mother's doctor, who would soon retire, was also stubborn about her moving, although by that summer of '95 she had not been downstairs for a whole year as she had become terrified of negotiating her own staircase, even with help.

Despite my belief that she should now be looked after by those who specialised in Alzheimer's, in a place where she would be less isolated, I did not ultimately have the confidence to make that decision on my own.

I was also having more problems with my son, who was now at another special school. He had never played with toys, had only one friend and was quick-tempered and obsessive. A year later, on his thirteenth birthday, he would be diagnosed with Asperger's Syndrome – a condition on the autistic spectrum, the main symptoms of which are lack of social skills, overriding obsessions and intense anxiety and frustration.

I don't ever remember telling my mother about my son even before she got Alzheimer's – protecting her peace of mind was paramount. In the car to visit her when Nicholas was twelve I told him, perhaps unwisely, that I wished I could solve all my worries about my mother with my word processor: *SAVE: YES/NO*. I wished that I could simply press the *NO* key and my mother would disappear. I wished it could be as simple as that.

On that occasion, in my mother's double bedroom, where she'd slept alone, except for various dogs, since I was seven – my father was in a single room, divided from hers by a bathroom – Nicholas sat on her bed beside her and gently touched her shoulder. My mother, with a violent gesture, shouted: 'Get off me, boy!'

No one told her off. The excuse was that she was too far gone. She'd already had Alzheimer's for nearly three years. But no one would have told my mother off *before* she got it.

One of our cousins, Hamilton, a bachelor fifteen years older than her, said to me soon after my father's death: 'Your mother needed a firm hand. She didn't get it.'

After my mother's brutal rejection of her grandson, I went upstairs and looked at my old children's books. My mother's New Zealand carer, who'd taken my son with her to the kitchen, was sleeping in my old bedroom. I found a book I used to love, *Seven Days Wonder*, about a Victorian child who falls off a swing and is transported into England in the 1950s, to a family where the children are actually her own future great-grandchildren. I recalled how I had pictured the house where that cheerful 1950s family lived as being exactly like our house, North Heath, the home of a happy family – in those days, my own.

I went to say goodbye to my mother, feeling resentful, as she had been nasty to my son. She was asleep. As I left, I couldn't help noticing the two dark blue toy taxis on her mantelpiece. She put them there – Raymond's toys – after he died. They had been there forty years.

Two years later my mother's Alzheimer's was more advanced. But, instead of being put into a home, she was being moved into a smaller, modern house built in the 1950s: Camelot. It was being converted into two flats and Mrs Anderson and her husband would live in the one upstairs. They would not use the large family kitchen, which would only be for my mother and the carer on duty at that time.

When I went to see this house in early spring 1997, I felt guilty that it was going to be taken over by one mad old woman. The wife who was selling it with her husband was giving a tea party for her two little children and their friends. Surely another young family should have been moving into it. It seemed a waste of a good house. As usual, my mother's money had allowed her to be in an abnormal position.

Meanwhile my daughter and I visited her, still in her old house. A pleasant-looking black-haired girl let us in the back door. Whizzy, the little rescue dog that Molly had found for her, came skittering to meet us. My mother had fallen asleep just before we arrived. She was wearing a dark red cardigan, dark red skirt and slippers, ordered from a catalogue by Molly. I suggested to Mr Mainwaring that he wake her, as he had successfully on my last visit.

This time, though, my mother did not rally. She sat looking dazed, with her granddaughter on the bed beside her. Mr Mainwaring chatted in his usual friendly manner, then told me that my mother had had a visitor from the village. Mrs M, who in my memory had always been very cheerful, burst into tears as she was sitting next to my mother on her bed. She looked at the two large oval photographs of Raymond that my mother had had up on the wall since 1957, above a shelf containing his woolly toys, and sobbed uncontrollably. As Mr Mainwaring described this in a shocked voice, I felt sympathy for Mrs M. At least she was acknowledging, through her spontaneous reaction, one of the several tragedies of my mother's life. This once-happy mother of four young children was now asleep with her mouth open, teeth broken, hair awry and brain rotted by alcohol.

My mother carried on sleeping. My daughter seemed depressed and sat in the car after we left the house. I went alone to what I used to call the Big Lawn, to pick some daffodils. The grass was neglected, covered with molehills. I remembered how, long ago, every April, the ground under the big oak tree there was full of primroses. I recalled a black-and-white photograph of myself aged nine standing among them, my back against the tree. Was my mother's collection of photographs of us, her remaining three children, a valiant attempt to fill the void caused by Raymond's death? Was she trying to persuade herself that life went on?

I picked a few daffodils, stinging my hand on nettles. I remembered how I used to play here, often alone; how I'd had a rope hanging down from the big tree by the pond, how I had learned to climb the rope on my own, right to the top, how it was much stiffer than the one in the gym at school. How I had played alone in the fields, roaming all over the place, how much I had loved the country in the spring.

My brother had just died. I was only seven. Surely *I* could have fallen into the pond, or the fast-running weir in the water meadow, three long fields away from our house. Maybe I had not been properly looked after.

That evening, I told my son about my mother in her bedroom, her mouth open in an oval shape, eyes shut.

Nicholas said seriously: 'That must have hurt you very much. That must have hurt you in your heart like this –' and he indicated a space in the middle of his chest.

The move to Camelot was imminent. I drove over to see my mother; again she was asleep. Another New Zealand girl was sleeping in my old room. I removed my photograph of my mother and grandmother riding side-saddle together at a meet near Knowle, and a photograph of my Exmoor pony. I went through the small chest of drawers in my child's bedroom and cleared it of sweet papers. I took my picture of a dog and a cat off the wall.

Downstairs, my mother woke and seemed pleased to see me. She was making an odd noise – half-moaning, half-humming. I picked up her framed photograph of Nah, her beloved nanny. 'Who's that?' This time, unlike a few months earlier when she'd got it right, my mother replied: 'It's "Gigy"' – her pet name for Gig, my grandmother's Scottish lady's maid, who, with Nah, had helped bring my mother up. I said no, it was Nah, and she seemed to register this and be pleased. I then showed her Gig, holding Raymond's hand on the deck of the *Queen Mary* as we'd all arrived at New York Harbour in 1955 on holiday to see our American cousins, he in a brown velvet pixie hat that Gig, a trained dressmaker, had made for him. Then I handed my mother a picture of my father as a young man in naval uniform. 'Who's that?'

'It's Dad, isn't it?' she replied cautiously.

Mr Mainwaring indicated two objects with blue stickers on them, ready to take to the new house. These were the two large oval photographs of Raymond which hung on my mother's bedroom wall, one with him smiling, about to throw a ball. I longed to say: 'Now's the time to end this morbid obsession with a dead child! This has been your excuse for not facing anything, for not dealing with day-to-day life, for neglecting the rest of us!'

Instead, I pointed out to Mr Mainwaring that my mother should also take the smaller framed photos of Nah, of Gig and of her American cousin Peggie, all of whom she loved. As I drove off, I felt relieved that my childhood home was to be cleared at last.

I felt like smashing the photographs of Raymond, my dead brother, with a hammer.

On her eighty-third birthday, my mother moved into Camelot. Molly, who helped her move – I did not – reported that on her first afternoon there, although normally she rarely uttered a coherent sentence, she remarked: 'I like this place much better!'

At last I felt vindicated. She'd never been happy in her home, unlike my grandmother was at Knowle. I was her daughter and I knew her. I had to remind myself of that.

Soon after that I had a scare, another lump which had to be removed, in my left breast this time. I went to the hospital where I had all my other treatments, for one night. My daughter came the next day – it was the school holidays – and I prepared to drive us to Sussex. The woman in the bed opposite asked suspiciously if I was driving, as I wasn't meant to after an anaesthetic. I pretended I was only going ten minutes up the road. However, when I was in the bathroom, my daughter innocently disclosed that we were going to Sussex. As we set off, I joked that the patient had probably sent the police after us. I did feel light-headed, but I told myself that, with my daughter beside me, I could get there. And I did.

It occurred to me that my mother, who, apart from old age and Alzheimer's, had not much physically wrong with her, was waited on and had no more duties, ever. I had had cancer, and now might have it again. I was divorced with two children, one with difficulties, and was ultimately responsible for my mother's legal and financial affairs, for which I had no training.

Ten days later, I am in Hope Cove, Devon, alone with Nicholas by the sea. It rains all the time but for some reason I don't mind. I'm waiting to find out if I've got cancer, this time in my left breast. Anticipating my death, Nicholas says he couldn't bear for me to be 'frozen then cut up and your bones ground'. This is what the ancient Egyptians did, he says. (I thought they had mummies.) He doesn't want me to be cremated either.

He asks about the afterlife. Would I be scared to meet my brother Raymond? He thinks that Raymond would still appear as a child, not as an adult. He asks if I am 'ghost-scared, child-scared', of the crippled child in my recurring nightmare.

At Hope, I have a disturbing dream about my mother's old house. I am clearing up there – as I will have to, in reality, when it goes up for sale. I am outside my mother's garden, in the old moat. I look up and see a row of half-grown children standing in a circle, very high up, on the threshold of a big spaceship or aeroplane. In my mind is the idea of how daring my mother is to have produced, or be associated with, these children, who at any moment might jump off the rim into the sky. One teeters close to the brink, as though she is going to jump. I then realise that, far from it being exciting, if she jumps off she'll be killed. But, although she sways dangerously, she doesn't do it.

Later in the dream I stand at the edge of my mother's garden and look into the lanes around it. In my dream they're wild and beautiful, more like the lanes here in Devon. I am surprised to find that I associate such beauty with my childhood home. I even feel guilty, at first, for misjudging my mother's environment, for finding it unpleasant when it isn't.

Also in the dream is a tall glass jug and glasses in a cabinet, all very close together, and in my reaching for them, one of them breaks. I feel guilty then, as I see my mother appearing with one of her carers. I am aware that my mother has more strength in her than I had realised and is angry that we are interfering with her things.

Nicholas's interpretation of my dream next morning is that the circle of adolescent children represents me and my brothers. I am the only one who's escaped. Even so, he says, I still find it difficult. The other dream, about the beautiful lanes surrounding my old home, is even simpler to interpret. It refers to my mother's money. It means that other people envy it and think it a marvellous thing, but I know the truth, that it has helped destroy my mother.

At seven thirty, my doctor rings from his surgery in London. 'Good news.' I have nothing malignant. Nicholas looks very pleased. I thank him for being with me.

Some months after this, I started walking regularly again in the Knowle woods. One Monday morning I drove my daughter to school, then went on to Knowle. But of course I no longer had the right to use the front gates. Instead of my grandmother, Katherine and Violet – Mr Tash's widowed sister who cooked, and helped Katherine look after my grandmother – three families were now living in the divided house. I drove past the Knowle main entrance and pulled in by a hidden gate.

I liked this secret access. I drove in and parked beside a woodshed – white doves flew out – then I started walking into the woods, keeping our dog Toby on a lead. A herd of small deer bounded away from me into the chestnut trees. On my right was the Glebe, where I would go often with my grandmother to see the baby pigs, and where I had walked with her that day with Raymond.

Pushing my way through mud and brambles, I reached the edge of the large field that looked across to what had been my grandparents' house, grey, perhaps a little forbidding. But it was where I was taken first as a baby, then often as a small girl, then as a schoolgirl, to visit my grandmother. Then in my twenties I would go alone, often, to stay. I realised as I stood looking at the house that I felt more territorial about it than I would ever feel about anywhere.

I was by a small clearing with a plantation of rhododendrons – 'Our Village' – where I played with Nicky just after Raymond died. I walked deeper into the wood, cautiously keeping Toby on the lead. I turned along the upper woodland path, which ended below Knowle itself. I passed a large hollow called 'Chow's Pit' after my mother's stepfather, whom she called 'Chow', that at various seasons was full of giant leaves, bright green and yellow, scarlet American maples, golden and coral azaleas and purple zinnias. A camellia was blooming now in spring, a deep pink. Twice more I saw groups of small deer leaping away into the wood. Now I was very near Knowle. I climbed over some broken wire and walked into the bottom of my grandmother's garden, where I stared at the masses of daffodils, some like bright yellow trumpets, others pure white, then more delicate narcissi with pale yellow petals and orange centres like fried eggs. My grandmother planted all of them. Some had spread and covered the grassy area where the swimming pool once was. The new owners had filled it in.

On my way back, I was about to skirt 'Our Village' when I saw a man and a woman enter the big field from Knowle and start striding across it towards me, with two large dogs. I ducked back into the trees. I felt invaded, though I was the trespasser. Those strangers now owned the field where my grandmother used to go each day with her dogs, where she had once walked with my grandfather, with my mother as a little girl, and, forty years later, with me. She and I saw a lamb being born there. Now, I was just a visitor.

Soon after her eightieth birthday, before Camelot was found for her, my mother had stood at the top of her old staircase, afraid to come down, repeating: 'I want to go home!' Eventually she was persuaded to walk slowly downstairs, holding on to Mrs Anderson's arm, a puzzled, slightly fearful expression on her face.

Later I asked Mr Mainwaring: 'When she keeps saying, "I want to go home", what does she mean? Does she mean Knowle?'

Mr Mainwaring replied: 'Oh no, she means where she is now.'

But my mother was already in her own house.

After revisiting the Knowle woods, I thought again about what she had meant. Was she referring to her own confused state of mind, where 'home' was some imagined place of safety where she'd no longer be disorientated, or did she really want to go back to Knowle, her childhood home, which I'd always thought she hated after Raymond's accident? Soon after that unsatisfactory visit to Madrid in 1992, Molly told me that my mother had gone with her to my Sussex house and photographed the garden ornaments that used to be at Knowle – a lead urn with mice crawling up the sides, a little boy holding a duck, and a little girl kneeling, one arm stretched up, yawning. Then she went inside and photographed the Spy drawing of her grandfather Michael. Perhaps she was trying to prompt memories with these images from her old home, before she forgot everything. Maybe she *had* been fond of Knowle as a child, even as a young woman. I found myself hoping that she had.

Chapter 5

The house went on the market in September 1997, a few days after Princess Diana's death. Its contents had to be sorted out. Luckily I had help from Molly and from Mrs Anderson, who had already moved with her husband into the converted upper floor in Camelot to help look after my mother.

I felt that again my life was taken over by my parent. I recalled all those years after my father's death and later, including the whole period of my marriage, when I would come home and find disturbing messages on my answerphone. One said: 'Pamela's husband has died!' (Pamela was my father's cousin, whom I had met once, at my father's funeral; my mother did not know her well either.)

My mother's voice on the tape was usually so slurred that it was unrecognisable, though of course I knew it was her. There was often a tone of self-pity which made me recoil. Once, she left a message saying that she had posted me a poem about old age. She must have hoped this would make me feel sorry for her but it had the opposite effect. Afraid of being dragged into her chaos and despair, I hardened myself against her.

Now, I wished that she had sorted out her own affairs in advance, while she was still compos mentis, like other women did, women who acted like adults. I compared her to June, the former Wren whom my father met when he was a young midshipman. June drove sailors round Liverpool at the beginning of the war and my father told me that he had proposed to her, years before meeting my mother. June, widowed after her last husband died in a car crash, ended up living down the

42

road from me, and we became friends. She told me that my father, after she'd turned him down (partly because he was Catholic), had then given her bad advice on her future first husband: 'You won't get very far with *him*. He only fucks dukes' daughters!'

When June became frail, she sold her house and went to live near her daughter, as did my aunt. These women tried to make it easier for their offspring.

At first, I found my mother's acquisitiveness disgusting. In the cupboard outside her bedroom were over seventy pairs of shoes, most of them unworn, many of them *alpagatas* (cheap rope-soled shoes) from Spain. Then I found in the attic a box of beach clothes that Raymond and Nicky and I wore as children – Aunt Dita had bought us three matching swimsuits, white with little blue flowers, when my mother took us to see her in Palm Beach in 1955 – and in a wardrobe outside my old bedroom was a brown leather Hungarian coat, waisted, double-breasted, with a full skirt. There was a green tartan shirt that my mother wore on a ranch, a bookcase of her children's books – *The Gold Thread and 'Wee Davie', Greyfriars Bobby, Teddy Lester's Schooldays* – all of which I remembered reading with pleasure, her bronze Red Indian, and, in a chest of drawers, heaps and heaps of old postcards.

In a small cupboard on the landing was a pale grey cotton bag with a drawstring, like those bags my mother used for prawning. I opened it and found it full of what appeared to be German passports. I looked through them and saw that many belonged to Luftwaffe pilots from the Second World War. I was shocked – and fascinated. My first thought was that my mother, whose wartime experiences I knew little about, except that she was a WAAF and had worked at Bletchley Park, had stolen them. Should she not have handed them to someone higher up in the organisation?

These passports were the first real physical evidence of my mother's working, adult life, before she met my father, a life that I knew almost nothing about.

I left the bag in the cupboard – a sweetmeat to be tasted later.

Next day, Mrs Anderson showed me some loose black-and-white photographs. They were of me and Raymond, with Nicky lying beside us in his christening robe. I stared at my darling little brother. I recalled how, after visiting him in hospital just after he was born, on 22 December 1953, I stood by the lift in my grandmother's London house and triumphantly recited my newborn brother's names: 'NICHOLAS – JOHN – PAUL!' I felt that he was mine.

I said: 'I absolutely adored him.'

We both glanced at a little pile of books on drug abuse that Mrs Anderson had unearthed. My mother must have been reading them when Nicky was a teenager.

I said: 'Both my parents were alcoholics. They should have been addressing *their* problems as well.'

In a disused flat above the old stables, I found portraits of various ancestors. My great-great grandfather, a barrister, came over from Ireland in the 1830s and bought a small farmhouse, then called Knole, in East Sussex. (The 'w' was added later, by my grandmother, to distinguish the house from the larger Knole in Kent, owned by the Sackville-West family.) Some of the portraits had hung less than twenty years ago in our Knowle dining room. Their faces had stared down at me when I looked in at my birthday tea, the day Raymond disappeared. The women had high cheekbones like their descendants – like my mother's Aunt K, like my mother and like me. Unlike me and my mother, they had receding chins and yellowish waxy skin, so that my grandmother called them 'The Banana Faces'.

When I was thirteen and my brother Nicky was nine, we were playing in this area above the stables. The thin floor broke under my brother and he crashed through. I remember shouting: 'Darling Nicky, are you all right?' I was terrified he was dead. Now on that repaired floor lay ornaments, stacked plates, a bowl of false fruit and two pictures, one of a hare under a full moon and one of a shepherd boy lying on a hill in moonlight, which I recognised from the London house where my mother was born – 40 Belgrave Square, which my grandmother's father Michael took on a hundred-year lease after he became rich.

Back inside my mother's house, outside her old nanny's room, was a small box of Nah's things. Nah died in 1963, but these must have remained there ever since. In an envelope were receipts, neatly clipped together, of Nah's copies of *Woman's Own*, delivered every week, and illustrated Easter and Christmas cards drawn by me and by her niece Rosemary, who called her 'Auntie Lye'. I found the little box of her things touching in its modesty. Nah was almost the only person in our household who did not go off the rails. As an adolescent, I spent almost every evening in her tiny bedroom. We watched *Emergency Ward 10* on TV and listened to her radio – Wilfred Pickles with his wife Mabel at the Table; 'Have a Go, Joe! Come and Have a Go!' I lay on Nah's narrow bed reading her newspaper's accounts of the Profumo case. The most sinister word to me was 'osteopath'. What sort of perversion could this be? Nah didn't know.

Nah never complained of having me in her room night after night. She used to offer me Callard & Bowser's Cream Toffees from her tin, two per evening. I felt it was the only safe place in the house.

Things were always going wrong at my parents', going out of control. A few months after Raymond died, my mother bought two donkeys, and the female gave birth to a foal that I named Shamrock. But the enchanting baby donkey died. Soon after that, my guinea pigs, which I'd had at North Heath, were torn to pieces by a fox. Years later, my pony got laminitis – she ended up being shot by the farm manager – and, when I was a teenager, a cob that my parents had bought, which they hardly ever rode, attacked and killed an old horse belonging to my mother's friend Angela from Knowle. Another incident concerned a cook, whom I hardly knew, because I had left home by then, but which I nevertheless heard about and recorded in my diary as a sort of narrative: the entry is undated.

The cook died on Thursday. Her bedroom was filled with bloody sheets that she had used to mop up her own blood. Towards the end she had been taking thirty aspirins a day. She had not cashed a cheque for four years.

'She looked really bitter. I always thought a corpse would look peaceful, but she didn't,' said the young man who sometimes drove my parents' car.

'I suppose she'd had a hard life,' I said.

'A refugee, wasn't she? Turned out of East Germany – her dad had a farm there. She saw him drop dead in her path. They just marched on and left him.'

Mrs N, it emerged, had led a solitary life in the kitchen and in her bedroom in my parents' house. When she had her day off she would never go far, and refused to go away on holiday. Instead she would walk on her own, carrying a staff, striding through the fields, humming softly. It seems terrible now to think of her sitting alone in her bedroom bleeding heavily. Surely someone should have noticed if four years of cheques had not been cashed? Perhaps my father had died by then. And my mother certainly didn't like to occupy herself with what didn't interest her.

The day I started clearing out her house, I was attacked by a violent stomach ache, which recurred each day. There appeared to be no physical cause and, after a visit to a doctor, I decided that the pains were psychosomatic. Indeed, when I no longer had to go to the house regularly, they subsided. Even at forty-seven, I could not dispel the feelings of anxiety, of danger, which I associated with my childhood home – and with my mother.

One afternoon, I found a box of things relating to Raymond; they appeared to be mostly his drawings and school books. My mother must have put them in the attic when we moved to Sussex soon after he died. I wasn't sure what to do with them. One idea, suggested by a friend, was to burn them in a ceremonial bonfire on top of the Sussex downs. But instead I took the box back to my workroom in London. Only then did I look properly at the contents.

The first item I took out was my brother's school satchel. It still looked very new. I had one exactly like it. I had the disconcerting feeling, passed on from early childhood, that we were interchangeable in the minds of the adults who looked after us. I remembered the way they talked of us always together, in what sounded like one word – ElisaandRaymond. In a shoeshop where my mother was buying us Start-Rite sandals, the assistant asked: 'Are they twins?' We both had light-brown hair and were almost the same height, although he was eighteen months younger. My eyes are grey, while Raymond's were blue like my mother's – another reason to make her prefer him, I thought, even then.

Looking at his arithmetic book, I noted that my brother was doing sums right up to four days before he died.

He had a Hornby train. Here was a certificate from the Hornby Railway Company, dated 1954. This was the kind of boyish prop, like his Dinky cars, toy soldiers and little tractor, that sometimes divided him from me, though, despite being a girl, I was bolder than he was. He was frightened of fireworks and always had to watch them from a window, and I also recalled that, at Comillas, he was afraid of the sea.

I went on looking for something that would awaken a personal memory. Here was his writing exercise book, which also had illustrations: 'I am Raymond, I am a tall boy.' In the drawing of himself, he was all in blue, his hands like bunches of bananas. Further on were other drawings, with his captions underneath: 'I played with my trains', 'I went to a circus' and 'We went to Hope'.

Then, with a shock, I saw some of my own drawings, which I remembered doing, and even a short story I wrote, about a farm. (I had longed to live on a farm, like the one at Knowle.) Here was an illustration by me, of myself and my two younger brothers and a line of other children, all holding boxes tied with big bows. I had depicted myself as much the biggest. I was giant-sized and was eating a box of chocolates. When I looked closer, I realised that the scene was meant to be my own future birthday party, and that those other, much smaller children were lined up to give me presents. How different that birthday, and every one of my birthdays ever after, would turn out to be – my birthday would always be the day of Raymond's death.

Why were my drawings shut away with his? I was torn between rage and pity – pity when I picked up a postcard he wrote to our mother in hospital, where she was having her last baby in June 1956. *Dear Mummy, I am doing 100s, 10s and units at school.*

Five months later he was dead. Now that I had had small children myself, this postcard, with its poignant message, reminded me that he was just a little boy who should have had a future like I had.

Also in the box were some loose sheets of paper in my mother's hand-writing. When I looked closer, I saw that it was part of a diary, dated 1936, but none of the pages was numbered. It must have been written at the time of the Abdication Crisis, as there were several references to Wallis Simpson and the King. Most of the diary was written in the USA – places such as Maryland, Virginia and Shenandoah appeared. A few sheets were headed with a little painting of the *Queen Mary*, with her three red funnels, and the blue sea beneath her. My mother must have travelled back to England on her that autumn.

The loose sheets were muddled up. I turned to one written in October.

October 14th 1936. Tallwood, Lutherville, Maryland.
Fife insisted on taking me for a walk . . . walking back through the cornfield he suddenly told me he was so much in love with me that it drove him nearly crazy and that he had never felt like that about anyone before although he had had lots of affairs and he asked me to marry him. I didn't know how I felt at all, but he looked so attractive and was so perfectly sweet saying he would live anywhere or do any-thing in the world. I had never had anyone love me with quite such an unselfish love before and it made me happy.

I said I couldn't become engaged to him and raised all sorts of objections about different nationalities and living in America which

I don't think I could do although I am half in love with him I believe, anyway we finally left it that we would discuss it later the whole thing rather frightened as well as surprised me, although I had half suspected it and knew he was in love with me before he did! I felt terribly nervy and Fife noticed at dinner and insisted on taking me home. He was most terribly upset and phoned the doctor. I went to bed and Doctor Buck came and talked to me calmingly and said I was alright, merely exhausted he gave me a sleeping draught and Nancy came and slept in the other bed.

October 15th 1936. Virginia.
Left with Fife still very concerned about 11.30. After Washington we stopped and discussed things, finally deciding that he should go back to Rio and that I should go out there, he kissed me two or three times, I don't know whether I love him or not. I wanted him to kiss me and I am very fond of him indeed.

I had known already that Fife – brother of Leith, my American godmother – had proposed to my mother. I also knew that he was very blond, which my mother had always found romantic. (When, at twenty-four, I had brought my blond boyfriend to meet my parents, my father declared later: 'Your mother's nearly having an orgasm over him!')

I had met Fife, then an elderly man, while staying at our cousin Peggie's. His blond hair was white and he had divorced the wife he had married after my mother turned him down. He had reminisced to me about my mother and seemed to still regard her in a romantic light.

Now, reading these bits of her twenty-two-year-old's diary, I found myself half-wishing that she *had* married Fife. Surely she would have been happier in America, near her cousins and Aunt Dita, who was more maternal than my grandmother? Aunt Dita, like my grandmother, was very generous; during the war she had insisted on opening her house in Long Island to over forty children from England, to escape the bombing.

In my experience, my mother was always extremely uncomfortable around small children, despite having had four. In this diary of 1936, however, she had written tenderly about Dita (then known as Deedie), who must have been about five.

October 21st, Westbury, Long Island.
I walked round the garden with Aunt Dita and Deedie, Deedie is really very sweet and Aunt Dita wasn't spoiling her a bit, in fact being quite stern I thought. Later Dita found a little toy car in the garden and all in one breath asked me how many gallons of gasoline I thought it would hold and then said she thought a fairy must have left it there!

This was Dita whom my mother had tried to attack with a walking stick in 1995.

The next day I was back at her old house. My mother was peaceful in her new home a few miles away but my stomach pains had started again and I felt overwhelmed by the tasks ahead. My brother had not come when we arranged, and I spent another day sorting, Mrs Anderson and Molly on one floor and me on another. In the late afternoon, as I was about to leave, Mrs Anderson and Molly came down from the attic with a large box. I opened it to find that it contained over thirty exercise books. My mother's handwritten diaries.

I placed them, with the bag of Luftwaffe passports, in the boot of my car and drove away.

Then an offer was made for my mother's house, by the first viewers. That night I had a dream – I was springing over snow at my childhood home, several yards high in the air. I bounced upright over fields and streams. I was leaving all that sludge behind me. That picturesque house, with its undercurrent of unhappiness, had had, for many years, an atmosphere of emptiness, of nothing much happening – and also a kind of brooding quality, something unpleasant waiting: my father's illness, his alarmingly quick death, Nicky's going downhill, my mother's drunkenly falling and breaking her limbs, her incoherent phone calls to me, her aggressive dogs – the last basset bit Mr Anderson in the arm, resulting in eighteen stitches.

But the house was full of books, most of which I had enjoyed at a young age – volumes of Proust, my father's Evelyn Waughs, Jessica Mitford's sophisticated memoir *Hons and Rebels*, Diana Holman-Hunt's charming and funny autobiography *My Grandmothers and I*.

However, a kind of disorientation persisted under the veneer of civilisation offered by these, and by other objects in the house – my mother's Spanish bulls, her palomino china horses, her watercolours of Venice. There was her wardrobe of elegant clothes: suits from the exclusive boutique Lachasse, two fur coats, evening dresses, one of peacock blue. There was her dressing table with lipsticks, scents and powder compacts (although my mother, in later years, wore little make-up) and the silver ashtrays, candlesticks and cigarette boxes in our cold blue dining room. My mother had a lovely garden, with ancient walls, an old moat with two little towers, yew hedges, lavender, white and red roses, peonies and delphiniums. It was even used in a children's TV film, *Tom's Midnight Garden*, and I'm sure many envied it. But inside the house, the piss-stained carpets and the endless supply of alcohol were indications of my mother's despair.

Now, at last, that place where she spent so much time drunk and unhappy was sold. And I had her diaries.

Part 2

Running on Stones

Chapter 6

July 1st 1914 I was born, 1915, my father was killed, during the war we were in London, Mum working in a canteen and in a hospital, all I remember is in the night being taken out of bed and carried down to the kitchen where I slept on the table. Mum feeding the dogs with biscuits but they refused to eat, sitting shivering with fright . . . me seeing a huge silvery grey shining object in the sky and being told it was a zeppelin.

Armistice Day. Buckingham Palace, the pram was squashed in two by the crowd. I sat on a man's shoulder. I remember the Royal Family on the balcony, and thinking that Princess Mary was waving to me especially, I remember the streets lined with flags, when the man put me down Mum asked me why I hadn't said thank you and I replied: 'I have not been introduced to him.'! My age was then 4.

The thrill of reading this almost gives me vertigo. Suddenly I'm looking down a magic kaleidoscope, I'm tasting the sweet centre of a honeycomb. This, at last, is my mother's life that I never knew. I did not remember her ever recounting these memories; perhaps she forgot them later. I felt privileged to read them.

The scraps, which she wrote aged sixteen, just after starting at Madame Boni's finishing school in October 1930, last for three pages and, as often with such very early memories, are not totally chronological. The little girl seems to have lived for a while with her Aunt Lin (one of my grandmother's sisters) in Sussex, about ten miles from Knowle. Lin's second son David, a few years older than Anne, wore *a dress of bluish-mauve silk: every evening we used to be dressed up and sent down to the drawing room. I was so shy I hated it; I used to look upon David as a hero. We ate porridge out of fascinating bowls in the nursery and David had a real Jaeger dressing-gown which I envied very much.*

Then, back to when Anne's brother was still alive: *Knowle – a tent in the grass where we used to have tea. Nah and my little brother Raymond in the tent.*

My mother never told me that she had any memories of Raymond. I knew only that, like my brother, he had died very young and Nah, who had looked after him, told me that he had never been able to sit up. Then the diary jumps forward, to my grandmother's wedding to Anne's stepfather. Anne, at five, is the only bridesmaid: *standing during the service near Grandma and Grandpa, carrying a bouquet of blue delphiniums, bigger almost than me, Grandma taking it from me and me sitting with them.*

I was glad that she had her grandparents' protection on what must have been a difficult day. By now, she is an only child again.

Driving from station in old Ford, always used to start on the 3rd crank, 3 was my lucky number. Raymond died aged 3, so made it unlucky, so changed it to 4 . . . Someone had told me that little boys were found in tulips, I always longed for a little brother, and I used to pray for one and go and look in the tulips every morning. I remember wondering why anyone ever died, why they didn't just keep on moving so that they couldn't.

When I read about her searching for a little brother, her own having died, I pity that little girl, almost against my will, for the first time. My mother and I, I realise with a shock, have a tragedy in common, the death of a brother when we were still so young ourselves. But I did not remember her ever commiserating with me directly over *my* brother Raymond's death. She always talked of him as *her* possession. It was her tragedy, hers exclusively. My father went along with this. It was sacrilege in our family to think otherwise.

Hearing about Grandpa's death driving along Frant Road. I was singing 'Oh Gin I were a baron's heir.' I said I would always keep that tune sacred to him.

She had told me this anecdote more than once, about her maternal grandfather Michael dying when she was six, almost boasting, it seemed to me, and I had cringed at her sentimentality. But now, when I read about it in her diary, it seems sincere.

Always loved getting to Knowle . . . Aunt Elisa gave me my ivory monkeys . . . Angela and Mollie in tam o'shanters, green and red . . . Hated when time came for them to go home.

Angela, two years older than Anne, lived across the road from Knowle with her parents, brothers and sisters. Angela's father had been a great friend of my grandfather. My grandmother, I knew, had encouraged Angela to be friends with Anne, clearly anxious that her only child should have a companion to play with.

The memories continue – my mother is handing me a beautiful, fragile thing, a fan full of colours like a peacock's tail – here is Nah, all in blue, on her first night at Knowle, by mistake putting the delighted child in the bath still in her *bedslippers*. Nah lends the little girl a woolly dog that she had bought for her nephew: *I loved it so much that she had to give it to me instead of the donkey brooch which she had got for me.*

Was this the beginning of Nah spoiling Anne, thus setting a pattern for life? It was certainly an example of the child attaching herself to possessions. Perhaps my grandmother was preoccupied with pleasing her second husband, supporting him in his army career, planning with him the Knowle gardens with their crazy paving, the row of white rose trees she nicknamed 'The Bridesmaids', choosing with him Italian urns, planting the apple orchard and the little box hedges leading to the swimming pool. Together they had designed the house's new wing with its green and white bathrooms, their huge tubs with feet like lions' claws. Maybe my grandmother, despite making a beautiful home and garden for Anne, did not spend enough time with her little daughter.

In 1922, Anne attends school at Camberley – her stepfather, Chow, is still in the army and must have been posted there – and he, Anne and her mother go home many weekends. (She writes, I noted with pleasure: *always loved getting to Knowle*.) In 1924, Chow is in another army posting, near a Roman camp. Anne recalls larks singing on the downs, and riding on those downs with Chow – perhaps she did sometimes enjoy being with her stepfather, whom she later clashed with. That year, aged ten, she goes to Palm Beach – this must have been when she stayed in America for nearly twelve months with Aunt Dita; I knew that Anne went to school there, as she'd recounted how she had had to swear allegiance to the Stars and Stripes each day at prayers. More memories now, of America: trips up the Loxahatchee, *Nah fell out of boat*, the American song *Swanee, Annie Laurie*, then, finally, back home in England: *Hope Cove, Susan ate all the biscuits. Angela and David frightening me about tidal waves . . . teasing me, escaping from them by running on stones – they couldn't run – then bursting out crying, just like a girl.*

This image, of the little girl, pluckily running on pebbles, then bursting out crying, seemed to sum up some of the disparate elements in my mother's character: her physical bravery and defiance but also her vulnerability and loneliness. And perhaps also that rueful comment – *just like a girl* – betrayed even then her ambivalence about being female.

And was not that secure sandy beach at Hope Cove, with the child's imagined threat of the tidal wave, more unsafe than it first appeared? For sometimes, even in the sheltered bay itself, I knew that there would be wild storms, and enormous waves would crash over the sea wall on to the road, hitting the harbour master's white thick-thatched house the other side. And the old lifeboat house, at the top of the slipway so close to the beach, was evidence that the lifeboat would often have to be launched at a moment's notice. Indeed, just beyond the Bolt Tail, so beautiful in June, with pink thrift springing up all over the grass, its red cliffs and blue-green silken sea beyond, was 'The Race', a dangerous current that my mother often spoke of, treacherous to boats. On my own holidays there as a child, my mother, despite loving Hope Cove itself, would talk darkly about Bantham, a few bays along, where she would take us at low tide to play in huge sandy pools and, when we were older, to surf. She warned us often of the dangerous undertow at Bantham and would announce, almost with relish: 'A whole troop of Boy Scouts was drowned there!'

One summer after my mother got Alzheimer's and could no longer come to Hope Cove, my own daughter and a fourteen-year-old schoolmate of my son's got into trouble while body-surfing. The girls had gone out too far and were in danger of not being able to swim back. I had already warned them, as my mother had me, about the undertow, and I remember my feeling of impotence, yelling at them to come in, all the time knowing that they couldn't hear my voice over the roaring waves. I understood then the undercurrent of fear that was always present in my mother. That little girl, bravely running on stones, was ostensibly in a landscape that appeared calm and safe but which had already – and would again – deliver terrible shocks. The teenage Anne knew of the fate of her Aunt Elisa; during her first few days at school in Rome in October 1930 she wrote in her diary of a cancelled excursion: *Madame Boni has discovered that Aunt Elisa was drowned at the place where the villa is, she is the only person ever to be drowned there, I am glad I am not going there now.*

Luckily, the girls were scooped out of the sea at Bantham by two lifeguards, but others in my family had not been so lucky.

When I tell friends and acquaintances that my mother has written over thirty diaries, eighteen of them about the six years of the Second World War, they express amazement. How wonderful! Did she write them every day? How did she manage it? To me, this feat is nothing special, since I too have been writing diaries, like her, from the age of fifteen, without knowing that my mother had done it before me. Maybe I am more her daughter than I had realised. What matters is that when I had thought it was too late, my mother has, unwittingly, thrown me a lifeline, linking herself to me.

I have no qualms about reading her diaries; not one has the word PRIVATE on its cover. Perhaps she did secretly want them to be read, even to be published. In that case, who more suitable than I, her only daughter, a diarist myself, to be their reader?

I feel that I have the right to scrutinise every word, perhaps because my mother has never communicated with me properly in person. I quickly discover that I feel so strongly about her diaries that I know I would fight for possession of them, I would try to rescue them from fire, I would barter my other things for them. Instinctively, I know how important they were for my mother, as important as my own diaries are for me. They are the one creation of her life that is really hers, the most personal thing, her true voice. And, unlike so many other aspects of her life, they haven't disintegrated.

I am soon convinced that, like me, my mother wanted to be a writer, but she was too shy to talk of it and did not have the willpower or confidence to persist. However, it took determination to write those entries nearly every single day of the war, besides doing a full-time job, often involving night duty. I find myself experiencing admiration, something new for me in connection with my mother.

When I visit her now at Camelot, I find a vague old woman in slippers, a semi-invalid who is given mushed-up food on a spoon. But in the diaries, I find a different person; first, a lively and mischievous girl, then, before and during the war, a vigorous and dynamic young woman. At first, in these new guises, my mother is a stranger to me, but steadily she walks towards me, becoming more and more visible as I immerse myself in her past, her inner life. I am aware that, had she not lost her mind, I would not be reading these diaries now. I would not be getting to know my mother.

There are twelve war diaries, then three written in Germany after the war in Europe ended. I find three after that, in lined school exercise books, then others written in America, from May 1946 till January 1947. But, to my disappointment, there are no diaries following these, none about how my mother met my father, nor their courtship, nor their wedding. And I can find only one about my early childhood in Spain. Dismayingly, this even starts in mid-sentence: . . . *flowers that smelled exactly like heather honey.* On its cover, inside a little frame of ivy leaves, my mother has written 'SPAIN Volume VI, Anne Segrave'. Unlike the other diaries, all with beige or black covers, this SPAIN diary is purple with a red border, and very long and narrow. This, seemingly my mother's only surviving written record of my very early childhood, at once seems sweet to me, like heather honey. But it turns out to have no entries about our life in Madrid. Instead, it begins on 26 August 1952, at Comillas, that seaside village in the north of Spain. I read that, instead of returning to Madrid after that summer holiday, on 9 September 1952 Raymond and I were put on a ship, *La Reina del Pacifico*, at Santander and sent back to England with Doreen, to stay at Knowle. My father was winding up his job as naval attaché and would return home after two months. I am so disappointed that I don't even read this diary right through. Where are the other five diaries about our lives in Madrid? Where are the diaries of 'the old days', when I was a little girl?

Although I am burning with curiosity about my mother's life as a young woman, I'm also apprehensive. Maybe this is why I don't delve at once into all her war diaries – those most representative of her adult life – and why I don't tackle them chronologically. Instead, I glance through different ones at random, fastening on certain sections. I'm almost reluctant to read them right through, for fear of what I'll find.

A few years ago, Molly told me that she had thrown away letters to my mother from a woman she had almost certainly had a love affair with after my father died. Molly said she was so shocked by the contents that she didn't want me or my brother to see them. What other secrets has my mother hidden?

Chapter 7

Iknew that Anne Veronica Hamilton-Grace was born on 1 July 1914, to Raymond Hamilton-Grace and Gladys Grace, distant cousins. Gladys, my grandmother, had longed for a son. She had told me without shame that when the nurse handed her her firstborn, she had looked at her baby girl and declared: 'Oh, I don't want *that*!'

I discover, with the diaries, a letter that Anne's father, an officer in the 13th Hussars, sent her from Flanders, for her first birthday.

June 29th 1915.

My dear daughter,

Very many happy returns of your birthday. May you grow up into just such a woman as your mother is, in this you will have a hard task for she is a perfect woman in every sense of the word. She is more beautiful than a wild rose, and more educable in character than any woman I have ever met or believe to exist. Still, you are lucky to have such a pattern.

You should be a strong healthy child too – children of a love match always are – I think there never was a match more concerted by love than in that of your parents. You will be lucky to have grown up in an atmosphere of love because the love of your parents will always last and you will be spared the sight of father and mother nagging at each other.

If you are wise you will see and learn how to create such a life for yourself in the future because it is the best that this world can give. First and foremost you must not be selfish and you must never say something that will hurt – for those things though forgotten always leave their mark. You must try to see the other's point of view and remember that the upbringing of your husband was probably quite different from yours and you must make allowances.

It is the little things in life which count – things that happen every day. Your mother much prefers that I should remember to write to her on every day and show that I have not forgotten her when I've been away for a day, than, say, once a year, I should give her a diamond necklace then forget her the other days. And when you are married do not forget that your husband will want to be petted sometimes and will want to see that you love him. He will not care to be the appendage of a beautiful successful hostess who is always too busy to talk and play with him. There is only one way to be happily married that is for you both to have the same aims in life, to be absolutely frank with each other, to respect each other and not to be ashamed of showing how you love each other. If you are not prepared for this then don't get married.

I have said 'the sermons' don't forget to have an aim in life people without them are always unhappy – besides which you have no business to help consume the world's produce and give nothing in return. As to religion for heavens sake don't parade it but if you work up to the idea of trying to make everyone a little happier because of your presence in this world you won't be far wrong.

Lastly as to your conduct and learning. If you follow the example of your mother you won't go wrong – don't forget you have the name of a very old family of which you may well be proud but don't be merely proud remember that it carries its responsibilities and to belong to an old family carries the responsibility of never staining its escutcheon. Others will judge you by your own estimate, so it will be well to have plenty of self-respect – but above all avoid being proud with nothing to be proud about. Let your motto be 'Play the game and make life for others happier by your presence.'

Goodnight and kiss your mother. I miss and love her very much for she went through a lot to give you to me.

Your affectionate father.

That was the only letter he ever wrote to her. Five weeks later, he was in action in France on his way to Dunkirk, when the soldier driving him drove into a farm cart. The soldier survived, but my grandfather, due home on leave for the birth of his son, died shortly afterwards.

My mother never talked to me directly about her father's death, nor had she shown me that letter. I did not even know where he was buried. But, just before my fortieth birthday, my daughter, then eight, had opened the drawer beside my bed and brought out an exercise book. It must have come to me from Knowle after my grandmother died, and was full of newspaper cuttings about the death of her husband. During the collision, one of the cart's shafts pierced my grandfather's ribs. He regained consciousness for two hours on the way to the hospital. His only son, named Raymond after him, was born five days later.

I look through the old photograph albums which also came to me from Knowle. On 15 July 1915, a fortnight after my mother's first birthday, two snaps taken in the garden at Knowle. My mother has written under them, much later, in her adult handwriting: *My Father's Last Leave*.

Everyone is sitting on the grass, including a white bull terrier. There is my grandmother, bare-headed, supporting Anne, a baby of twelve months, in a white dress and cardigan. My grandfather, in his soldier's uniform, is looking down at his little daughter. In the second photograph, the baby Anne is standing, in the same white dress and cardigan, but this time her father has one hand up (probably shielding his eyes from the sun) so that his face is hidden, turned away. He will never again be part of that little family.

In the next photograph, taken a year later, my grandmother, a young widow, is sitting with her two small children under a tree at Knowle. She is all in black, except for her white sun bonnet. Its ribbons hang charmingly down each side of her pretty face. My mother, now a little girl, also in a sun bonnet, is standing behind, her hands on her mother's shoulders, and there, on my grandmother's knee, is my mother's little brother, lying on his back, his puny legs bent in an odd position, a sort of rictus grin on his face. What was wrong with him? Everyone's dead who might have known. I remember again Nah saying that he never sat up, and I know that he died aged three. How pretty my grandmother is! But when I look closely, I see that her smile is fixed, like that of her disabled son. She is still mourning her beloved husband, and must be horribly aware that her son, who bears his name, and was born a few days after his father was killed, is not quite right. How much does my mother, nearly three, understand about all this? In this photograph she looks such a robust, happy little girl. Please let her go on being happy! I find myself wishing.

In earlier albums are photographs of Knowle, taken before my mother was born. There is my mother's father's sister, (Aunt Kathleen), with her high cheekbones and pear-shaped face, hands in a fur muff, standing with a distinguished-looking old man with thick white hair, outside what was once the front door. That old man must be Aunt K's father, my great-grandfather Sheffield Grace.

A wing was added to Knowle after Colonel Joseph Benskin – Chow – married my grandmother in 1919. Would she have led her life differently, more simply perhaps, if my grandfather had lived? I prefer the look of the old house without the extra wing, unfussy, as it was when she saw it as a bride in 1912.

Here are my two grandparents having breakfast together on the lawn outside the old front door. My grandmother has her hair in a single plait down her back and is in a long white dress. He is in his soldier's uniform. I recognise their little round table with the teapot on it. I have it in my flat in London.

Here is my grandfather again on the lawn, towering over his girl-wife, jokingly pushing his pipe into her mouth, both of them laughing. How happy they look!

There are even older albums, of Knole, as it was spelt then, in the 1900s. My grandfather Raymond and Aunt K were raised there and, judging from the theatre programmes pasted into the album, Aunt K acted in amateur theatricals at home and in the nearby village. There are photographs of picnics at Knole, even a snap of Aunt K as a young woman haymaking in the field near the house, with a woman friend called 'Bird', and others of horses, polo ponies belonging to my grand-father. I see that in those days there was a wide gravelled terrace along the top of the garden, where, twenty or so years later, my grandmother planted 'The Bridesmaids'.

In another album are photographs of my mother as a baby. The baby has a strong face and does not look happy, unlike photographs I have seen of myself at that age (also taken at Knowle), where I am usually smiling.

My mother's very first existing diary starts on 1 January 1930, when she is fifteen. She is an only child, living at Knowle with her mother and stepfather. Her life is that of a girl who has everything done for her, clothes washed and ironed by maids, stockings darned by Nah, a fire lit in her bedroom, meals cooked, beloved pets, horses to ride cared for by a groom. There's a beautiful garden with a croquet lawn, tennis court and swimming pool, there are walks in the woods, golf lessons, indoor and outdoor games, frequent holidays abroad, dances, even a car for her to drive when few cars were privately owned.

I am excited by the diaries' density, the hiddenness of a whole period of my mother's life – and, more importantly, her inner life – that I knew nothing about.

Jan 10th 1930. Knowle.
Went to Burdett-Coutts' dance, enjoyed myself tremendously. Danced every dance . . . Saw pretty girl with lovely green fan. Discovered she was Lady Ann Cole. Two disgusting snaly females horrified me, very bad types, Mum thought so too . . . Snaly Female's name was Kitty Duval, they live near Wadhurst. Another girl with that party Mum thought the most vulgar of the lot, I am sure I have seen her some-where before. I think it was on the boat going to America.

Jan 11th.·
Feet jolly sore after dance. Went hunting. Meet at Black Ham. Mum drove me there in the Austin, arrived late, saw Lady Ann again, she is staying with Miss Foster so is Lord Mulgrave who I danced with

last night. I am very taken with Lady Ann, must get to know her some time. Very good run, jumped lots of hedges, lots of people fell off. Looked up Lady Ann and Lord Mulgrave in the Peerage, she is the eldest daughter of the Earl of Enniskillen, her name is Ann Florence, she was born in 1910, so she must be nineteen or twenty, has two sisters, one born in 1914 the same year as me, her name is Frances Jane and the other in 1917. Their seat is Florence Court, Enniskillen, Co. Fermanagh, Northern Ireland, so she is Irish like I am, the old Peerage gives this as the seat of her grandfather who is now dead and their residence as Pettypool Hall, Sandway, Northwick, so I don't really know where they live.

I shall go to the meet instead on the chance that Lady Ann may be there again.

Jan 13th.
Lovely day for hunting, meet is at Park Corner somewhere near Groombridge, I do hope Lady Ann will be there but I doubt it, however I will soon see. Simply masses of trees have blown down in the night one fell right across the drive just missing Billy as he was walking home. One fell on the stables and one on the cow-sheds. Lady Ann was not at the meet, so I presume she has gone home. Had great fun in spite of this though it was a great disappointment, lots of jumps.

Jan 14th.
Golf Lesson today at Nevill. Was tired so did not play round after lesson, I drove home alone in the Austin, the first time I have driven alone except in Scotland, it was great fun. Saw Mrs Sprague who looked horrified at seeing me driving silly fool! Hang it all I am fifteen and a half. Golf with Angela great fun, saw Billy there, he seemed quite annoyed I called him Billy still I don't care. Lost one ball and two tees, drove one Angela lent me into the pond luckily it was a floater, Angela also drove one into the pond. We discussed the Burdett-Coutts' dance. Apparently she is gone on Mrs Freeman Thomas who was Maxine Forbes Robertson of the great acting family, a sister of Jean Forbes Robertson's, she was at school with Jill

and she has a glass eye, I didn't admire her at all. Personally, she didn't touch Lady Ann in my opinion, but a lot of people seemed to admire her. Anyway Angela liked Lady Ann too, she also hated the snaly females whose name is not Duval but De Valois, they are wards in Chancery so that partly explains why they behave as they do, no one looks after them, the other one is called Judy. What seems funny to me is that I heard one of them at the dance talking about her father, which is extremely odd if they really are wards in Chancery. Tonight Mum said she would like some false eyelashes and that she would then look like Lady Ann Cole, so that beastly Gig must have told her that I am in love with Lady Ann. Secrets are never kept in this house worst luck!!!! Today Mum suggested that I should join the dancing class at school, I think I will as I wish to dance well, in fact I wish to do everything well now in order to be able to when I next meet Lady Ann, for I am sure I will sometime, I can ride and play Tennis quite well, my golf is bad but I am trying to improve it, I can swim and play Croquet quite well too, and I am learning Bridge, but I certainly dance badly but that will be remedied by next winter. Mum suggested my taking a few Spanish lessons at the Berlitz School in preparation for our trip to Spain at Easter. I should simply love to do so. I am sick of the thought of returning to school, gosh won't it be boring, I want to go to more grown up dances where I meet people like Lady Ann, everything is too babyish.

Jan 16th.

Ha ha I should have been at school this morning. Thank goodness I am not anyhow. Apparently we are going to lunch with the Potters today. Had a very amusing time at the Potters, Lally and Joan are awfully nice and very amusing, they are coming to lunch here tomorrow and then going on to a Movie in Tunbridge Wells. They asked me to go too but dash it all I am playing golf with Henry Havard. Dash Henry I am sick of him. Have just heard from Miss Houghton she returns to the flat on Monday at 6.30pm, she is going to Chester, cheers and laughter!!!!!!!!! I shall write at once and ask her to get all knowledge possible about Lady Ann. On the way home I saw a grave-stone in a churchyard with what looked like Ann Cole on it, it gave me such a fright, it is a funny coincidence though, I must look next time I pass that way and see if it really was Ann Cole on it.

Jan 19th.
I can hardly believe that I go back to London tonight, worst luck . . . Have started writing a new story entitled 'Three's None' which is a sequel to 'Two's Company' that Noreen and I started writing together. We wondered what we were going to do this afternoon but the dogs settled that problem for us, Jerry and Polly went hunting and Nah, Gig, Mum and I went to look for them. I wandered all over the woods . . . It was lucky we got Jerry because he would have certainly come home with that lung trouble again and we could not have brought him up to London. I just hate being back in London again. Gosh won't school be boring? I can hardly bear the thought of it, in fact I am miserable, I simply must see Lady Ann again soon or I shall die. Never mind, the thought of her cheers me up I'll see her alright if I make up my mind to by Jingo, and I have made up my mind alright. Hurrah, I am quite cheered up already and so Goodnight!!!!!!

These passages revealed much about my mother as a teenage girl. As well as showing me her privileged life among the country gentry, it describes her fascination with a young woman she meets at a local dance. Lady Ann Cole, with her long eyelashes and lovely green fan, seems to have been the spur for Anne to start her first diary, and for me it is also the first indication of my mother's lifelong romantic interest in other women.

I wonder too about those snaly females. Was not fifteen-year-old Anne, who presumably had invented the adjective 'snaly' just for them, more interested in them than she admitted? On one hand was the nine-teen-year-old graceful and demure Lady Ann Cole, whose family was in *Debrett's*, and on the other were the snaly females, rumoured to be wards of Chancery, temptresses, serpents in the Garden of Eden. Even then, I believe, Anne's conventional side was at war with the experimental, sexual part of her nature. These De Valois girls did intrigue her. Anne's playmate Angela had also hated them, according to Anne's diary. The two snaly females do come across as more confident than the ladylike Ann Cole, who sounds shy and ethereal. Several of the women that my mother would later become interested in would display the self-assurance of those two. Lacking in confidence herself – certainly when I knew her, though not, it would appear, in these very early diaries – she seemed to need that quality in others.

After that dance, and indeed for many months, Anne romances about Lady Ann Cole and tries to see her again, enlisting the help of her Aunt K, who has a friend who knows the girl's mother, Lady Enniskillen. But Lady Enniskillen is rumoured to be a religious fanatic who attends an odd church called The Sanctuary behind Harrods and is therefore considered unapproachable. Anne also consults her Aunt Lin, who reports that Lady Enniskillen is in an asylum – *isn't that the absolute limit? She must have got hold of the wrong end of the stick.*

Anne also heard the *filthy news* from her old governess, Miss Houghton, that Lady Ann's grandfather was a *disreputable penniless Irish peer* who had done nothing for the county of Cheshire, where he lived most of the time. (My teenage mother then sensibly wrote in her diary that he could not have done much for Cheshire if penniless, adding that she didn't care about Lady Ann's relations, she loved her anyway. She had confided in her mother about Lady Ann's father and I was amused to read that my grandmother had said that she was sure she would have liked the penniless old roué.)

At fifteen, Anne attends Queen's Gate School in London as a day girl; my grandmother has a flat in Carlton House Terrace, 40 Belgrave Square being occupied by her widowed mother, Margarita, known by Anne as 'Grandmoods'. But that January of 1930, for no stated reason, my grandmother allows Anne to return five days late for the spring term – the girl even goes hunting on what should be her first day back. Still at Knowle, Anne plays badminton, has golf lessons, hunts and enjoys herself with her dog Jerry, her pet squirrels and her turtle doves.

And she has Nah and Gig to go for walks and play indoor games with, and indulge her. Back at school several days later, despite getting up at *the unearthly hour of night, cold dark awful UGH!!*, Anne appears to enjoy many aspects of it, not least the companionship of the other girls. She is pleased to be sitting next to Zoe, worried that Noreen is absent, and looking forward to the *Bandarlog*, a school activity involving amateur theatricals. She chucks blotting paper pellets in class and throws herself into the dancing lessons, despite admitting in the diary that she is by far the worst. However, after only a few days, she develops a sore throat and temperature and, on the doctor's advice, is again off school and back at Knowle. She then does not return to school for seventeen more days. The last few days, when she's better, she goes hunting with Will, the Knowle groom. Unfortunately her mare Kitty falls on her and injures her leg – resulting in another delay. She finally returns to school on 10 February, and is soon writing of how glad she is that her leg is better – now she can play in the school team in a lacrosse match. She still often dreams of her heroine – *I do want a green ostrich feather fan like Lady Ann's* and admits – *I never felt any attraction to any of the male sex . . . I only think of boys as friends and no more . . . in fact as a whole I utterly scorn men and boys. I suppose I am very odd and old fashioned or stupid but I can't make myself feel any different, I am sure I can love too, because I have always had love affairs, only with women, never men. Isn't it odd?*

It is clear from the innocent tone of this that Anne sees no reason to be ashamed of her attractions towards other girls. And indeed, because of her comparative isolation, she probably does not know that many girls of her age experience them.

She does, however, perceptively guess that her negative attitude to men may arise from her experiences of her stepfather: *I should hate always to live with one man, they're so boring and fussy, of course Chownie is the example I have of this, he drives me mad always, I can hardly bear to be in the same room with him sometimes and he has hurt my feelings dozens of times, once at a dinner party at Aunt Lin's, I shall never never forgive him for that.*

Again, I felt sorry for her never having known her own father. It was unlikely that she would have regarded him as boring and fussy. I knew from various cousins that Chow had been irascible, and my mother's former playmate Angela had told me that the young Anne felt constantly undermined by her stepfather's criticism. My grandmother once confided to me that she had hoped that her second husband and her daughter, both interested in the arts, would have that in common. But Anne, I realised, perceived her stepfather as controlling and harsh, and he could not get anywhere with her.

I have a photograph of little Anne at her mother's wedding to Chow, where she was the only bridesmaid. I showed it to my son when he was twelve. He looked carefully at the little girl in her white dress, with her artificially curled hair, glaring at the camera, then declared, with absolute conviction: 'Your mother was away from love.'

My mother, at only five, had lost her father and her little brother. She had then lost her mother to a stranger – a man.

Chapter 8

In April 1930, Anne holidays in France and Italy. She and her mother go from Dover to Calais on the Golden Arrow boat – the *Canterbury* – then, in France, meet up with my grandmother's sister Dita, Dita's husband Jay, and their daughter Peggie. All five of them then travel on the famous fast 'Train Bleu' to Cannes. There they lunch and bathe, and try to visit Grandmoods, who is renting a villa near Monte Carlo, but she is out. Later Anne's mother goes with her sister Dita to see their mother while Anne, Peggie and Anne's Uncle Jay explore the town.

That evening, my grandmother and Peggie, who puts a photograph of *a youth called Gordon Douglas* out each night in her hotel bedroom, try to get Anne into the casino at Monte Carlo. Anne, cross-questioned at the entrance about her age, pretends that she can't understand French. They bring an interpreter – *the game was up*. The doorman concedes that 'the young lady' can wait in a room alone, while the others go in and gamble. My grandmother, drawing herself up, declares: 'Do you think I would leave my young daughter alone at a casino in Monte Carlo?' and they leave, with much mirth. (Anne writes, presumably using an expression learned from her American relations, *Gee, we did have some fun this evening!*) They proceed to Genoa, then Pisa, then Florence, where they receive a telegram – Grandmoods has died suddenly of a heart attack. They return to her rented villa and Anne's Aunt Lin, her husband, Suirdale, and Chow arrive from England. It is decided that Grandmoods will be cremated in Golders Green and her ashes scattered on her husband Michael's grave in the churchyard

The Girl from Station X

at Battle. Anne is allowed to choose whether to return home for the cremation with her mother or to resume the Italian holiday with Aunt Dita, Uncle Jay and Peggie. (I imagine that Dita did not go to her mother's cremation because, Peggie told me, her mother was always mean to her.) Not surprisingly, Anne chooses Italy. She does, however, write in the diary that she is upset by her grandmother's death, and by the idea of her household and staff being disbanded. She begins to feel ill and her mother tells her that she can still go home if she wishes. Then, before her mother leaves with Chow, Lin and Lin's husband, she tells Anne that she need never return to Queen's Gate School.

I am furious when I read this. What did my grandmother think that she was doing? The diary had made it clear that Anne was doing well at the school, both in her lessons and at games, and had made several friends. Perhaps it actually suited my grandmother *not* to have her at school; maybe the practicalities of having the child stay up in London five days a week were inconvenient. Or possibly, like many women of her era, for whom marriage for a daughter was the ultimate aim, she simply did not see the point of Anne having any academic qualifications. Even so, the casualness with which she delivered the news to Anne of her schooldays being truncated must have given the girl a skewed notion of commitment. Here is Anne's diary again after Grandmoods' death:

May 14th 1930. Rome.
Peggie's very nice to me, I like her awfully. I had a letter from Mum, Yvonne and Nah today, Will has mumps, apparently he was quite ill and Frank [the chauffeur] *and all the children have it. Nah is in quarantine for them. The baby rabbit died and Jerry has bitten lots of people and it is very cold. I heard today that a bomb big enough to blow the whole building to pieces was found concealed in a lavatory in the Casino at Monte Carlo with a fuse to it, it must have been there when we were there, it is supposed to be someone inside the building who has done it as no one is allowed to go in with any sort of package and six men have been arrested, it is rather thrilling considering*

we were there such a short time ago and it might have been blown up while we were there and our hotel was within a few yards of the Casino.

May 17th. Knowle. We had a lovely crossing and arrived at Folkestone at a quarter to nine, they were very good at the customs and opened nothing. The car met us and we arrived home at 10.45, pretty good I think. I miss everyone awfully, especially Peggie as she was so awfully nice to me. The garden is lovely, it is being opened to the public on Wednesday next. I am going in twice a week to Italian Lessons in Tunbridge Wells and a French woman is coming out twice a week to talk French to me, rather more work than I anticipated still never mind, we are meeting Miss Houghton in London next Monday, what a pity. Everyone is well here which is good, no mumps in the house thank Goodness and the weather is quite warm.

Anne, no longer obliged to study with her peers, spends an enjoyable summer with tennis lessons, tennis tournaments, swimming in the Knowle pool, walks in the woods and excursions to London to buy hats and to see the Trooping of the Colour – and does some lessons with her governess. But what of the school friends Anne has left behind, with whom she still exchanges letters? Did her mother not realise that these friendships were important, particularly for an only child? Having Angela, who was two years older, come over to play at Knowle was not the same for Anne as spending hours each day in class with other girls. I was sure that this rash decision of my grandmother's to remove Anne from school had helped sow the seeds that made my mother feel so often that she was a special case, that she was exempt from the boring duties of life, that she did not have to muck in.

On her return from that holiday with her American relations, she misses her older cousin.

May 18th. I <u>do</u> miss Peggie so much I think she was awfully nice to me considering I am seven years younger than she is, she must consider *me a mere babe, I adore her and I would do anything for her and all I have succeeded in doing is forgetting to bring her statues home, oh dear life is really too hard. My silver pencil is lost, I hope we find it soon.*

The American relations seemed to be always changing their plans:

May 22nd. I don't know where Aunt Dita is or anything, Uncle Jay is supposed to be sailing on the 24th, heaven only knows if he is or not. Jerry killed a large mouse this evening. Mum comes home tomorrow anyhow and I shall know everything then thank goodness. I think I shall go up early on Monday and have my hair permanently waved and buy a hat.

May 24th. Mum has heard from Aunt Dita, she arrives at the Ritz tomorrow. I am having my hair permanently waved for the first time next Monday, I am thrilled about it. We are going to the Trooping of the Colour Tuesday week Admiral Rushton has sent us 3 tickets for his room at the Admiralty, it ought to be rather fun, I went last year and sat in the Horse Guards Balcony.

May 25th. We played Tennis most of the day and Billy came to lunch . . . This morning I was going to drive the car to take Aunt Kathleen to church but unfortunately we met that damned Martinet Chownie in the stable yard and he wouldn't let me go, he is a fool, and Clancy contradicted me when I said that people under age could get a driving licence by passing a test, he is a fool too. Aunt Dita is not arriving in London now until Monday.

I noted the entry about Anne's conflict with her stepfather. She does appear self-willed, and a bit spoilt, but does not actually get her own way.

May 26th.
I went up to London on the 9.50 today and was 10 minutes late

for the Hairdresser's appointment, I had a man called Mr John and a woman. First of all they washed my hair and dried it, then they twisted it into long things and tied it with string, then they twisted it up in blue papers which smelt of ammonia, this process hurt most terribly, it was agony and I felt like screaming with pain, after that they fixed the papers to a machine and steamed it for 5 or 6 minutes and then the papers and ******* were taken off and the hair washed again dried and set, it was rather a hateful process really but well worth the trouble as the hair looks very nice.

Mum rang up to say would I like to spend the night at the flat and see Aunt Dita, but I said no as I shouldn't see much of her, and she would be tired after the journey and my dear Peggie wouldn't be there anyway and I am glad to be away from Chownie too as I hate the blinking Martinet, I don't think Peggie likes him at all either I am sure she thinks him a perfect fool by the way she behaves, I don't know if Aunt Dita likes him or not, I don't think she does much, Uncle Jay is indifferent I think. I am going to back Lansdowne in the Derby if it runs as I landed on that with a pin 3 times tonight.

May 27th. Mr Mears gave me the tip of 'Knight of Lorn' for the Derby, I am going to back that, Lansdowne and Ballyferis all 'To Win'. My French Lady came today, I did not see her but Mr Mears says she is old but very nice, quite a different type to 'Inkey'. I wrote to Noreen telling her to send me the books I want from school. Mr Mears played Tennis with me and Miss H this afternoon.

Mr Mears, I gathered, was the Knowle butler then. I noticed that Anne's 'playmates' were now Mr Mears and Miss Houghton, her governess, instead of her teenage contemporaries who were still at Queen's Gate School.

May 28th. Noreen rang me up tonight, Gwyneth has got measles, Zoe is coming down to her Grandmother's two weekends after half term and lots of people are asking when I am coming back. I wonder if

Aunt Dita will come down here, I <u>do</u> hope she does. I rode again this morning. I think I have found the Turtle Dove's nest, it is in one of those two firs on the drive where the white gate used to be, we found a sweet little nest in the broomy field. I am sending five Doves to London, and I am trying to mate Micky with Boy Blue. Miss H has calmly ordered the car to take her to the Station and to meet her in the evening, she has <u>no</u> business to order <u>our</u> car to meet her whenever she wants, the bus is quite good enough for her. We saw a fox quite close this afternoon. I wish Peggie would come down and stay with us here but I am afraid she won't.

Anne here again seems spoilt and unpleasantly stuck up in her remark about Miss H and the car. I could not help thinking once more that she should have stayed at that school.

May 29th. Miss H left for London this morning and returned this evening + 13 shillings for doves. I sunbathed this morning and swam in the pool, the water was much warmer than I thought it would be. I played Tennis with Mr Mears this afternoon and played disgracefully. Knight of Lorn is scratched from the Derby, so I shall back Ballyferis 2/- to win.

May 30th. Mum came home last night, Glorious news!! Aunt Dita and Peggie are meeting us at 3 Bridges this morning if it is fine, we are going to see dogs and have a picnic lunch and then go on to Leonard's Lee, won't it be just too glorious, I <u>do</u> hope it doesn't rain, it has been nearly all day. Aunt Dita may come on here afterwards but Peggie leaves for Ireland tonight, she didn't go to Germany after all. I don't know whether Uncle Jay is coming tomorrow or not, I hope not though I do like him but men are always in the way, they are so stupid . . . Uncle Jay sails on Saturday but Aunt Dita is staying on to be near Peggie. I learnt the truth about her and Gordon today, here it is:– Gordon is younger than her and Peggie herself is <u>not</u> in love with him but she is bored and all her friends are married so she says if she *doesn't fall in love with somebody she will marry Gordon, of course it would be a great mistake to marry him it obviously wouldn't be a success, so I am glad she has gone to Ireland otherwise she might have gone straight back and married him. I think she's being too silly, it would be madness to marry anyone she's not in love with marriage is enough of a gamble even if you are in love with the man I think, so I hope she gives up the idea. Aunt Kata* [Anne's Peruvian godmother, mother of Meg] *has sent the most lovely green silk shawl, she really is most awfully nice to me and is always giving me the most lovely presents.*

In late June, Anne was deprived of her little dog. He had been missing all night after running off to chase rabbits in the Knowle woods. *Could not write before, too upset. Jerry is dead he was found the next day but died after, I pray to God that he is free of all pain now and happy but I am miserable.* She was so unhappy that she had not written her diary for eleven days. I felt very sorry for her when I read this. I had loved my own dog, given to me shortly after Raymond died. Jerry's death just before Anne's sixteenth birthday, and her reaction, made me remorseful over my dismissive attitude to each of the deaths of her three basset hounds when she was old. When the first one died, a strange patch shaped like an ugly flower appeared on my right breast, long before I had breast cancer, which my GP said was due to 'stress'. I had guessed even then that it sprang from empathy with my mother. I had tried to brush aside her anguish about the dog, but my body had stubbornly reflected it. Again, I was closer to her, in certain ways, than I wished to be. But this was not acknowledged by either of us.

On 1 July 1930, Anne celebrated her sixteenth birthday at Hope Cove with her mother, Nah, Gig and Angela. Her mother gave her a long evening dress. However, Anne was more interested in another type of apparel:

two girls went on the cliffs dressed in long white trousers, everyone was shocked. When they saw everyone staring they ran for shelter to a hedge and once behind it ran on till they reached the garden of 'the Hope Cove Hotel', we saw them bathing, the smaller one has a very nice figure and wears a silver cap in the sea, we watch for them every day now. We could not make out who they were, we thought of Chorus Girls, Typists and Oxford Students . . . but have now decided that they are the proprietor's daughters. We saw them go out with two young men one night. When we moved their bathing wraps out of reach of the incoming tide the youngest did not even say 'Thank you' which I think was very rude.

I just long to have a beach suit now, like 'The Trouser Girls' were wearing, they looked awfully smart.

The errant females, in their modern get-up, represented the emancipation that Anne would not experience herself for several years.

In August 1930, Anne was treated to another holiday, on Brioni, a fashionable island on the Adriatic side of Italy which was later taken over by Tito and used as his summer residence. On Brioni, Anne developed another crush, on Mary, an American girl staying at the hotel with her sister. Mary sounds similar to Lady Ann – delicate and faun-like. Lady Ann's fan and ostrich feather were green and Mary's eyes were *greeny hazel flecked with brown very expressive, always looked rather sorrowful.*

Anne seems to have fallen head-over-heels for Mary, but only after Mary left – she had never actually spoken to her. *Oh dear I am so upset, my darling little American girl really has gone . . . I do want my Mary.* She went on to describe Mary in great detail, from memory:

very daintily made, eyebrows small thin but unplucked, eyelashes rather long, nose longish and straight, a well shaped small pretty little mouth, pretty teeth and a pretty smile . . . quiet and inconspicuous. Her hair was done in a small bun fairly low down behind with curly bits coming over her ears . . . It was her smallness and delicateness that made her so attractive with a small dainty face and pretty *expression and she <u>must</u> be nice as she helped Lena* [a friend of both my mother and grandmother] *oil her back without being asked to do it. Her colouring was rather pale though sunburned to a charming colour. I loved her so much I <u>do</u> wish she hadn't gone.*

Anne rhapsodised about Mary's clothes: *a black lace dress with which she wore longish diamond earrings and a diamond necklace, a yellow chiffon evening dress, a pink afternoon dress and a green Jantsein bathing suit with low back and dark green trousers (all in one) and white painted on belt and a green cap to match, besides beach suits.*

An hour or so after Mary's departure, Anne searched her empty cabin – *all I found was remains of Olio di Noce and 2 cigarette ends, I examined them.*

This action, which to others might seem pathetic, came across to me as frighteningly predatory, in the light of other disturbing things that I half-knew about my mother and her secret longings for members of her own sex. And indeed, the sixteen-year-old admitted: *it <u>is</u> funny how I have absolute passions for people I have never even spoken to and I feel <u>so</u> miserable when they leave.*

That same morning at Brioni, a young man broke his neck by diving into two feet of water. The diary's reaction seems a bit callous – Anne writes more than once that she cannot understand why he had dived just there and expresses irritation that an American guest, who didn't know him, wept on the hotel housekeeper's shoulder. However, the details that she records – the man *limp and unconscious . . . bleeding . . . I felt sick* (her stepfather helped wash him before he was taken away; later they heard that he had died) – imply that the incident made more of an impression on her than she admitted. Certainly, she often told me this story and warned me against ever diving without first checking the water's depth.

Anne's long summer holiday continued. In late August 1930 – bemoaning her departure from *darling Brioni* – she and her mother and Chow travelled to Ireland, to the coming of age of John McGillycuddy in County Kerry. This was the John who, for many years when I was a child and adolescent, would stay at 40 Belgrave Square while working for Schweppes – his wife was in Ireland running his inherited estate.

After that, Anne and her mother and Chow proceeded to the Highlands to fish; Aunt K, then Angela from Sussex, joined them. Here is my mother, aged sixteen, in September 1930, five months after being taken away from Queen's Gate School, writing about herself during that long fishing holiday:

September 1st 1930.
Angela beat me 21–15 in the Ping Pong Tournament, I got in an awful temper and was beastly to everyone especially her, I felt miserable and I knew how badly I was behaving too and yet I was too proud to show that I was wrong and had to wait till the others approached me first, I really have <u>the</u> most loathsome character, I can't think why anyone likes me at all . . . I am spoilt that is the truth of it, thoroughly spoilt and selfish only thinking of self self self all the time and how badly treated I am and how I hate everyone else, I can see all this bad in myself and yet I make no effort whatsoever to stop it and behave better.

There is no more mention in the diary of American Mary.

Chapter 9

In October 1930, Anne's first term began at Madame Boni's finishing school in Rome; these establishments, where girls from privileged families would learn languages and be given a background of art and culture, were a rite of passage.

At Madame Boni's Anne was kept busy getting to know the other girls, studying Italian and French, and going on outings, cultural and otherwise. She and fellow pupils shopped for presents for a classmate's birthday, thereby learning the Italian words for 'address book' and 'silk'. They strolled in the Borghese Gardens and were taken picnicking to Ostia, the ancient part of Rome, where Anne was particularly fascinated by the remains of Turkish baths with their heating apparatus. In the evenings she romanced about a pretty woman and her husband whom she and her two roommates could see from their window:

October 18th. 1930. Madame Boni's, Rome.
Last night we had great fun, it started by my seeing a quite nice looking Italian officer looking pensively out of a window opposite, presently we saw he was joined by a girl of perhaps 20 or so, with fair hair and a fair skin, small, about the size of Peggie with a very pretty slight figure, she was rather pretty as far as we could see and looked rather American, certainly not Italian, they talked together and then went in, of course we were thrilled scenting a romance at once, she came and looked out of the window several times, she was biting her fingers and looked extremely worried, she had a ring with some blue stone, I think it was a sapphire and diamond ring on the fourth finger

of her left hand, she wore a tweed dress with hat to match. We can see a bedroom with two beds in it and we saw her unpacking assisted by a maid and patting down the beds in a most professional style, another room we believe to be the dining room and third on the left a sitting room. I can see both the dining and bedroom from my bed. They are really rather exciting, we think they arrived last night and that they had a terrific love affair and married against the will of their parents and this is the beginning of their married life, she is either English or American we think.

October 24th 1930. Madame Boni's.
I saw the young American wife opposite last night, she was staring out on the street in the same terribly melancholy and unhappy worried way that she always does, she was dressed in black. I am <u>sure</u> that they are very unhappy she always looks as though she were going to cry any minute and at the Tennis he was sitting on a seat with the little American, I know <u>not</u> his wife. No: I am now sure she is sorry that she married a foreigner and he is sorry too.

Anne obviously enjoyed these speculations, usually about young women she hardly knew, and making up stories about them. There was that earlier reference in her diary of January 1930 to a story that she had composed with her schoolfriend Noreen. She had also written a play called *The House Party* – my grandmother had made some suggestions for the plot.

And in Rome Anne's curiosity about other worlds meant that she was not satisfied with mixing only with her English and American fellow pupils. She quickly expressed in the diary a longing to meet some young Italians and, at the riding school, she made friends with Minervina, a half-Italian Catholic girl of her own age who led a protected life.

November 19th 1930.
I had a long discussion with her on religion. She told me that the Catholics believed in hell, purgatory and Paradise and that if you

84

committed a mortal sin such as murder or not going to church when
you ought to (This is really one!) you went to hell and once there you
could <u>never</u> get out. (God, what a thought, I don't believe there could
be a God like that, I said so and she said yes, He was just.) She also
believes that her sins are absolutely forgiven after she has confessed
and she feels very light hearted afterwards. I asked her what you said
at confession and she said Oh things like 'I have been disobedient' . . .
I'm sure she wants me to become a Catholic but not for me, how could
I believe in a God who sent one to hell for ever and ever? It is entirely
against my ideas of God. She advised me that if I married a Catholic
to study the Catholic religion and then change if I like it better, and
stay my own if I preferred it. Her mother was Protestant and became
Catholic. She tried to impress upon me that sins really were forgiven
if you confessed them because you feel so happy afterwards; perhaps
they are, if you believe. I don't know.

My mother would have been brought up a Catholic if her Irish
grandfather Michael had not lapsed. I was impressed by the way she
was thinking for herself. Her curiosity about other religions was evidence of an enquiring mind.

She also seemed to enjoy wholeheartedly the Italian culture and history she was introduced to at Madame Boni's. The girls were taken to
the opera, and to Venice and Florence, where Anne enthused about the
Medici collection: *vases, pots of precious stones inlaid with enormous*
pearls, emeralds, rubies etc. Tables of mosaic with pearls inlaid, little
animals made of pearl and precious stones, the richness and marvel-
lous workmanship of the whole collection is indescribable, suffice it
to say that I was simply astounded by it all.

I was struck by this passage, which showed the sixteen-year-old
responding to art treasures with sensitivity and intelligence. I feared
that my grandmother would not have been able to relate to this side
of her daughter, and I was annoyed on my mother's behalf when I
read how Madame Boni told Anne that she and Libby, an American
pupil, acted 'younger' than the other girls. It seemed to me that Anne,

intellectually at least, was more advanced than some of her classmates, who, by the sound of it, were more inspired by boys and clothes than by history and art.

The teenage Anne was not only interested in ancient history. She longed to get a proper view of Italy's Fascist leader. She had observed Mussolini from a distance – once with her fellow pupils at the opera, then at La Coppa di Mussolini, an equestrian event. A year after leaving Madame Boni's, her wish was granted. In April 1932, she and my grandmother, on yet another Italian holiday, were staying at the Excelsior Hotel in Rome, where Mussolini was giving a dinner for Franz von Papen, the conservative and monarchist German politician who two months later would be made Chancellor of Germany. A whole portion of the hotel was barricaded off, guarded by *fascisti in plain clothes.* Anne eagerly asked two waiters and a concierge if she could see Mussolini but they, and her mother, told her it was impossible. She then approached the hotel manager, who said yes – *I took Mum as well and we and three Italian people were taken round behind the kitchens and saw him quite plainly through the glass doors at the banquet, he looked rather fat and had a very determined face . . . It was very thrilling, seeing him as close as that. It is not often one sees him at all, especially foreigners like us.*

I couldn't help being impressed that my mother, who could be very shy – she always pushed me in front of her if we had to go into a room full of strangers – had overcome her timidity on that occasion. The girl's determination was that of a journalist getting a scoop. At only seventeen, she had an awareness of history in the making.

In October 1931, she had been sent to another finishing school, Ozanne's, in Paris. Anne went reluctantly to this new one, fearing that she would not like it as much as she had Madame Boni's. Just before setting off, she wrote:

my last day in England till Christmas, going to speak and hear French all the time, study till I am nearly dead and live shut in with no air and no exercise and with society girls who have no interests other than

boys, balls and clothes, what a prospect! Angela, Carla [the Italian
girl my grandmother had found to spend the summer with Anne] *and
I were so happy together, now it is over I realise what fun we had
but nothing happy can last for long. My dream now is that we three
should all meet in Rome at Easter, it would be heavenly.*

It is clear from this passage that Anne did not regard herself as a
'society' girl. Although she had loved her time in Italy, she also enjoyed
English country life and regarded herself as something of a free spirit,
finding the idea of being encouraged to be 'genteel' at the Paris finishing school restricting. She was not going to make an effort at Ozanne's.
After only five days, she wrote: *I don't like it here, whatever I do I must
try and persuade Mum to let me leave at the end of this term.*

Almost at once, my grandmother dashed over to Paris with Gig and
took her daughter on various pleasure outings – Versailles, the Bois de
Boulogne, the opera and a dress show, culminating with two nights in
my grandmother's hotel – all, presumably, while Anne was supposed to
be doing her lessons. I felt sorry for the two Ozanne sisters running the
school; my grandmother was undermining them by letting her insub-
ordinate daughter get her own way.

But despite her mother's efforts to convince her of the delights
of Paris, Anne did get her way. Her wilful obstinacy, and my
grandmother's compliance, gave me an insight into their relationship
for, on 12 December 1931, after only two months there, Anne was
allowed to leave Ozanne's and return to England. It was a mistake,
which she soon realised, for she wrote in her diary of the possibility
of going to America with her mother in January: *nothing is decided
yet. I should love to go in one way and in another I want to go back to
the Os'.* It seems from this that Anne was in need of an adult to impose
structure in her life. Gig, unlike Nah, had sent Anne a firm letter while
she was still at Ozanne's, advising her to stick it out, saying that she
would be glad in the long run. But my grandmother was not one to
enforce discipline and, in addition, Anne had terrified her mother by
having a fainting fit and several high temperatures while at the school.

Once again I lamented, as Anne often did herself, the early death of her father; I was sure that he would have been firmer, and he had certainly had more experience of normal life and its obligations to pass on to his daughter than her mother had. I thought again of his letter to her for her first birthday.

My grandmother indulged her only daughter. Anne was sent to Paris again the following spring – this time with Nah – to live in a hotel. A French governess came daily and Anne spent her leisure time with Vivienne Worms, a girl of her own age, half-English and half-French, whose English mother my grandmother knew. The girls enjoyed themselves riding, chatting, playing with Vivienne's family dogs, shopping, and going to films or to the opera, where Anne heard the famous Russian bass Chaliapin singing the role of Prince Galitzky in *Prince Igor*.

That April of 1932, while staying in the Imperial Hotel in Paris with Nah, Anne again started fantasising about a young woman, this time a fellow hotel guest, Contessa Oddone di Felleto. She and Nah examined with a torch the shoes left outside the Contessa's door for cleaning. The hotel manager then told them that she was a widow of a much older husband, and would often spend five weeks at a time enjoying herself in Paris.

April 29th 1932. Hotel Imperial. Paris.
I saw her again today on the steps of the hotel dressed in a green shirt and hat and black short fur coat rather made up, she looked as though she had fair hair and blue eyes.

I noted that the young women who fascinated Anne were small, like my grandmother, and had her colouring. Perhaps a psychoanalyst would say that her attraction towards them stemmed from her not having had enough attention from her mother as a very small child; Gladys, grieving for Anne's father, and perhaps for her infant son, had, when her daughter was five and needed her mother most, deserted her and gone abroad, to work in Sicily for the Mesopotamia Comforts

Fund, a humanitarian relief effort for civilian victims of the First World War.

After the Contessa left Paris, in an uncanny repeat of her behaviour on Brioni in August 1930, Anne managed to get into the young woman's vacated room. There, consumed with curiosity, she held up a piece of blotting paper with her writing on to the mirror to see if she could decipher what she had written, and pocketed a photograph of the Contessa that she had left behind.

Reading about my mother's early life was, for me, a look into a grand, now somewhat unreal era. Those who passed through the lives of her and my grandmother sounded like characters from a novel by Henry James: Princess Bibesco (daughter of Henry Asquith, former prime minister of England, who acquired her title when she married a Romanian diplomat); Contessa Suardi Patrizzi; Degna Marconi, daughter of the inventor of the commercial radio and telegraph system; aristocrats such as Lord and Lady Goschen, Lord Cavan, Lord Mulgrave and, of course, Lady Ann Cole and her mother, Lady Enniskillen. I assumed that my grandmother, who always maintained that she was basically middle class like her father, knew these aristocrats as a result of his social ambition, and because, through his hard work, she and her sisters were heiresses. My grandmother was also pretty and lively and, despite having been shy as a girl, had, my mother told me, later been dubbed 'The Asp' because of her quick, sometimes malicious, wit.

I had had a glimpse into this old-fashioned grand world during my own childhood, when I was taken every so often to 40 Belgrave Square. It was a mark of my great-grandfather's social ambition that he had taken such a house on a hundred-year lease, for Belgrave Square (laid out by Thomas Cubitt for the 2nd Earl of Grosvenor and constructed in the 1820s) was one of the grandest squares in London, occupied mainly by aristocrats. Number 40 became my great-grandfather's London house and the imposing Battle Abbey, also rented, was his country residence.

My main memory of that Belgrave Square house is of soot. I don't think it was ever cleaned. On the front hall floor was a mosaic of

Medusa's head, serpents weaving in and out. In the little sitting room were two brocade sofas, one dark gold, the other royal blue, and a bookcase full of old books, many about South America, where my great-grandfather had made his fortune. (My mother was furious when her mother later sold those books in a job lot without consulting her.)

On the dining-room walls were deer heads with antlers. A white linen tablecloth was always on the table. On the sideboard were little bottles of Schweppes orange juice with an odd metallic taste supplied by John, the family friend from Ireland who used to stay there while working for Schweppes in London, as a thank-you for my grandmother's hospitality.

Also in the dining room were two gloomy pictures, one of Highland cattle under a dark sky and another of a shipwreck. Underneath was written: 'The Sea is His and He made it.'

The house had six floors and most of its rooms were unoccupied. On the first floor was a ballroom, with an old sedan chair. Dances were still given there occasionally for young female relations.

Above was my grandmother's bedroom, which had been her mother's, with pretty painted green furniture and a bowl of false fruit. I had loved touching the cloudy purple grapes and the gleaming glass orange. Below the attic where maids had once slept were two adjoining bedrooms, for my parents and me, whenever we visited London. I used to love gazing at two paintings in my parents' room, one of a shepherd boy lying on his back in moonlight, another of a hare under a full moon. I had seen these two again in that stable flat at my mother's.

My high old bed at number 40 was brass, the wallpaper of garlanded pink roses. On the wall was a long tinted photograph of a cormorant on the bank of a river in Florida. I used to stare at it and imagine what it was like up that river.

In the basement was a bad-tempered old Scottish cook, Eva, and white-haired Bessie, her hair done up in a bun, in the traditional maid's costume of black and white. At full moon Bessie talked to herself in different voices. I would lie in bed hearing her close the curtains next door. The voices were just too low for me to hear what they said. If

90

Bessie was interrupted, she would stop at once and address whoever it was in her normal voice.

The ghost of my great-grandmother Margarita was supposed to have been glimpsed standing outside her old bedroom so, if I was alone, I would always rush past, bounding up the huge staircase with its mahogany banisters three steps at a time.

My mother recalled Grandmoods as a 'fun' old lady who stuck out her tongue at policemen from her carriage in Park Lane and at Christmas would always bite her liqueur chocolate in half so that the liquid shot out, despite everyone at the table shouting 'Stop!' My grandmother, however, found her mother a fusspot and said she had 'hated' her South American women friends, who 'ate sweet cakes and chattered like birds'. There was one called Paca she detested; Paca was always sticking her finger down my grandmother's throat and saying: 'The child's not warm enough.'

This old-fashioned world was part of my mother's heritage. Then there was her lifelong romance with Russia, which may have started when she went with her French governess to hear Chaliapin sing:

May 23rd 1932, Paris.
'Prince Igor' was really wonderful with Chaliapin in the part of Prince Galitzky, the place was crowded with Russians . . . Russian is rather a fascinating language, it sounds like a mixture between Italian and English . . . 'With a Smile you can get anywhere' is my new motto, it is especially so out here on the continent, people will do anything for you if you are amiable and pleasant and it is quite natural too. Nah was saying to Mademoiselle that I always get all I wanted like that and she said, 'Yes, I can quite believe it'.

Anne had missed the sarcasm in that remark. She had just written grandly in her diary: *I am accustomed to doing what I like.*

It was a Russian who had assassinated Doumer, the President of France, shortly before this, on 6 May 1932. Anne wrote excitedly of attending the President's funeral procession in Paris, of how she and

Mademoiselle had fought their way through the crowds to the first floor of a house in the Rue Souffroie, from where they watched the procession, which included the Prince of Wales – the future Edward VIII – *walking between the Duke of Aosta and Prince Paul of Serbia, he looked very small and insignificant, his busby made him look even smaller.* Women fainted and children screamed and the only people who kept their heads, Anne wrote, were the English Boy Scouts. Despite the assassin having been Russian – she wrote that she would have been deeply ashamed had he been English – her fascination with Russia continued, and that summer, at a dance near Knowle, she met her favourite dancing partner of the whole evening – Prince Serge, a Russian, *tall and fair with a kind smiling face. He told me he had only escaped from Russia in 1920, he has no money now.*

This obsession with Russians would sometimes cloud my mother's judgement later in life. (Four months later, Paul Gurvulov, the disturbed Russian assassin of the French President, was guillotined.)

At the end of May 1932 Anne left Paris, to continue her life of pleasure – not unusual for girls of that background. In the years before and after her nineteenth birthday – celebrated by a coming-out ball in July 1933 – Anne and her mother, sometimes accompanied by Chow, travelled to Cap d'Antibes, Portugal, Palm Beach, the Caribbean on a cruise, Switzerland and Austria to ski, and to Budapest the month that George V died.

I had known that my grandmother and mother had travelled, but had had no idea of the extent of it. It was almost like reading about the lives of strangers, it seemed so exotic. Besides travel, Anne had beloved pets, sporting and cultural activities, indoor games and a cast of playmates and relations. It would be easy to assume that the girl – well off, clever, athletic, good-looking and interested in so many aspects of life – had a golden future. But perhaps there was already something lacking. Was such a hedonistic existence suitable for someone with her nervous, volatile temperament and lively mind?

I found myself wondering what her life would have been like if her father had lived. After all, he had said in that letter for Anne's first birthday: '*don't forget to have an aim in life people without them are always unhappy – besides which you have no business to help consume the world's produce and give nothing in return*'. And Aunt K, his sister, had managed Knowle for her widowed father when she was only eighteen, whereas my grandmother was happy to let Chow, or her housekeeper, do it. As for Anne's stepfather, I knew that, after leaving the army, besides running the Knowle farm, Chow had sat on all sorts of committees and also on Lewisham County Council. He had never stopped working, even after he got cancer; Katherine had told me. Chow was also artistic – Knowle was full of his drawings and statuettes – and he had designed much of the garden with my grandmother, as well as planning the water gardens in the woods. If Anne had been his own daughter, he might not have allowed her mother to be so indulgent to the girl. But it was clear from the diary that Anne did not listen to him.

Here is Anne in Rome in 1931, still at Madame Boni's, after an Easter outing with her mother and stepfather. Another pupil, Esmé, and her mother, Mrs Mackinnon, had turned up at the same restaurant, with Madame Boni. Esmé's father, like Anne's, is dead.

April 7th 1931. Rome.
Mum went out to play golf with the others to make up a mixed foursome for a competition although she didn't want to go, I agree with Mrs Mackinnon who advised me not to give in to my husband all the time as it was very bad to give in always to men as they took all, and more, willingly. Both parties I think should give in equally, I can see I shall have to be careful who I marry but really Chownie is so getting on my nerves I could scream, all I do is long to get away from him all the time, always a row everywhere we go and grumbling all the time and I hate the way he speaks to Mum and he is so selfish too and Esmé doesn't see why I should be obliged to like him, after all he isn't my father, and I feel no blood ties towards him, Esmé thinks he is very tiresome too, it is such a relief to get away from him into peace and quiet with people who don't snub you and make you feel what a

fool and what a baby you are, I often think how different my life and character would have been had my father lived, how I wish he had, all my life I have almost looked on him as a god and spoken to hardly anyone about him and Esmé feels the same about her father, we talked together, the subject is sacred to both of us.

It appears from this that Anne, understandably, did hero-worship her dead father. Also, she must have been affected by her mother's lasting sorrow at his death – at every Armistice Day, on 11 November, Anne was made aware that her mother was thinking of him and Anne herself quickly learned to respect that date. All this must have made it more difficult for her to like her stepfather.

I now wondered why, since my grandmother had been so devoted to Anne's father, she did not encourage her daughter to see more of *his* family – the exception being Aunt K. On 18 June 1932, at seventeen, Anne *was* sent to stay with the Windhams – her paternal grandmother was a Smyth-Windham – and the young went punting:

A lovely hot day, we took a picnic and started early in the punt, Ralph, Ruth, Pixie and I, we met some other people who were to join us later so we started off downstream, it was <u>glorious</u>, I have never felt anything like it gliding on past lovely lawns, gardens filled with flowers and pretty houses right on the river, it really seemed to me like being in fairyland! . . . We got back quite late punting and paddling. Ruth had to get off early to go and help Mrs Windham lay and cook the dinner as they have no maid but do everything themselves. It was a glorious day.

June 19th.
It seems so funny that these people are my cousins, 'Cousin' Ashe is like a typical country parson (like the Maldens for instance). I can't believe that they are relations of mine, I have never thought of my father's relations at all before or connected them with myself in any way. Mum's relations seem the only <u>real</u> relations to me, I have their

outlook, their standpoint and yet I have unfortunately the others'
looks, the greatest curse of my life is that I did not take after my
mother in looks. I like the Windhams though, they have been very
kind to me, I like Ruth better than Pixie, I don't know why but I feel
I never could be real friends with Pixie, she seems cold and standoff-
ish, she seems somehow annoyed with me because I have nice clothes,
money etc, and jealous of it, we don't seem equal somehow.

That day Anne drove to Radley with Ruth in the old car, 'Knocking
Nellie', that Ruth had bought for £3

who is famous all over Wargrave and <u>quite</u> one of the family! She
went so fast that I was terrified and kept saying 'Madonna mia' and
'Mamma mia' over to myself all the time.
We played games after dinner. The Windhams have the same 'fam-
ily' obsession that Aunt K has, they showed me endless portraits of
Cousin so and so etc and when I told them that I wouldn't accept
Cosmo Rawlins as a cousin they were quite shocked, I <u>love</u> shocking
people!

I thought it was a pity that Anne had not seen more of these Windham
cousins. My grandmother, who was overly obsessed with her own family, probably could not be bothered to pursue the connection. However,
as a married woman, my mother did see Ruth and Ralph, and I recall
Ruth coming to stay with her two boys in Sussex.

Chapter 10

Knowle. July 1934.
I am keeping this book only for my travels abroad, as I would rather travel than anything else in the world. I want to have a written remembrance of them, so that I can live them over again in my mind.

I return to those loose pages I had found among Raymond's things, my first inkling that Anne had written a diary. How my mother loved travel! The diaries described Anne's visit to America in 1936, when she was twenty-one, and Fife had proposed. I read now of her return voyage from New York to Southampton with Gig that November, during the Abdication Crisis, which was by then all over the American newspapers but not the British – on 26 October, the *New York Journal* had printed an article headed *KING WILL WED WALLY*. Anne related that Douglas Fairbanks Senior and his new wife, the former Lady Ashley, were on board the *Queen Mary*; so was the actress Merle Oberon. I love the writing paper with its coloured picture of the ship.

November 8th 1936. Sunday. The Queen Mary.
Fairly rough, she is rolling a good deal and the weather report is gale. We walked round the deck and played Ping Pong. Everything cancelled, including 'Swingtime' which is disappointing . . .

Anne did manage to play a gambling game, Keno, during which a whole table of people fell on to the floor, slid the length of the room, then back again with each roll. All the furniture was roped after that.

A German freight steamer was reported sinking some way off and the *Queen Mary* rushed to her aid, too late – next morning Gig spotted a lifeboat with nobody on it. Another ship had got there, but had found only one survivor. Anne boasted in the diary that, despite reports of the roughest seas for forty years, she had never felt a qualm of sickness the whole voyage. Back at Knowle, she wrote: ***The papers here are full of terrific reports of the storm and stories of how we raced to the rescue of the Isis. I only wish we had been in time, I never realised before how terrifying and how awe-inspiring a tragedy at sea could be.***

In *The Times* of 9 November 1936, in my local library, I read about the doomed German ship, the *Isis*, and its survivor, found alone in a lifeboat – a deck boy, Fritz Roethke, of Berlin, too exhausted when picked up to be able to give any information. That boy, the only one left out of a crew of forty, had withstood drowning in wild seas against terrible odds, but my mother's son, twenty-one years later, had died in her mother's swimming pool, in a supposedly protected domestic setting.

But in the 1930s, Anne, in her early twenties – well off, curious and bold – had a life of adventure to look forward to.

In July 1937, she and Jean Whitaker – they had met at seventeen on the steps of a Mayfair house, both shy before their first debutante tea party – went to the Balkans. In Venice they waited while their respective mothers made enquiries about whether it was safe to proceed – there were riots in Belgrade; in Venice, Jean and Anne spotted the recently abdicated King Edward VIII and the former Mrs Simpson at the Lido, a month after their marriage. Anne's diary describes 'Wally' sitting in a bathing hut in dark glasses and blue shorts. The former king, in grey bathing trunks, sat beside her chatting, then had a dip in the sea with his equerry, Dudley Forwood. Anne and Jean soon decided to continue by train to Yugoslavia, where they were paying guests of a Hungarian family, the Tallians, in the village of Novi Knezevac.

August 1st 1937. Novi Knezevac, Yugoslavia.
We played a game called Marocco after dinner which is like Spillikins, there is one piece called Mussolini which if you take it first is worth 50

. . . They all got frightfully excited and chattered away in Hungarian, even the old Uncle trying to move some of the pieces . . . They talk about politics most of the time here . . . The Baroness has a horror of the Serbian peasants, they walk around in what used to be the Tallians' garden and are quite insolent, no Hungarians ever come there. There is a feast day almost every day here as there are Serbian, Catholic and Mohammedan feasts, all celebrated by everyone. The government are now taking about 1000 in 10,000 an acre to give back to the landlords whose estates were confiscated . . .

The whole mentality seems extraordinary to us and their outlook is quite another one. Whenever we come into the house here with dirty shoes, maids come with rags and clean them for us.

At Novi Knezevac, Anne had encountered people who led a more feudal life than hers at Knowle. But, unlike those of Anne and her mother and stepfather, the Hungarians' privileged lives were almost over.

Anne and Jean must have liked their new friends, because they returned the following summer, 1938, this time taking a Ford V8 from Knowle across the Channel, then driving it east, through villages in Saxony, where inhabitants were already making 'Heil Hitler' signs – four months earlier, Nazi troops had marched into Austria and annexed it to the Third Reich. Anne and Jean then drove to Novi Knezevac, where they picked up Bertha (Baroness Tallian) and her brother, Count Karolyi Magdelhelm, and went on, Anne and Jean still taking charge of the driving, as far as Hotin, a town on the border of Soviet Russia.

July 30th 1938. Cernauti, Rumania.
We went back on our tracks and got to the river which is the boundary between Bucovina and Bessarabia, then we went onto a ferry made of planks and were pulled across to the other side, where we struck on the stones and had to be pushed out by some peasants, when we found that we had a puncture and as usual an enormous nail stuck in the tyre. It has been the same wheel every single time so far, the back right hand one and we have lost the round thing in the middle and a

tool now! We put on a new wheel, which was fairly flat and drove into Hotin, hoping for the best.

I was surprised and impressed by Anne and Jean's practical ability. They had both had family chauffeurs. Perhaps these men had taught the girls how to change a wheel before they set off.

Hotin itself is a queer place quite unlike any other town we've been to. Karoly says it is completely Russian . . . All the houses were joined together in one long row, with the occupants sitting outside them. We were stopped by a policeman in the middle of the town, a very officious looking gentleman, who talked incessantly in Rumanian and a soldier who looked exactly like the Tsar of Russia, in a khaki uniform. The policeman, who resembled a very unattractive animal, both in looks and in mentality, wouldn't let us pass, but insisted that we go back to the Police Station, however Karoly saw an officer in the street and leapt out and the officer got a permit for us to go to the Russian frontier. Accompanied by the policeman and another Austrian soldier, we proceeded through the ghetto, which was rather interesting with wooden houses, obviously very old, down to a church, where we saw the Dniester, all my life I have dreamed of seeing Russia, but somehow I never thought I would do it.

When I asked Jean, in her eighties, and very compos mentis, about their trip, she told me of the abject state of the Jewish ghettos and of the anti-Semitism of their two Hungarian companions. My mother, it was clear, had not noticed these details, or considered them unimportant. It was Russia, which she would only visit for the first time nearly forty years later, which really caught her imagination.

We were looking across the river . . . at Russia. People were bathing on the Rumanian side, but very few on the Russian where there was a village with little white houses with thatched roofs. It all looked so calm and peaceful. As though nothing awful ever happened there. The soldiers on the Rumanian side were walking about, but on the Russian they never appear, apparently, but are quartered in the houses, so that they can watch the people better who are trying to cross the frontier. If someone swims out too far into the middle of the river both the Russians and the Rumanians fire at him, from each side. There is no bridge for miles here, and if they want to cross, signs are made by the soldiers to each other, and then a boat puts out. In the winter apparently, the peasants there haven't much to eat and they drive their carts across on the ice and live like that, then they are put in prison for a year and sent back to Russia, where they are all shot. The great fields outside the villages belong to the state and the peasants have to till them, and they each get so much but it is not enough in the winter, and the old people, when they cannot work, get nothing at all. There was a large building with two red flags in the centre of the village which was the local theatre and performances there are given three times a week, all free. The church too we could see, all shut up and used as an arsenal now. The peasants are now allowed under Stalin, since about a year, to have their own little field of Indian corn behind their houses, and a cart or two, so it is better for them, but before they were allowed nothing of their own at all and consequently starved sometimes. This large theatre in the middle of a small village looked so incongruous somehow. We were standing on the rampart of an old Turkish fort and a soldier told us not to stand there too long as the Russians were quite apt to shoot if they saw people there for long, as they might be taking photographs or something, in fact they had done it before, so we got down quickly. It all looked so peaceful I found it hard to believe that so near to us was Soviet Russia, yet it was incredibly sinister somehow. It was practically dark when we left Hotin and drove back to Cernauti (Cernowitz).

We are staying near the Residenz, where the pretty woman was this morning.

Another pretty woman in a hotel! I was interested to see that, despite her often over-romantic obsession with Russia, she was able to observe precise physical details of the scene in front of her and write it down as though she was a travel writer or journalist.

The journey back westwards was eventful: they were pursued by Romanian police for taking photographs, then on a mountain road in Montenegro an Italian chauffeur tried to bar their way, resulting in Jean scraping the Ford V8 on rocks. Before arriving in Dubrovnik, they were shot at by bandits.

My grandmother, I read, had travelled alone to Dubrovnik by boat and train from England to meet her daughter and Jean. Anne soon spotted her mother in a hotel dining room, flanked by two young admirers whom she had met on the boat. In those days, it seemed, despite their lack of shared intellectual interests, mother and daughter were often good companions.

I had long disliked my mother's travelling, as she seemed to prefer it to being at home with us. I had been uneasy about her fascination with White Russians, Polish officers who'd come over and fought with the Allies, dispossessed Hungarians; in other words, aristocrats who'd lost their positions, money and estates. (When, in my twenties, I challenged her about this, my mother annoyingly replied that she felt more sympathy for them, as they had had further to fall.)

Now, though, I was intrigued by those two diaries written in the summers just before the war, about Novi Knezevac, on the River Tisza, in the new Yugoslavia, which, before 1914 and the Treaty of Versailles, and the other treaties that followed the end of the First World War, had been part of the Austro-Hungarian Empire. I looked up my mother and Jean's routes of 1937 and 1938. I stared at the unfamiliar place names – Cluj, Vecs, Radauti – and pored over the photographs in my mother's albums, which my mother had meticulously labelled: *OLD SERBIA, MY LITTLE RUMANIAN SHEPHERD BOY IN THE KING'S PASS* – I noted the personal pronoun, something she was fond of – *GYPSIES IN THE VILLAGE OF BETHLEN, TRANSYLVANIA, FERRI* – a shaven-headed boy – *FISHING IN THE TISZA*. I was fascinated by the beautifully mannered old uncle, Willibacci, who had been at the

Spanish Riding School in Vienna, with whom Anne communicated in faltering German. He showed her and Jean a picture of himself riding behind the Emperor and Empress at Godollo and told them how, at the time of the Bosnian occupation by the Austro-Hungarian army in 1876, at only eighteen, he was the first Hussar to enter Sarajevo. Anne was bowled over by the romance of it all, and sympathetic to the situation of her new Hungarian friends, who explained to her how Hungary's territories had been drastically reduced after the First World War. *The flags were flown at half mast in Hungary as protest as well as in mourning for the lost land.*

In that diary of summer 1937 – Hitler had been Chancellor of Germany for four years – Anne had inadvertently described a world that was about to vanish. Novi Knezevac would be occupied during the Second World War, first by the Germans, then by the Russians. The old uncle would have died by then, but the lives of Bertha, Tibor, Lala and Karolyi – not to mention the gypsies and that little boy, Ferri – were irrevocably, tragically changed and my mother and Jean never saw any of them again.

Part 3

War

Chapter 11

September 10th, 1939.
I never expected to have to start this diary again under these circum-
stances. It makes everything I wrote before seem pretty futile and war
of course changes one's whole outlook.

The young woman had never made a cup of tea in her life. Left alone
by the corporal – 'I expect you'd like to make it yourself,' he had said,
mistakenly – with a gas cooker, a huge kettle of boiling water and a
canister of loose tea, Anne realised that she did not even know how to
tell when the kettle had boiled. She went off to find a handkerchief to
lift its lid but by the time she got back, the water had all boiled over.

By some miracle, the first cups of tea that my future mother ever
made turned out all right. Two officers came to drink it with her, out
of RAF mugs. *On the mantelpiece was a large photograph of a naked*
woman and one of the airmen rushed in, snatched it up and stuck it
in his pocket. I couldn't help laughing!

Anne had enlisted as early as March 1939; that year, the Women's
Auxiliary Air Force, founded after the First World War but then
disbanded, was re-formed. I found a letter she had kept from a Miss
Trefusis Forbes, saying that she was starting one of the first companies
of the Auxiliary Territorial Service (ATS), at Kidbrooke, Dulwich,
attached to No. 1, Balloon Centre, and that she wanted one section
composed of ex-pupils of Queen's Gate School. Anne had written
back at once, agreeing. Her WAAF number was 513. She would later
be proud of that, as it showed how early she had joined. She had,

I was delighted to see, without hesitation, shown a sense of duty, a willingness to help and a readiness to experience a life out of her ken.

September 10th 1939.
I drove to Kidbrooke, with Mum, Nah and Aunt K in the morning . . .
masses of refugee children, their gas masks on their backs struggling
about the roads . . . lots of soldiers speeding on motor cycles, although
why the general standard of driving should have deteriorated to such
an extent I can't imagine.

On that day, a week after Great Britain's declaration of war on Germany, Anne started in the ranks, in her first job, in 'supplies', at Kidbrooke. Here, in Dulwich College, requisitioned as the headquarters of No. 1 Balloon Barrage, after a lunch in the mess of greasy meat, cabbage and potatoes followed by prunes and custard, she found that she was expected to wash up her own tin, mug, spoon, knife and fork after each meal. This was a novelty, so much so that she even mentioned it twice in the diary.

The best side of Anne comes out in these early war diaries, her willingness to throw herself in, her curiosity and her sense of humour – *Someone said at breakfast this morning: 'When we about turned this morning, Clayton didn't 'arf go on my foot'!* Having to focus on the practicalities of life must in some ways have been refreshing; Katherine had told me that each time the girl wanted to do something for herself at Knowle, Nah would step in and do it for her. My grandmother was also no help in this respect, advising her daughter: 'Never do anything if you can get someone else to do it for you!' (My mother had told me this, seeming at the time to disapprove.)

Anne appears to have enjoyed Kidbrooke, where she did functional tasks such as making out a card for each man with his details, and filing – a more senior colleague was surprised by how quickly Anne grasped the essentials of the job, without having had any business training. Anne in turn was admiring of the different personalities she encountered, in particular the two office boys, Lewis and Perkins,

Lewis just seventeen and from a mining family in Yorkshire, Perkins hoping for, but then not allowed, the day off for his own seventeenth birthday. She was also impressed by Barola, a senior WAAF officer, twice widowed, who had driven ambulances in the First World War in France, for which she had been awarded the Légion d'Honneur and the Croix de Guerre. Despite having then lived in America for nineteen years, when war was declared in September 1939, Barola had returned home at once to pitch in. And unlike Anne, who confessed in the diary that she couldn't sleep due to fear of air raids, Barola seemed to disregard any personal danger. Having offered to drive Barola to her flat to collect some personal items, Anne had waited outside in the blackout, getting more and more nervous, only to see – and hear – Barola coming out singing, *completely oblivious*.

Anne differed in another respect from her female colleagues: *Everyone here is crazy about the men and they all dash about to pubs etc. with them and get clandestine notes from the officers*. Indeed, it is striking that, in all the diaries so far, Anne, now twenty-five, had not fallen for any man – she had written of how she had been flattered and touched when Fife fell in love with her in America, but did not really reciprocate. Since starting the diaries at fifteen, she had written every so often of romantic crushes on young women. But these were never acted upon, probably because she perceived active lesbianism as shameful, even sordid. Indeed, in this early war diary, she tells of an incident at a party given by a senior WAAF officer, a Colonel Barker, and the 'friend' she lived with, *a very pretty woman named Mrs M*. Mrs M was spotted through a half-open door hugging and kissing another woman officer, Cameron (not Colonel Barker!), on the sofa. Anne wrote that such a woman as Cameron should not be in charge of girls, adding *it revolts and sickens me*. Her disgust was, I think, genuine. Something as blatant as two women openly kissing shocked her, but, in view of her own romantic interest in females, there may have been some part of her that even then found it erotic. Perhaps she loathed that aspect of herself.

In this very early part of the war, 'The Phoney War', Anne see-sawed between her two homes and her job – one of the two family chauffeurs, Clancy, who lived in the mews behind 40 Belgrave Square, drove her back to work after her first half-day off. Then, after only one week at Kidbrooke, she was summoned by Miss Trefusis Forbes, who told her that a Johnny Hearn had asked for her to join his personal staff at Kelvin House, Cleveland Street, off the Tottenham Court Road; I imagine that he, like Miss Trefusis Forbes, was part of Anne's 'old school' or family network.

Anne was sorry to leave Kidbrooke and her co-workers expressed reluctance to see her go. She certainly did not show any sign that she felt superior or destined for better things as regards her work; instead, she seems to have been humbled by her new experience of working close to those who had not had lives like hers.

On 18 September 1939, eight days after she'd started at Kidbrooke, Anne became a WAAF driver, based at Kelvin House. Her new job, which she wanted to **make a success**, required her to chauffeur officers to balloon barrage sites all over London and its outskirts, often in the blackout.

31st October 1939, Kelvin House, Cleveland Street. A new experimental balloon being put up . . . We were given lots of hot Bovril to drink . . . Cleaned the car for hours – no hosepipe and no light, very difficult.

She was now performing tasks very similar to those of her family's two chauffeurs. Was this young woman really my mother, whose only practical skills that I could recall were tying on fishing flies and shelling peas – once a year – at Hope Cove? A few weeks earlier, in that same diary, instead of gratefully gulping Bovril and painstakingly washing a car, she had been sipping champagne and water-skiing in the South of France. There, she and her friend John M had been arrested during a police raid on La Bastide, a Cannes nightclub frequented by homosexuals. My mother found the incident amusing and was amazed at

John's naïvety in not having noticed the clientele when she and he, unknowingly, had first gone inside. Now, like so many others, she was caught up in the war.

I was burning with curiosity about my mother's life as a working woman, so that these early war diaries quickly became compulsive reading. I kept the first two with me, glancing through them often at random, with children's TV on in the background, skimming them at night and in the early morning before the children's school. Very soon I was greedily reading them everywhere: in trains, tubes and sometimes hospital waiting rooms. My mother, as she had never been in person, was quickly becoming, through her diaries, my closest companion. Still half-fearful of what secrets I would discover, I was also longing to know.

December 2nd 1940, Bicester.
Physical love is what I have missed all these years. It is lack of it that has made me nervous, terribly emotional and restless. Now it brings me rest and harmony and glorious oblivion and balance to the strained senses.

I was shocked – and excited – when I read this. How different were these sentiments from the previous year, when the inexperienced Anne had expressed disapproval of those two WAAF women kissing, and of a WAAF officer having an illicit affair with her RAF boss. Now Anne was, for the first time, physically attracted to a man:

. . . Alan says that we should be happy married, that we are twin souls . . . I do not know how much David loves me, I do not know him so well as Alan and there is always David's family . . . Alan . . . satisfies me utterly, he is so tender and yet sometimes rough with passion so that I am quite afraid.
I cannot describe the weakness of my will to resist. The strain of the last months seems to vanish and for a moment one looks at the world

with a happy face, as one used to do, long, long ago in that other life.
Glorious, glorious forgetfulness, glorious oblivion and peace.

I now know that I am a harlot, not for me all the rules I have
observed so long through cowardice alone.

In her teenage diaries, Anne had reiterated that she didn't like men.
Now, it seemed, in 1940, she was romantically involved with *two* men
– one passionately.

I knew that she had been engaged, long before she met my father, to
a David Heber-Percy. Clearing Knowle with Katherine two years after
my grandmother's death, I had come across a photograph of a clean-
shaven young man: 'We'd better keep this away from your mother!'
Katherine had declared. I had had the impression that it had been
David who had jilted Anne, rather than the other way round. Indeed, I
remembered my grandmother saying that she had found her daughter
in tears over it.

I had no idea when Anne became engaged to David. The Heber-
Percys, I knew, were a distinguished landowning family. This would
have pleased my grandmother, despite her own first marriage having
been to someone a notch down from the class that her ambitious
father, Michael, had wanted for her. Her three sisters had all 'married
well': Elisa and Lin's husbands were titled, and Dita's was an American
millionaire. Michael had even apologised to my grandmother, his
youngest, for not being able to provide the large dowry demanded
by some impecunious English lord. 'I can find my own husband – you
don't have to buy me one!' she had retorted. He had then suggested
some other aristocrat, adding: 'He has a great name.' 'I would rather
marry a great man!' she had replied. In my grandfather, she told me,
she had found one.

Anne did not have that confidence and, I suspect, still under her
mother's wing, had agreed to marry David partly to please her.

It was time to read the war diaries in their correct order, but this
proved to be frustrating as far as David was concerned. Anne did not
even state in her diary where they met and, during her job as Duty

Driver at Kelvin House, she wrote not of her fiancé, but of the minutiae of her life: a dropped treacle pudding served up again, now full of little bits of china; a drive to a balloon barrage site at Felixstowe, where she waited in a seaside café nursing a cup of tea costing 1s and 6d; and the return journey, during which, having driven them an hour in the wrong direction, she and her superiors stopped for drinks and a pie in a village called Hatfield Peverel: *Just like a play – locals with a wonderful Essex accent, sitting and drinking beer out of huge tankards and playing dominoes. Everyone was very cheery.*

Anne seems far more interested in these vignettes, in the delightfully Italian flavour of the little streets near her headquarters in Cleveland Street and in her colleagues, than in David. There is Mrs Chavasse – Chevvy – who has already lost a husband and a baby, and Dawes, an RAF 'Lothario', who had come over in 1914 with the 1st Australians as a Trooper, *joined the Royal Flying Corps and is as tough as hell. He was very badly injured in a plane crash and has to wear steel clamps and suchlike.*

When at last she writes of David – *You suddenly know they are the only person for you and it is marvellous* – it does not ring true. She adds: *You don't notice their looks or anything.*

What young woman would not notice her fiancé's looks? She adds obliquely that her friend Juliet's aunt wrote to congratulate her, meaning, presumably, that Anne and David are now engaged. I was struck by the contrast to her diary of four years earlier, of how excited she had been when Fife had declared his love.

There is a glimmer of this when, at last, in early January 1940, David sends a telegram announcing that he is coming to London that night on leave. *Was so thrilled. I rushed home. I never realised how much I missed him before.* Anne notes that she is about to accompany David to see his parents, but there is not one word after that about the visit – strange for such a conscientious diarist.

Her life then as Duty Driver – negotiating her way through the blackouts to balloon barrage sites, being chatted up in Soho Square in her lunch hour by a well-travelled ARP warden, whose company she seems to have enjoyed more than any encounter with David – contrasts with the life led by David's parents, who, judging by later diary entries, sound rather stuffy and unlikely to have approved of their future daughter-in-law being picked up by strangers. I enjoyed these anecdotes about Anne's casual meetings in wartime London. They showed a side of my mother that I appreciated.

There were a couple of aborted meetings with David that January of 1940 and Anne recorded that he had the new naval job he wanted, adding proprietorially: *I am not too pleased, especially as I heard Haw-Haw (for the first time) tonight saying that they proposed to treat the new ships as warships.* ('Haw-Haw' was William Joyce, who, throughout the war, had broadcast Nazi propaganda to the British from Germany by radio. He was tried, found guilty of treason and put to death in 1946.) Nor was David the most eager of suitors, leaving longish intervals between his telephone calls. Still a virgin, Anne had a long talk with her older widowed colleague about sex and marriage:

I told Chevvy that I thought it a good idea to sleep with someone before you married them and she agreed . . . and said that for success in marriage there needed to be a great physical harmony or it could be hell . . . She asked me: 'Does the physical side frighten you?' To which I replied yes, it did a bit and that I couldn't reconcile the mental with the physical. She said that married life might do that for me and remove any repressions that I suffered from and that I should only marry somebody kind and who would understand me . . . She asked me too if I had any photographs of David.

Anne, it appears, had not.

I told her that I had been discontented with life for the last two years and she said that it must have been amazing for me to come to K. Hse and see life from the bottom up, instead from the top down. She suddenly said to me too: 'You keep everything to yourself, don't you?' To which I replied yes.

CHAPTER II

Anne was *not* keeping everything to herself – she had her diary. The fact that she wrote it nearly every day of the war, despite a demanding work schedule and an often hectic social life, shows that, as an emotional outlet alone, it was essential to her. She also expresses in it her first sign of personal ambition, stating, after a couple of months at Kelvin House, that she is sick of always being in the ranks, and could do a whole lot better.

In late March 1940, having been encouraged by her boss, Mrs Welsh at Kelvin House, she completed a Code and Cipher course at Harberton Mead, Oxford. When I read about this – she was hopeless at arithmetic, as I am – it was with delight that I saw how she improved each day, encouraged by the teacher, nicknamed by the girls 'The Flying Flea'. When she listed everyone's final exam marks, with herself two-thirds of the way down, with 75.6 per cent, I found to my surprise that I was extremely disappointed that she was not in the top three.

Immediately afterwards, Anne started a new job, at Bicester, as one of two clerks. Bicester was an airfield used by the RAF, from where the two main types of aircraft, Hudsons and Blenheims, were sent out to bomb Germany. Anne had to receive and send messages from Bomber Command headquarters in High Wycombe. She enjoyed using her new skills. *A Type X came. A.M.* [Air Ministry] *excelled themselves with 5 Corrupt GPs in 10 lines, which I succeeded in working out, before the amendment came and was v. proud of myself!* – and she was particularly thrilled by one secret message which she recorded in her diary, surely against the rules:

A thrilling Type X case in today, the 1st really interesting message so far from Bomber Command Headquarters. To say that the RAF in France were making V. important reconnaissances today and that if any planes landed at our aerodrome a report from the crew were to be telephoned to Bomber Command Intelligence at once. They say that on this reconnaissance depends a lot of our next moves.

Not until early April does Anne meet David again, in London – *I was so glad to see him.* David and Anne do not appear to have known each other well when Anne agreed to marry him. It is clear also that she did not know herself.

I see her in that period being pulled in two directions, by the old world, represented by David and his parents and by the old-fashioned country life that my grandmother wished her to lead, and by the new world of work, in a setting where many of the old class barriers were being broken down. Because of the war, she and many other girls like her who had had leisured lives were now using their brains in a disciplined way.

Anne was also meeting a wide range of people. There are several references to class – she often repeats, as though to convince herself, that she feels more at home with people from her own background. However, judging from her accounts of daily life, and having known myself some of those with whom she made lifelong friends during the war – Mrs Hunt, her landlady in Leighton Buzzard, Ida Knott (Knotty), with whom she first worked at Bomber Command, High Wycombe, and Rita Davics, a Communist from Glasgow encountered at Bletchley Park, and countless others – I am not sure that this was the case. I suspect that one reason for the frequent references to feeling 'at home' with those from *the same world* was that my mother, unlike my grandmother, did *not* feel socially secure.

My grandmother was the daughter of a man who had made a fortune in less than twenty years. He had carved a place for himself and his family in British and American 'society' and had lived to see his four daughters successfully married. He had provided for them and for future generations. He could hold his head high and my grandmother and her three sisters were proud of him. My mother, however, was an only child with no father to protect her and, because of the early death of her brother, a sole heiress. She was the granddaughter of a self-made Irishman ('squireens from Queens County', my grandmother said of her father's antecedents), who had founded his fortune on the back of the guano trade. Michael's effort and hard work were certainly

114

something to be proud of and, on Anne's father's side, her ancestry could be traced a long way back in Ireland and a cousin, Raymond Grace, was featured in *Burke's Peerage*. However, her fortune was relatively new and she was not of the same aristocratic class as some of her smarter friends, such as Rosemary Bowes-Lyon, a close relation of the Queen Mother, or the daughters of the Duke and Duchess of Rutland, with whom Anne had occasionally socialised in Paris in 1932, and when 'doing the season'.

Jean told me that Anne had confided to her that she felt she was an heiress by default. If her brother had lived, he would have had Knowle and at least half of the inheritance.

On 7 April 1940, Anne, with twenty-four hours' leave, accompanied her fiancé David to one of his family homes near Warwick Castle, where the basement was now occupied by boys from one of Dr Barnardo's homes. Anne found it sad going round upstairs, with everything shut up and falling to pieces. *Often I still can't believe that the war won't end tomorrow and we shall all be happy again . . . It could really be very attractive I think if a lot was spent on it.* She added that there were about 7,000 acres, including two villages, but no electric light or central heating, and she doubts that they could ever afford to live there properly. It seemed that she was trying to play the part of a suitable future wife.

Judging from her inability, or refusal, when she was married to my father, to run a far smaller country house, it would surely have been a disaster if they had gone ahead with the marriage. Even if they had not taken over that huge estate, my mother would have been expected by David, and his parents, to run her home like any upper-class wife of that period. David might not have been as long-suffering as my father proved to be in taking on duties that traditionally belonged to a wife.

After my father died, my mother had for several years a cook who was a physiotherapist by training. My mother didn't care about food but my aunt and others who came to stay were astounded by Mrs S's 'cooking'. My aunt told me that for supper one evening all they'd had was a slice of old pâté and some lettuce leaves. Surely this was not what you employed a cook for. One Christmas, I recall Mrs S telling me proudly that she had sliced the vegetables for the Christmas lunch two days in advance. When finally my mother asked Mrs S to leave, she did not dare do it in person but instead wrote her a letter which was delivered by the driver who picked Mrs Stubbs up from the station on her return from her annual long holiday. Mrs S refused to accept a written dismissal and marched in to talk to my mother. My mother was terrified.

Like other young couples in wartime, Anne and David must have found it difficult to get to know each other better. His short, infrequent leaves from the navy did not coincide often with hers, and he seems then to have always felt obliged to visit his parents. Maybe he was simply being a dutiful son, but it appears that he was in thrall to them.

After that visit to his home, Anne drove alone in the blackout back to Bicester, while David went by train, to return to his ship. He wanted her to move back to London, so that he would be able to see her more easily when he did come on leave, and had begged her to ask about a reposting.

Two days after David's departure, after Germany had invaded Norway and Denmark, Anne did show concern, writing of her fears of David's possible involvement in the ensuing long naval battle. Like many in wartime, now it seems that she felt the pressure to marry because events were hotting up in Europe and at home. It was almost as though she thought that marriage would allay her unease about her country's general situation.

April 21st 1940. 40 Belgrave Square.
I think of David constantly, I never realised quite how much I am in love with him, until this naval warfare really started. Came to London tonight, the train packed with soldiers returning to work, mostly the West Kents. The moon looked marvellous, just rising, as we came along, but we had to have the blinds pulled down as it was blackout time, although quite light. I always miss the lights most as

they used to look going over the river. I always used to look forward to it at night and with all the lights reflected in the water it used to be very beautiful just there. London seemed very empty tonight, and as beautiful as I have ever seen it, a brilliantly clear night with myriads of stars in the sky and the moon, absolutely full lighting up the whole sky. I walked round the square to enjoy it, with Mum, when we came here. Every now and then, if you looked hard enough up into the sky, you could just make out the dark form of one of the balloons, which seemed to be flying rather higher than usual and there was one which appeared to be almost touching the moon itself with its fins outlined clearly in the moonlight. I thought if London were bombed, how terribly I should mind and how I should never forgive the Germans. I love London, in a way new to me now. I used to know only a tiny bit of it, but now I feel that I begin to know it more and I have seen it in so many moods. I love every stone.

The following day, she tried on her half-finished wedding dress. She still was able to escape, sometimes in the Knowle woods, where she had been earlier that day:

April 21st 1940. Knowle.
The most perfect day. Rode, the woods are full of primroses and the sunniest banks are a mass of cuckoo flowers, with celandines and a few violets too, filling in between. In one part of the wood there are thousands of anemones. It was the hottest day since last summer by far. Almost without a cloud and it made me think of all those marvellous days of the past . . . It made the war seem worse than ever somehow and so remote from the calm of today.

On April 22nd, Anne was stationed at Bicester – 13 Operational Training Group – and was soon enjoying being in the thick of the action on a Bomber Command station, where planes were flying in and out. She felt, in this job, that she was contributing to the war in a more direct way.

On 5 May 1940, she was again on leave, at Knowle. That day began with another lyrical description of the spring, which led me again to believe that she had once loved the place:

The most perfect day in the world. I lay in the orchard in the baking sun, looking up through a mass of blossom to a blue sky beyond . . . bees hummed all around me. I love the smell of summer, the amazing greenness of everything in England at this time of year never ceases to seem like some miracle to me. No other country has quite this almost liquid green and it is a most beautiful thing. We cooked our lunch in the woods, amongst primroses and violets. Later played croquet and Ludo. I long for David so much sometimes that I can hardly bear it.

David seems then to have been the focus for Anne's general yearning, restlessness, and excitement caused by the spring – a season when one often longs for a romance. But he remains indistinct, and there is no indication of mutual passion. However, she went dutifully off to London for another wedding-dress fitting – having initially not wanted a grand ceremony, she wrote that she now longed for a big peacetime wedding with lots of bridesmaids.

On May 6th, she made a special trip to Kelvin House to say goodbye to her former boss Mrs Welsh, who was about to leave her own job there. However, Anne did not request a transfer to London, as David had asked, even though she records Mrs Welsh wondering if the younger woman had come to ask her about *something special*.

Anne may have had a little crush on Mrs Welsh, though she probably viewed her mainly as a mother figure. She had worked well for the older woman and wanted to please her. Unlike my grandmother, who had let her fifteen-year-old daughter give up school, Mrs Welsh, who already had a senior position and three and a half years later was made 2nd Director of the WAAF, had encouraged Anne and seen her potential. She had urged the younger woman, while they were both still at Kelvin House, to do the Code and Cipher course, instead of remaining just a driver. My grandmother, who told me once that she had been perfectly happy working in a canteen during the war, would not have thought of it.

However, it is clear from her diary that Anne was finding her new job exciting and absorbing.

May 10th 1940 Bicester.
We heard that Germany has invaded Belgium and Holland in the early hours of this morning. Events move so quickly these days that it is almost incredible. People will wonder one day perhaps in the future exactly what it felt like to live through these days and the answer would be difficult to give, in my case at any rate it is definitely delayed reaction. I just daren't let myself think about it. We seem to be in an awful way with the split in the Government and tonight we heard that Chamberlain has resigned and Churchill is Prime Minister. People thought that Halifax would be but everyone has such confidence in Winston these days it is amazing and I feel it myself. The traffic was fast and furious today and all RAF personnel were recalled from leave. Over 48 hours leave was cancelled and orders came back to man all the gun posts and be prepared for air attacks and descents by parachute troops. We also had a request for the list of planes we could supply for operational use and we are expected to supply 18 Blenheim and 7 Ansons. Mr. Gunn thinks we are planning a colossal air attack on Germany in the near future. Brussels and Amsterdam have been bombed and British and French troops are in Belgium arming the frontier this morning. Now we thought Chamberlain would resign in the face of this crisis. All the civil defences in this country are standing by. We had a message from 'Puma' saying that bombs had been dropped with varying time limits, several hours in most cases, before they exploded. Una was supposed to be on duty tonight, but Mr. Gunn did it and I went into Oxford with Buller. We went to the Rathbones' party in the Randolph in a private room ... The Rathbones again asked me to go tomorrow with them to 'The Gondoliers' but I didn't know whether I can get off or what is happening at all. I rushed straight back and Mr. Gunn was inundated with Type Y messages, so

I stayed down in the office until 2.15 am having eaten nothing since lunchtime today! . . . Rathbone wore his gas mask throughout the evening, even sitting in the theatre, to impress the A.O.C.!

Anne went into Oxford with a young pilot, Sandy Buller, to see a production of *The Mikado. He really is rather sweet*, she wrote. Finally, after more weeks of hearing nothing, on 21 May she received a letter from David, sent, she guessed, from *the Med* – the first time he had contacted her since their visit to his old family home in early April. She does not refer to the letter's contents, but by 1 June was writing, *Sandy Buller is going away . . . I long for David so much sometimes, especially when I am tired or depressed. I haven't seen him for years it seems.*

On 5 June 1940, five days after the retreat across the Channel by British troops from Dunkirk, she wrote: *Rathbone went over to West Drayton today, where he saw Sandy, who sent long and tender messages to me . . . I long for David so much sometimes specially when I think what our life might have been like in other circumstances.*

It was surely Sandy – who, during their short acquaintance, showed more warmth and affection towards her than David – whom she really missed.

Then, on 10 June, David's birthday, she heard that Sandy Buller had been killed 'On Active Service'.

I felt quite ill and my knees could hardly hold me. He was so especially nice, the one person here that I really was fond of and he is only 20. I cried, it all seems so futile and he loved life and things so much. Such a waste of a person like he was, so full of charm and sweetness of character and fine too. I kept thinking all the way to Oxford of the times we had driven along that road together and of all the things we talked about and it was only a day or two ago now that he sent me these messages. I regret terribly never having said goodbye to him. He wanted so much to be on the staff here too . . . I sort of can't believe he is dead at all and he had only just begun his life. He had qualities that reminded me of David, I think that is why I almost loved him, the same quiet charm and individuality, only Sandy was more viva-cious. He loved the stage and wanted to go in for Producing . . . At such moments I long to see Aunt Dita walking towards me and like a child I would like to rush into her arms to be comforted. To be fêted and spoiled once again and to know peace away from all this ago-nised suspense.

It was her aunt far away in America from whom she wanted com-fort, not her mother. I am almost certain that Anne never wrote or spoke so tenderly about any man again as she did in that passage about Sandy – not, I fear, about my father. I found myself crying as I read it.

At home I had always heard my father making cracks about 'Brylcreem Boys' and delivering other insults and jokes about the RAF. After reading of Sandy, and my mother's subsequent accounts of life on bomber stations, I saw how belittling these remarks must have been. She rightly admired the pilots and always remained proud of having been close to them.

I had never read anything before which made that period so real to me. It was different from histories of the war, which of course were written with hindsight. My mother was writing from *inside* the experi-ence, day after day, not knowing whether Britain would be invaded, which parts of London would be demolished, or whether Knowle, which was on the flight path to London of the German bombers, would go up in flames.

I knew that I would have tried to do the same, record each day in my diary, as I did about my own life. But it was my mother who had gone through the war, not me. It was my mother writing, but in the diaries she was a different person from the one I had known. Again, I found myself experiencing admiration, something which was foreign to me in relation to my mother.

The most surprising aspect was how she took responsibility, something that I had hardly ever known her to do.

On 19 July, she led a parade of WAAFs past King George VI when he came to Bicester on an inspection:

When I got a few paces from the King I gave the order 'Women's Auxiliary Air Force, eyes left!' and I saluted myself till we marched out of the hangar and I said 'Eyes Front', 'Right Wheel'. I marched them down and got to the Gas Centre where I halted them (on the right foot!) and said 'Officers Fall Out!' then I said 'Flight Dismiss!' and most of them turned with their backs to me and none saluted, partly my fault I suppose but I'm not certain. Anyway there were no awful muddles. We cheered the King away at the Gate.

Was this young woman leading a parade past the King really my mother, who couldn't even switch on the TV when my father was alive, who always shoved me in front of her when we entered a theatre, hissing: 'You take the tickets!', who had never once cooked in her own kitchen and whose favourite cry was: 'I can't struggle any more!'?

Sometimes in the diary Anne would look back on her pre-war life, with its freedom, its absence from care. Every so often she would have little tastes of that life again. In early August, she and my grandmother, in an echo of those pre-war Devon holidays, went to Thurlestone, where they stayed in a hotel, as the house at Hope Cove nearby was full of evacuees. The golf course above the Thurlestone cliffs, where my grandmother and her daughter and their friends had spent so many enjoyable summers, was now dotted with posts, to prevent German aircraft landing. *The watch on the coast is full of romance and takes me back to the days of the Armada, although often, I can't believe it is true, when I lie sunning myself on the beach and look up all about me to see a soldier's figure silhouetted against the sky gazing out to sea.*

At Knowle, she witnessed some of the most dramatic scenes of the Battle of Britain. She and my grandmother stood beside the swimming pool on 2 September 1940, watching through field glasses.

There was a faint roar in the distance which grew and grew as it approached us until it was almost deafening and one of the most menacing sounds that I have ever heard . . . a huge formation of Bombers came into sight, flying in magnificent order, the whole sky was black with them and above there was another mass of fighters. We were watching these, when I suddenly looked up and saw that the sky directly above the house was agleam with silver Messerschmitts, darting about the sky. I stepped under the shelter of the verandah, still with my glasses and counted seventy-five Bombers in the formation, which was speeding away towards London . . . relentlessly while we stood there helpless to do anything. It seemed impossible that one stone of London would be left standing.

Chapter 12

Anne had again not heard from her fiancé David for nearly six weeks; not a word since that letter from 'the Med'.

While he was away at sea in the early autumn of 1940, and Churchill was issuing warnings of a German invasion, Anne first mentions Alan, a pilot. She writes that he is *charming*, used to be on the stage, and is South African. He takes her to visit some friends, one of whom runs a private printing press. *I always feel so at home with these sorts of people and in my heart of hearts adore the artistic world.*

Away from her mother's influence, Anne was introduced to an environment to which she was perhaps more temperamentally suited, where creativity and the life of the mind were uppermost. Alan also possessed other qualities that she admired – physical courage and daring.

I was aware throughout my childhood of the importance that my mother attached to these attributes. She was a good tennis player, skied well in snow and on water, and often boasted of how, as a child, she had climbed the rocks with bare feet in Hope Cove, outdoing the fishermen's sons. I remember that she was particularly excited by the anecdote of a man who had skied down the Cresta Run – sheer ice, only for professional tobogganers. My father's courage in having commanded destroyers on the North Atlantic must have impressed her. I recall how, after a holiday with him in Greece, my mother described to me how she had looked out of the window as their plane was landing at Athens and to her alarm noticed one of its engines on fire. She alerted my father, who replied: 'I've seen it already' and continued to do the *Times* crossword.

Several times in the diary my mother writes that she would have loved to learn how to fly a plane.

On 29 September 1940, Anne had news of David, via his mother. *I am thankful to hear something at last . . . Sometimes I feel unless I see David soon I shall go mad.* But she was soon being courted by Alan and I do not blame her; David had become remote. She and Alan grew closer. She took him to dinner with her first cousin Michael (Aunt Elisa's son), at Wotton, Michael's house near Oxford. The following day, she watched Alan *messing about with his motor bike.*

When a young woman is content just to watch a man messing about with his motor bike, it usually means she has fallen for him. But Anne did not appear to be familiar with these warning signs.

On 17 October, she went up in a plane, an Anson – she does not mention whether this was with Alan. However her description – *brilliant sun . . . great billowing mountains and valleys . . . the great power and strangeness of the universe* – tallies with her exalted state. She was falling in love. Two days later, she admitted: *He is the person I like almost most in the camp.*

Alan took her to Oxford where she met some of his stage friends. They attended a party with the then popular writer and journalist Godfrey Winn and Felix Hope-Nicholson, who would be my future husband's landlord in Chelsea, twenty or so years later.

On 4 November, there was a farewell party for Smithie – Donald Smythe – one of the Bicester pilots, whom Anne would make my godfather. I was surprised to read that Smithie kissed Anne in his car after the party. On duty that night in the Signals Office, she discovered, rather too late, that her mouth was smeared with lipstick.

She wrote ecstatically of that earlier Oxford party with Alan, after which they had had long talks about literature and the stage. This atmosphere, she confessed, was harmonious to her and she had always *secretly longed for Bohemianism which . . . now, I suppose, will never have.*

Presumably she thought that she would have to eschew 'Bohemianism', because she was marrying David.

*

Meanwhile Steeles Road, off Haverstock Hill, Hampstead, where Aunt K and her artist husband Matthew did live a somewhat bohemian life, was badly damaged by bombs. Anne went to see her aunt that November at her house, number 39. The street's main sewer had been hit and sewage ran everywhere. Anne recorded that her aunt and other locals had no gas or phone lines, the animals were still in the Zoo nearby, which she thought cruel, and there was a large bomb crater near the BBC headquarters. Aunt K had even heard that eighteen bombs had fallen on Knowle, but she and Anne could not get through by telephone to verify this.

That day, Anne went on to lunch at the Cordon Bleu restaurant, where several women, she observed, were smartly dressed. She saw a car with the new pre-Christmas warning sign, '*Tree lights for all at your own risk*', and visited Woollands store, where she was pleased to see her friend Mr Wright, still selling spectacles. *Everyone is tired but they carry on just the same.* She then returned home, to Belgrave Square. West Halkyn Street nearby had been badly damaged, and one house had had its entire centre removed, leaving the top floor suspended in mid-air, attached to the houses each side of it, *forming an arch resembling the Ponte dei Sistii in Venice*, while in Belgrave Square number 4 had been hit, as had the houses of the Duke of Norfolk and the Howard de Waldens – the latter family's whole house-front had gone. Anne, recalling the house's magnificent staircase, thought nostalgically of how she had danced at a pre-war ball there with an Austrian archduke.

When she arrived at the other side of the square, at number 40, the house where she had been born, she was shocked. The glass above the front door was smashed, and so was that of one of her sitting-room windows. There was no glass left in any of her, or her mother's, bedroom windows and there were no shutters. She hastily packed some things into a suitcase, *moving as though in a kind of trance, steeled against what might be to come and yet listening and looking as one always is these days, never wholly at rest.*

On her way south to Knowle by car – she almost ran out of petrol but managed to get some near Sydenham – she saw more wreckage, of countless little houses and streets. One village had its walls and roofs bespattered with earth from a bomb that had fallen in a garden, and another village, which she had watched being built over years of travelling that route, had lost several of its dwellings. She spotted a German bomber flying off in the direction of the coast, then eight RAF Hurricanes flying back towards Biggin Hill, *black against the reddish sky.*

She reached Knowle at teatime, thanking God that it had not been bombed as Aunt K had thought, though an Italian plane had dropped one bomb near the big Shernfold Lake in the woods, and in the Lost Field there was *an H.E. bomb crater, 30ft. by 10ft.* The following day, she was getting out of bed when she heard shouts and saw from her window Tash the butler and some of the evacuees from London gazing at the sky. *I rushed out and saw a trail of black smoke over the trees towards Mayfield and there was a parachute miles up right above the house, coming down quite slowly. There was a very high wind and the man was swept from side to side, swinging about 40 ft, while the parachute twisted and turned in the air. We thought he was coming right down onto the house.*

The following morning, they heard that that German pilot's plane had been shot down near Heathfield, about forty minutes' drive away. Later, Anne observed a large twin-engined bomber making off towards the coast, in and out of the clouds, *with one of our fighters right on its tail.* The previous week, on the Manor Farm estate, which my grandmother and Chow had bought some years earlier, only a short walk through the woods from Knowle, 160 incendiaries had been picked up, and in the county of Sussex 12,000 bombs had been counted.

My mother recounted in her diary how she walked with Gig to look at the bomb crater in the Lost Field. They searched the woods for shrapnel but found none. *The colours of the trees down here are simply wonderful and they have not begun to fall yet, as they have in Oxfordshire. It is much softer air here too, it was raining this afternoon, but Mum and I went for a walk all round the woods.*

Even in wartime, Knowle was a place of beauty and stability. But it provided only a temporary respite, for Anne was now enmeshed in her new and complicated emotional life.

Soon, despite being engaged to David, she was sorely tempted by Alan's advances. At first she sought to excuse her susceptibility: *a tremendous urge fills one to create as much happiness as is in one's power, especially for men in the RAF, who go straight from here to operation work, and stand an even chance of being killed.* She mentions again how much she and Alan share, books and *all the artistic and beautiful things of life.* Had she anything in common with David, apart from a love of dogs? I wondered. She states, surely correctly, that in wartime they were all slightly unhinged and goes on to admit that she finds her admirer physically attractive, something that she had never said about David, then the proof: that at Woodstock one night, *I let Alan make love to me.*

Despite 'make love' not meaning what it does now – Anne was still a virgin – the situation between her and Alan had progressed beyond a point that was seemly for a young woman engaged to another man. Anne was aware of this, but tried to justify it to herself:

Is this wrong, I began to wonder. All my upbringing says; you are engaged to someone else and you betray him when you flirt with Alan and let him make love to you and yet do I really do so? I think not, because David is all the time the centre of my life and this is only an interlude, giving pleasure to Alan and giving peace to me while it lasts.

I have cut love out of my life almost entirely and it has been the biggest mistake that I could have made. It has made my life, instead of being united and evenly balanced, abnormal and dissatisfied and I know am sexually starved, which in its turn even affects my mind. I think it altogether wrong, that women should not sleep with men now and again, without having to marry them and I suppose most people do it. That is an entirely different matter from giving oneself freely to right and left. There is a lot to be said for living with people now and again if one is in love with them and were I to go away for a weekend with Alan, I believe it would do us all the good in the world. How David would view this I have no idea, but obviously I do not expect him to remain celibate when he is away from me. Our upbringing is all wrong, a wicked travesty, left over from puritan days and unreasonable and does not fit me for life as it really is. After all, why draw such a line between actual physical love and the platonic side? That in itself is a grave mistake. I admit that I do not know the answer to this problem, nor that I have gone so far, it is difficult to draw back without being a fool and I am carried away too. Being in love with David has made other sensations even more poignant to me and I feel sensitive, far more than I ever did before.

Let her go on deceiving herself about loving David, I thought, but I did not blame her. I was sure that I would have had an affair with Alan myself. He sent her books, a love letter when she had a cold, then they attended a birthday party which ended with Alan getting covered in her lipstick. But then she received *marvellous news*, via David's mother, who had received a letter from her son saying: *I am on my way home.*

At this, Anne seems content, albeit briefly, to play once again the part of the dutiful young fiancée. However, the diary reveals her conflicting emotions: *I have always been an escapist . . . murmuring 'manana, manana' to myself whenever a decision appeared over the horizon, too weak and too stupid perhaps to see that failing to take that same decision when it presented itself, a decision far larger and far more difficult would arise, that might cause much sadness.*

This self-description was all too familiar to me and I marvelled at her sudden perspicacity.

'You must make a decision!' I recall her saying helplessly, many times, to me or to one of my brothers, tacitly admitting how difficult this was – for her.

Now she had to make a choice between the two young men, Alan, the handsome RAF pilot, and David, her sailor fiancé. She is harsh on herself, accusing herself of *having no life pattern*, of *wafting hither and thither*, of being *unsure and unequipped* and of having *no discipline to face life*. 'The one thing I regret is that my mother never taught me self-discipline!' I recall her saying to me, and I felt, impatiently that, yet again, she was letting herself off the hook. But now, knowing how my grandmother had arbitrarily removed her from Queen's Gate, then given in to her about that finishing school in Paris, I understood a little more what she meant.

I realised also that my grandmother's expectations of life had been different from those of her daughter, less complicated. She had hardly ever wanted to experience another world from the one in which she was brought up. Anne was not like this.

December 1st 1940. Bicester.
At times too, I have been driven by an insane desire to experience things . . . I have failed lamentably, as I was always held back by the fear of what my mother might think. The Bohemianism in my nature was at war with my upbringing . . . For the first time in my life, I was really living . . . there was some point to my existence. That alone made life worthwhile, together with the kindness and cheerfulness of everybody I worked with. Being part of the WAAF too was a great help, as I felt that we were all working together and the spirit of the Balloon Barrage crews all through that first terrible cold winter and deadly job was magnificent.

This passage surely showed my mother at her best. She really had tried hard, she had indeed been *really living*.

At least she had stood firm in one aspect. David's parents wanted her to give up the WAAF, so as to be available each time their son returned on leave. But, she put in her diary, she had promised to stick to the service when she first joined. Also, she could not bear to have someone dictating to her, and certainly did not intend to be regarded just as David's fiancée.

I had great sympathy over this. My mother was an instinctive feminist; she really believed that women were capable of doing everything as well as men, or better. She was so unlike her own mother in this respect. My grandmother, an agnostic, was independent in thought – 'I don't know if it's true but it's such a sad story!' she once said of the Crucifixion – but in her actions, like so many women of her time, she was happy just to be a husband's helpmeet. My mother, despite her frequent lack of confidence, was not.

And at Bicester, she enjoyed being treated as an equal rather than as an ex-debutante, an upper-class girl on a pedestal. And she admired the men's courage, and found it attractive. *If they want to make love to me now and again and are going straight from here to an operational station, where the chance of getting killed is so high, who is one to refuse them at such little cost to oneself?*

I had not before heard my mother express such generosity towards the opposite sex. She tried hard to understand those young pilots and to adapt to her new life with them – *I began to see a bit below the surface and got fond of the people, who were so good-hearted and gay!*

But she remained inexperienced, frightened of a full sexual relationship with Alan. She agonised: *What was morality except a safeguard for women? One does not think much of the woman who is not prepared to give, especially in such times of stress . . . I was utterly inexperienced in the ways of love . . .* She wrote of how she *had* almost given in to Alan, of his first 'making love' to her in the moonlight among *the silvery trunks of birch trees*, of how she was powerless, *and abandoned myself to its delights.* She stopped short of sleeping with him, however, particularly after he had burst into tears and told her that he was past flirtation and wanted to settle down and have children. She realised then *how unfitted I was to deal with such affairs . . . This sex business is impossible, it is this urge that I am unable to fight against and it is such a natural thing and should be satisfied, I am convinced.*

She was intellectually convinced, certainly, but she still held off giving herself to Alan completely, also because Alan himself had abstained – *he says that it occasions so much unhappiness that he would not do it to me and I do not know if he is right or not. On top of that we have done already, I cannot see that it would make much difference.*

My mother, in my hearing, would always poke fun at couples who were physically affectionate in public. And, for as long as I could remember, each time my father put his arm round her, she would push him off. This was certainly very different from the passionate way that she had acted with Alan and I felt cheated that she had always presented such a prudish front to me. Or was it simply that she had changed unrecognisably from that young woman in her twenties – mad about a man for the first time?

Throughout the winter, the romance with Alan went on, alongside her engagement to David. Alan stirred her inner longings, spiritually and physically. The following passage expresses fear, hope and a sense of something beautiful at the heart of life, even at its most grim. She was ripe for an affair:

The sky is dull grey and the smoke from the chimneys of the Mess is blown into little tufts into the air, to drift away towards the Hangars. In the distance the engine of an aircraft roars and every little while there is a burst of machine gun fire from the range. Miraculously it seems in such a day as this, a bird is singing near my window, so sweetly, we might almost fancy that it is Spring and if one shuts one's mind to all but that, it is no longer an illusion. I cannot see my bird and I am glad I can imagine him to be what I will, decked in gorgeous array, a Cardinal perhaps, flashing scarlet amidst the Palms, or a Kingfisher, a sapphire skimming over the water, there is no limit to what he might be and for me he is all of them. The most magnificent, the sweetest and the most rare bird that exists in all the world for he brings all these untold visions into a winter day.

On 4 December, she and Alan went to the Trout for lunch, where they drank Scotch ale and talked beside a huge log fire – *pretty heavenly*. The following day, she heard bad news – Alan had been transferred to

Operations. Alan's posting, to Swanton Morley, seems to have shocked her. Apart from her emotional attachment to him, he was a kindred spirit – unlike David – and her closest companion at that time.

I felt awful all day, exhausted and so strung up. I hardly knew what to do. I felt I just couldn't bear the war any more. It is so awful when people leave here and the next thing you hear is that they have gone. It is the first two raids that are the worst, if they survive them, they have much more chance. You just come into the Mess here one day and someone says 'Have you heard old so and so's gone, pretty bad show,' and then no one is sad and one just has a kind of sick feeling inside and one sees their name still on lists on the notice board and scribblings on the telephone box and their letters still arrive and lie on the hall table, no one quite knowing what to do with them. Sometimes, I feel awed by the awfulness of it all, at others I feel I must rush madly somewhere shouting 'Stop, Stop for God's sake before it is too late and the people who are alive and who are decent and fine are all dead in this madness.' Alan left after lunch and I have never felt so lonely as I did for the rest of the day. Everything reminded me of him and of what we had said and done together in that particular place, so that I thought I should go mad and could hardly bear the Mess. Every time the door opened I expected him to come in and instead, I sat down trying not to think. Thank God I am going home on Wednesday.

After returning briefly to Knowle, she did not write the diary for eleven days. By the time she resumed it, her engagement to David had been broken off.

On 15 December 1940, she had received a message to telephone David's parents. He had, at last, come home on leave, but instead of contacting her, had gone straight to see them. The following day, it was his father who rang her, not David. *I went to Wotton and was rung up there by Capt. Heber-Percy from Hull, who told me that David arrived here yesterday and was at Osmaston. I felt so hurt that he had gone there and had not even, the day after, tried to come and find me, but*

I couldn't get through on the phone. Finally, in the evening, David did telephone, and two days later they met in London. He arrived late and the meeting was strained and cold. She conceded in the diary that it was partly her fault, as she felt *nothing much.* She drove him to the Admiralty, where he was then told that he was to get command of a new destroyer, the *Quantock,* around 1 January. He did not seem enthusiastic about anything and said that he must go north that night to see his father. *I felt very depressed at him leaving again so soon and at his apparent lack of feeling for me.*

She motored back alone in the blackout, went to bed and was very sick. Alan, on short leave, came to see her at Bicester and the two of them dined again at the Trout. She could not get David on the telephone, so decided to go home for her short leave.

At Knowle, she admitted in the diary to feeling *furious* with David. When he finally rang, she told him that she was tired of *following him round England.* On 21 December, she sent a telegram asking him to meet her in London. She seems to have been uncharacteristically decisive, wanting to bring the relationship to a head.

She returned to London, travelling by Green Line bus, through the badly bombed areas of Lewisham and New Cross – *some of the houses look very pathetic with bits of furniture, pictures etc., lying amongst the wreckage and I saw two old ladies wandering in the garden of a completely demolished villa.* When David finally arrived – his train was three hours late – my mother, perhaps for the first time in her life, emerged as the stronger: *he told me how he was suffering from nerves which affected him so that he was only happy at sea and wanted only to get back to the ship and to have no more ties. He seemed quite unable to make up his mind as to what to do and was like a child in trouble.*

A woman who was more experienced with men, and more compassionate, might have been able to help David, but she could not. Also, to be fair, he may by then have realised that he was not in love with her, but lacked the courage to say so. At least she was trying to get him to declare his real feelings.

They went together – again on the Green Line bus – to Knowle. There, David had a long talk with my grandmother, after which Anne wrote: *He is fast heading for a nervous breakdown and is frightfully weak.*

My grandmother sent for the local doctor, who said that David was in danger of a collapse but that his new command of the *Quantock* and the consequent change of scene might pull him together. *We decided definitely that the only thing to do was to break our engagement. It is all v. sad . . . there is no bitterness on either side and we remain friends.*

Anne went on seeing Alan after that Christmas and in early 1941, but her broken engagement knocked the stuffing out of her; back at Bicester she recorded: *awful waves of depression . . . I feel very futile and of no importance to anyone.* She must have been relying on that future marriage more than she realised. Her gaiety and youthful enjoyment of life, displayed when she first joined the WAAF, were now not so evident. Also, once the obstacle of her engagement to David had been removed, she seemed unable to commit herself to Alan.

Incendiary raids on London continued, with enormous damage inflicted on the City; its fires, my mother reported, could be seen from Knowle, over thirty miles away. Retaining her diarist's curiosity, she went by tube to look at the bombed area round St Paul's. Her depression – surely like that of many of her compatriots during that phase of the war – continued, and she wrote of *lack of colour*, of *feeling nothing*, of being *terribly tired*, of having *no will left*, and wanting *only to sleep and forget the war.*

In mid-January 1941, Alan rang to tell her that he had been promoted to Flight Lieutenant, which, she judged, was *pretty good.* By now, four men were attracted to her: Alan, Peter (no surname provided), who came down to visit her and stayed at the Randolph Hotel in Oxford, John M and, finally, Joe, her senior at Bicester, who declared *he was forgetting all this fatherly stuff and was falling in love with me himself.* None of this, however, seemed to cheer her up.

She was taken by Alan to meet his parents. She records feeling quite out of her depth, *very nice really, but a different world.* I suppose she meant that they did not know the sort of people that she and her mother mixed with socially. She admitted then in the diary to being physically in love with Alan, *but again there are setbacks.* Her lack of confidence had returned: *What a muck I have made of my life . . . I should have someone to lean on, to cling to and admire . . . this ghastly invasion hanging over us is too much to bear at times.*

Anne was in a fragile state. That meeting with his parents seems to have been a turning point for her. She probably did not have enough confidence to marry someone who was not of a similar background. Perhaps she was already falling out of love with Alan and looking for a let-out. Certainly, her broken engagement with David played a part; she must have felt guilty and blamed Alan, as well as herself, for the termination of that prospect. After all, the marriage to David had symbolised a conventional life after the war, a secure future. Marriage to Alan would be something more unknown.

A month after being introduced to Alan's parents, she was posted to Hucknall, in Nottinghamshire, where she immediately met a young woman she liked, Babe Turnbull, who was half-American. Alan is not mentioned so often now in her diary, but he was still madly in love with Anne, judging from what happened in late February 1941 at Knowle, when things came to a head dramatically at what must have been, despite the war, a weekend house party. (It included John M and Anne's friend Cynthia.)

Perhaps when he was staying at her family home, Anne decided for good that Alan didn't fit into her world. Maybe she had already fallen out of love. At any rate, after that weekend she wrote: *Alan now frankly bores me and I have never met anyone so introspective before. He is the way I used to be at the age of 18 or so and does nothing but talk about himself, the entire time.*

Poor Alan, it emerged, had left a note in her bedroom the first evening asking her to come down and talk to him alone; she refused. However, due to his *awfully nervous mood,* she later felt obliged to comply.

Some of what followed was uncannily like what had occurred with

David at Knowle only two months earlier – the local doctor was again summoned and Alan talked to him all afternoon. He later confided to Anne that he was exhausted, needed weeks of rest, and she was the only person who could help him – *he became worse and worse and burst into tears two or three times. Then he asked me to marry him all over again and I said No despising him terribly by this time, although I feel mean at having led him on in a way, except that when I did it I was genuinely in love with him or at any rate thought I was.*

Anne appears to have been unable to cope with the emotional young man, when, at 1.30 a.m., he appeared at her bedroom door in his cap and greatcoat saying: 'Something has gone here!' and pointing at his head. He told her that he was going away and had wanted to see her once more first, then rushed downstairs. Anne woke Cynthia and the two young women went down to find Alan standing by a loaded revolver on Anne's stepfather's desk. Cynthia tried to be flippant, but Alan seized the gun and rushed outside. The women then woke John M, and the three discussed what to do. They heard Alan come back into the house and all crept back upstairs, Anne moving into Cynthia's room, from where she heard Alan go along to her empty bedroom. *I suppose I am to blame as well, but we are all slightly mad these days and crave for affection of any kind. Life is such hell that one turns instinctively to love and friendliness and most people's nerves are all on edge as well.*

She added that she doubted that Alan *had the guts* to shoot himself. This seems unfair, when for months he had been flying bombers over Germany, a feat that she greatly admired. These young pilots were expected to go on their missions often with little or no sleep, and the likelihood of them being killed was high. Alan was probably suffering from nervous and physical exhaustion.

The following day, she was even more unsympathetic, and seemed glad to get rid of Alan, refusing to go and talk to him despite a message from him imploring her. She was even more infuriated to find his note saying: *It's all right, darling, I missed.* She said goodbye to him in the company of the others on the lawn at Knowle, then John M drove him to the station, where, he told Anne later, Alan had threatened to throw himself off the train. Alan had by then written her another note, apologising. She wrote coldly in the diary that it was *all very unpleasant.*

Trying to forget the experience, she went for tea with the others to Hastings, which was practically deserted, but they had *lashings of butter and chocolate (an untold luxury) to drink in a café on the front and enjoyed ourselves quite enormously. There was barbed wire all along the front, on the way we crossed 'The People's Moat' anti-tank ditch and our fighters were making the most wonderful designs in smoke.*

She does not appear to have connected those fighters with Alan's own dashing achievements in the air. She again wrote cruelly: *He bores me.*

Anne does not come out of the episode well. She was unable to offer sympathy to Alan, on the brink of suicide. As seemed to be her wont, she retreated into trivia, to escape dealing with difficult emotions. Her account of that outing to Hastings only an hour or so after Alan had left Knowle, reportedly threatening to throw himself under a train, describing *lashings of butter and chocolate*, does seem callous.

There are many examples in her childhood – indeed, throughout her life – of my mother turning to treats and possessions for solace. I read again some of those earliest memories: *Nah had bought a sweet woolly dog for her nephew Freddy for Christmas and she lent it to me to play with one day. I loved it so much that she had to give it to me instead of the donkey brooch which she had got for me . . . my cousin David had a real Jaeger dressing-gown which I envied.*

And I read in another, later diary how, soon after Grandmoods had died in 1930, Anne was taken to 40 Belgrave Square to look at her grandmother's possessions, which were to be divided: *Aunt Lin has marked 6 Inca pots for herself including the bird one, I <u>did</u> want it, I <u>must</u> GET IT, I <u>will</u> get it.*

That acquisitiveness was something that I disliked in my mother. However, now I tried to understand it. She thought that toys, possessions, gadgets – special bottle openers, battery-operated wasp swatters, which she used to acquire in America before such things came to this country – would save her, would lessen the hard blows of life. And indeed, when her newly widowed mother had abandoned Anne, removing her from her home, Knowle, and sending her to live with her Aunt Lin, the child, by her own later account, had, each evening, envied her cousin David's Jaeger dressing gown. Was it surprising that the little girl, fatherless, temporarily motherless, and whose only brother had just died, had turned to possessions for comfort?

I visit my mother at Camelot. It has just started to rain. As I get out of the car, I can see her through the window sitting in her armchair. She looks more alert than usual. Through the glass I signal to Fiona, her carer from Scotland, that I'm going in through the kitchen.

My mother has already walked into the kitchen by the time I've got there. She is led by Fiona, who is holding my mother's hands and arms out straight, walking backwards, to stop her falling. My mother looks delighted to see me. Her old charm is back. I recall other occasions when I've been pleased to see her – on the beach at Hope Cove when I was with my small children, and she would unexpectedly appear over the sea wall with her fishing net, crinkling her blue eyes, waving to us. How much of my life has been spent trying to awaken that magic, to get my mother to smile again, to laugh happily with me like she used to in Spain, in our garden with the apricot tree, to dance with me as she did long ago in that other garden at North Heath – 'Grey Lady dancing! Boop boop-a-doop!'

Back in the bedroom, in her armchair beside the TV, she keeps putting out her right hand and grasping mine. Her toys – another woolly dog, a donkey, the pink teddy bear that she handed to her cousin Dita placatingly that day after trying to hit her with a walking stick – are on the bed. Fiona says she's having 'a very good day' and has been mentioning her cousin Peggie a great deal. I tell Fiona that I've been reading my mother's diaries. As we sit there, it begins to snow, very thick flakes. Fiona says it won't lie, but it does, just for a few minutes.

I suggest ringing up Peggie in America. I get Peggie on the line and my mother grabs at the telephone's cord, missing the receiver, which I then hand to her. I worry that Peggie might be put off by her talking gibberish, but she doesn't seem to be. I then take the telephone myself and say that my mother wants to visit. Peggie says: 'Let her come!' I explain that my mother might panic in the plane. Also, she wouldn't be able to communicate with Peggie when she got there.

My mother is very excited and has understood it was Peggie. She seems in a very good mood altogether. Fiona says she sometimes sings to her, Scottish songs. Probably she recognises some of the tunes, I tell Fiona, as Gig sang them to her when she was a child. Perhaps Fiona's soft Scottish voice reminds her of Gig's. Then I look out of the window and see that the snowflakes are about one inch wide. They look odd beside the flowering tree with its white blossom. I do not have the feeling of dislike towards my mother that I sometimes have and I wonder whether this is because I've been reading her diaries.

Chapter 13

February 26th 1941.
It is 12.30 a.m. and I have the impulse to write. As I came up the stairs tonight, a wealth of memories seemed to envelop me, making me feel unreal, as though I was a stranger surveying the scenes which someone else had lived and felt. Suddenly, I did not know which was real, me or these familiar scenes. How could they be reconciled with what I had become? And yet was I not as much the real person than the being who had lived her life, who was but half alive, being a life of pleasant unreality?

My mother has called her fifth war diary 'STILL MORE WAR', instead of just giving it a number. Eighteen months now into the war, these diaries were proving a unique source of comfort to her.

Weeks into her recent posting at Hucknall, with the dramas of David and Alan behind her, she was ready to meet new people. One was George Widowski, a Pole brought up in the Ukraine: *These foreign men have minds like women and yet they are not effeminate.* She adds that it is difficult to find an Englishman on a woman's emotional wavelength, unless he is Jewish, physically unattractive or homosexual.

Maybe she *would* have been better with a more feminine man. She may have often found my father's relentless masculinity exhausting. Her entry about preferring men on a woman's emotional wavelength also suggests that perhaps she really yearned, even then, for the emotional closeness of other women.

WAAF Officer's Mess. RAF Station
Hucknall, Nottingham
No. 1 Group Headquarters
February 23rd 1941.
In the sky, which was absolutely clear blue, The Fighters were up very high and all we could see were these trails of white smoke twisting and curling about as though drawn with a pencil across the stratosphere . . . this war has the strangest effects on one and I enjoy almost anything now, and yet when I am not working for long, or have some point to my existence, I feel rather lost, and the very fact, whatever we may feel about the WAAFS at times, of belonging to a service is a great help.

Apart from the stability of being in the WAAF, she also enjoyed the companionship of the other women in it; at Hucknall, her new friend, Babe, *makes me laugh till I cry.*

Babe Turnbull – married, half-American, half-English upper crust – was yet another female friend who was more confident than Anne; indeed, Anne was even unsure at first whether Babe liked her for herself, or was simply being friendly because they had ended up in the same posting.

Her new friendship with Babe, and the change of location, undoubtedly gave Anne a new lease of life. She began taking Italian lessons, and on 1 March wrote happily of the sun shining despite the cold and of birds singing in the woods behind the house. She slept much better, though admitting that she sometimes dreamed of dive bombers – *one gets the feeling when one is half awake that there is something rather unpleasant in the background but one can't remember quite what it is.*

She added that she had made three decisions: one, she did not want to marry John M, who had proposed to her again, as *he did not understand women*; two, she did want to get married, to *someone*; and, three, she desired a job requiring more initiative and with less routine – she had not grasped that getting a more exacting job would be incompatible with marriage.

My mother also noted in her diary one of Babe's remarks that pleased her: *You and I ought to have been journalists!* Sadly, it did not occur to her that this might still be a possibility.

The German air attacks on London went on. Anne learned of the bombing of the Café de Paris on 8 March, where thirty-four people, including the jazz performer 'Snakehips' Johnson, were killed and another eighty or so injured. She had often enjoyed herself there. She wrote that now she could understand, vaguely, what it must be like for people such as the Poles who had lost everything – their country and the people they loved. *To me, the world of imagination has always been more near than that of reality itself and I am therefore a fool when it comes to practical things. Only since the war have I been forced to come face to face with reality and to live in a way that I never did before.*

Despite her sympathy for the Poles, her reaction to a letter from her Hungarian friend Tibor Tallian seems insensitive. He had written from Novi Knezevac in December, but she did not receive his letter for three months. Tibor, his wife Bertha, his sister Lala and Bertha's brother Karolyi were, like the Poles, now under threat, from the Germans in the west and the Russians in the east. *I don't envy them their position, but they are so used to a life of sheer hell and misery, that perhaps it doesn't affect them much any more.*

This, considering that she and Jean had visited Tibor and the others for two years running, and travelled with Bertha and Karolyi, seems almost on a par with her callousness about Alan's and David's near breakdowns.

Her affectionate feelings towards her cousin Peggie, however, were consistent. Peggie's concerned letter from America, received soon after that one from Tibor, reduced her to tears and on 1 April 1941, after noting that Roosevelt had seized all Italian, German and French boats in US waters, my mother was able to write triumphantly about the country of which she was so fond: *America is awake at last!*

She also appreciated the effects of the war on ordinary Londoners. There was the old lady in the newspaper shop in Soho who had lived there through the last war. *There is something pathetic about all the people and they are so courageous. She was awfully pleased to see me and asked me to come in, whenever I was passing by.*

My mother often had problems with intimate relationships but had genuine warmth and sympathy towards those whom she met casually. And I was pleased to read that on that same afternoon she and my grandmother, then seemingly good friends, had walked together through Soho trying to buy Player's cigarettes. Anne had also bought a typewriter, perhaps dreaming of becoming a writer, and they had lingered outside Vaiani's Italian restaurant, which had a notice on its door stating: *The proprietor is a British subject.* Anne wanted to have a meal there, to show that there was no ill-feeling towards the Italian owner.

The German bombing went on. In late April, after what was said to be the worst raid on London so far, Aunt K's house in Steeles Road in Hampstead was hit for the second time, so badly that it was rendered almost uninhabitable; sixty people nearby were killed.

Three weeks later, my mother recorded shocking changes to the area where she was born.

May 17th 1941.
I wandered round Belgrave Square. The garden gates are no longer locked, for fear of incendiaries, and the grass is all overgrown, the centre greensward is now planted with vegetables and the tennis court is ruined too. I wondered what had happened to the gardener who used to take such a pride in his garden there. In Eaton Place, there was a house on the corner which had had the whole of one side removed by a bomb. On the sidewalk lay pieces of furniture, of sofas, curtains, and other things and a gold winged chair looked out rather forlornly from the midst of the rubble. The stairs were intact and lead up and up into nothing at the top. In the rooms the mirrors, unsmashed, were still hanging on the walls, with a sheer drop to the street below them and the lift was still there with its criss-crossing plating. A bookcase stood rather sadly with its side removed but all the books still in place

inside and looking through a door into what had obviously been the kitchen, I could see all the cooking utensils and china standing on the table ready for use. It was this that seemed to bring home to me suddenly what it all meant and I felt quite sick and hurried away feeling somehow that it was indecent to expose people's private lives and their things and not daring to think about the people themselves. I was only to be confronted by the damaged St Peter's, Eaton Square, where the clergyman was killed, and which, although all the walls still stood, was labelled as dangerous. It seemed really like a nightmare and I was glad to leave.

Her parents had married in that church on 12 December 1912.

These accounts of the devastation of London occurred more and more frequently in the diary. It was as though my mother was handing me a pack of cards, one by one, each illustrated by her own highly coloured images. Unwittingly, she was enabling me, over fifty years later, to experience history in the raw. Indeed, sometimes I felt, or hoped, that she had written the diaries for me.

At the end of April 1941, Anne left Hucknall for a new job. Just before that, Smithie, her pilot friend from Bicester and my future godfather, paid her a visit. He had been awarded the George medal for pulling someone out of a burning aircraft.

My mother was now at Leighton Buzzard, at 60 Group HQ, an Intelligence Centre. This Leighton Buzzard office dealt with all overseas traffic and was a part of the Air Ministry. Anne described it as *the most interesting of all the cipher traffic places that exists . . . there are about 10 of us on a watch . . . quite a few nice ones – Angela Griffiths, whose father is a mining engineer in Rumania.*

Events that spring were discouraging. On 27 April, the Germans had occupied Athens and Allied troops were about to be evacuated from the rest of Greece. A few days later, Iraq declared war on the Allies. The evacuation of Greece was now almost complete, though with 3,000 still left behind.

My mother relished learning these facts through her work, ahead of the public, and putting them in her diary, feeling thereby that she was experiencing *history in the making*. She also recorded changes in the roles that women were now permitted to play. On 1 May, she saw her first woman porter and observed that there were now women ticket collectors and women attendants on trains, though usually a man was still in charge. This last fact would have disappointed her. Anne was so unlike my grandmother, who had admitted to me that she would not have felt confident under a female doctor. My mother always felt more secure *with* a woman in charge. She must have been excited by these particular changes brought about by the war.

Meanwhile American planes were arriving in Britain, their pilots to instruct British pilots in flying the new types of aircraft which, Anne wrote, could bomb from 30,000 feet. She wrote excitedly (and indiscreetly) about a cipher from the previous night, during which she had worked a nine-hour shift:

someone in command at Abyssinia asking for freedom to bomb the bases of the Iraqi air force as Iraqi planes had bombed our aerodrome that afternoon and done a considerable amount of damage, it was giving a raspberry for the orders forbidding them to bomb Iraqi bases and they also said 'due to our shortage of fighter aircraft'. Later on, we got the answer. Giving him a free hand to bomb as he liked. It's all rather thrilling in a way being so much in touch with things.

She was now billeted to Silver Birch, Plantation Road, Leighton Buzzard, Beds, the home of a Mr and Mrs Harry Hunt. They would become lifelong friends.

On 11 May, Angela Griffiths failed to reappear in the Leighton Buzzard office after a short leave in London. The air raid on the capital the previous night was reportedly the worst yet; Anne wrote that Whitehall was enveloped in smoke from the still-raging fires, Westminster Abbey and the Houses of Parliament had been hit, the Alexander Hotel had been bombed, and those trapped in the shelters there were heard crying while rescuers worked to get them out.

Angela eventually turned up in the Leighton Buzzard office, having been in a London flat which had had a direct hit. Her eyes were red from burning cinders and her hands cut by broken glass.

Despite these awful events – including more damage to the City of London – Anne seems to have been almost enjoying this part of the war. She comes across as quick, responsive and on her mettle. Her emotional life also seems intense. Here she writes of coming up to London by train from Knowle:

As we approached the City there were more and more signs of the devastation of the last air raid. Practically every street had a yellow diversion sign and others were all roped off. There were masses of police about and people stood about in little groups watching people working amongst the debris. For the first time I felt a terrible feeling of tragedy everywhere and although people were going about their business as usual they looked tired and had set faces. There was an indescribable feeling of depression in the air, which I have not felt before and as we were turned this way and that like in a maze, I began to realise the extent of the damage. I saw that it would be impossible to reach Cannon Street and so I got out and started to walk, carrying my suitcase, which seemed to weigh a ton and it was only then that I really saw what it was like. You could not go literally more than a 100 yards or so without passing some damaged premises, either shops, with no fronts to them at all, or great blocks of concrete fallen from a portico, or the now familiar white notices, 'Dangerous Building' stuck onto a wall or door. Everywhere lay heaps of rubble, broken boards and charred beams, smoke was pouring up from heaps of rubble in a number of places and the fire brigades were busy. I could not believe that they were still smouldering since the raid, but was told that they were indeed. There was dust on everything and as I walked on in a part of the city near the river, that perhaps I had known once but in any case could never have recognised amidst the gutted and ruined buildings of which it was mostly composed. Mercifully, to me, the glimpses of reality are few, and the tragedy of what was the city only dawns upon me at moments. Here I seem to live in an unreality and cannot seem to connect this devastation with the London that I love, then some little thing seems to bring it home to me with a sickening flash which makes one want to cry out with the sudden pain of realisation of what it means. Outside some business premises were piles of books, the pages blackened by fire and the remains of a burned typewriter stood forlornly in the street. People seemed to hurry on about their business quietly, mostly on foot, though a few buses were running in some of the main thoroughfares. I went through a fish market and up to the monument at the edge of London Bridge, then as I crossed the river, I got the most wonderful view up to Tower Bridge, the light was reflected in the water and the barges were chug chugging up the river. Rivers have always fascinated me, there is an atmosphere about them that leads me to wild fancies. I got back to 40 Belgrave Square from London Bridge and of course I had missed my train by half an hour at least. On Birdcage Walk, the flowers in St James Park were more beautiful almost than I have ever seen them, perhaps they seemed so in contrast to what I had just seen.

Here Anne was able to see beauty amid the horror of war. She was also enjoying her new job. Her work at Leighton Buzzard was as a signals clerk. She learned how to use a Typex machine, a sort of large typewriter on to which you would type a message in plain text and it would churn out an encrypted version. This would then be sent out by radio using Morse code. It was a labour-intensive way of transmitting information but was necessary for security.

Anne, working as one of ten clerks, was amused by her colleagues' behaviour: *Nina, bawling just like a schoolmarm . . . several thousand BAs etc and lets you know it too, Musso, knitting on top of the Typex lid, then suddenly decides to do an OPS summary or suchlike, about six pages long, which she does almost without a mistake,* Gardenia, with her *grand sense of humour,* 'Smithie' (another one, this time female), Maureen McWaters, the Irish girl at the teleprinter, Topsy Stevenson *banging away on the Typex about 100 to the dozen . . . never seems to make a mistake. She is a BA law . . . Angela just sits doing nothing and saying 'Bloody' and 'My God' every moment and looking at the clock endlessly.*

Angela Griffiths appears to be the only one not pulling her weight. Anne, though, seems to have revelled in being part of the group, perhaps even too much, for after drinking Pimm's with one of her new women friends at the Swan, she fainted, in front of Mr and Mrs Hunt. I couldn't help wondering whether this was an early indication of her alcoholism.

In late May, Anne and her mother stayed at Thurlestone, as they had done the year before. The house in Hope Cove was still full of evacuees – at least twenty in a house that normally slept nine. Anne was ecstatic about the cliffs, the light over the sea, the noise of the waves breaking against the rocks and the cries of the seagulls. *Bluebells were everywhere and larks were soaring . . . the gorse was in bloom. The smell of the sea made me feel a kind of yearning and a wild desire for adventure in far lands . . .* Coming back to reality, she declared: *When I look back, I am horrified at the futility of my existence.*

She meant her life before the war – skiing, fishing in Scotland, Palm Beach in winter, cruising in the Caribbean – all of which she had enjoyed but now suddenly perceived as shockingly hedonistic.

She went on to write seriously of the current war situation – the sinking of the *Bismarck* on 27 May, then, by 1 June, 15,000 Allied troops evacuated from Crete, the Allies having lost the island to the Germans. In April there had been the bombing, then disabling, of HMS *York* while it was being repaired in Souda Bay off Crete – Anne had read about it in a cipher before it became general news.

In early June, she visited Aunt K again and experienced a scene in the local tube station of Londoners preparing to bed down for the night: *people sitting on sacks in the passages leading down to the platforms and there was such a wind blowing that it almost blew their skirts over their heads and I thought what it must be like to spend a whole night there in that cold combined with the inevitable smell of the tubes.*

In contrast, there were visits to Knowle – haymaking, the sweet smell of lavender, the garden full of roses. And she still had her own bit of garden there, *full of bloom* . . . Even in wartime, Anne found stability and relaxation at Knowle, as I had often done myself. *Home, every smell and mood of it is familiar to me since I was a child . . . The cream pink rose which grows on top of the stoke hole roof is perfectly lovely. They are cutting the hay . . . we spent some time turning it ourselves and by the time I left it was almost all carted.*

Here were my mother and grandmother 'turning the hay' as Aunt K had done as a girl at Knole, with her friend Bird, thirty years earlier.

Anne first heard of Bletchley Park on 21 May 1941, through a friend who

is in a most interesting job and is in a place known as a 'war station'. I gather they translate things and that it is a combination of all 3 services. They are thinking of having WAAF officers there and she is going to make enquiries about it for me. Of course she can't tell me much about it which is tiresome. They are connected with Transcom [a branch of US Defense] *AMC* [Air Military Command] *on private wires. All rather exciting, though at present some of the stuff at Transcom is thrilling and you really feel that you are doing something. I am more thankful every moment that I am in the RAF and not in the army. 3000 parachutists have landed in Crete and half of them have been rounded up already.*

Anne was curious, even enthusiastic. On 5 June through the intervention of this friend – who never appears in the diaries again – she was interviewed at Bletchley Park itself. Its main purpose – though it is doubtful as to whether Anne would have known all this then – was the breaking of enemy codes and ciphers. Other related tasks included the study of enemy wireless systems, the translation and clarification of decrypts, the communication of this intelligence to the government and a discussion with them of the significance of such intelligence.

In the diary she does not mention the appearance of Bletchley Park – also known as Station X – which she later found grim, but concentrates only on the interview, in which a Captain Edgar asked her to read out a passage from an Italian newspaper, then translate it. She was then handed a test paper by Group Captain Humphreys, her future boss, containing information about planes, which included the phrase *'retractable undercarriage'*. Despite her recording in her diary that the interview had been **terrifying** and that she didn't do very well, her stint at Madame Boni's, and the Italian lessons that she had just taken in Nottingham while based at Hucknall, must have helped.

Her next interview, six weeks later, at the Air Ministry, with *a most charming man who spoke v. good Italian and French*, more or less clinched the job. She was told that she might be wanted soon, after just one more interview at Whitehall.

This final interview was on 11 August, with a Squadron Commander Hill, who said that she might have to go down to the country that night, but must first report to a Miss Hogan in Broadway, SW1, after getting some photos of herself. *Off I went to get the photos done, did some shopping and then went to lunch with Gig and then back for the photos, took them to Air Min and off to Broadway. They gave me the wrong address.* This was an incident that my mother would relate in later life, still wondering even then whether she had deliberately been sent to a butcher's shop as a test of initiative – *I found it none the less in the end and was taken to see the Grp Cpt, the CO, a most charming man, in fact they were all charming there and this is the HQ. They gave me petrol and the GC told me to stick to my billet at all costs and not to go down till the morning. They seemed to have found out all about me and the whole interview there was very nice. I came out pleased but shattered with exhaustion and nerve strain.*

Before starting at Bletchley, Anne went on leave in early August with her mother to Craignure on the Isle of Mull, off the west coast of

Scotland. Here, in this beautiful setting – *the air soft and sweet . . . lilies and Marsh Marigolds in full bloom* – a person intrudes in the diary in a way that is shocking and disturbing. I had been half-expecting this character to show herself, and had been on the lookout for her, without knowing her name. I assume that my mother was writing about her now because, on holiday, away from her work routine, she had more time to reflect on a subject that, for her, was important and complex.

When I was a teenager, my mother had told me with some relish how, during the war, a lesbian had propositioned her. 'But I told her: "I'm sorry, I'm not that kind of person!"'

She seemed very proud of her reply but I sensed that there was something not quite true in the story. I suspected that, susceptible to flattery, and also perhaps attracted to this woman, my mother had led her on and, shocked when something physical was suggested, had then done an about-turn, taking the moral high ground.

That August 1941, Anne romantically describes Stirling Castle: *standing on a high crag in the half light before the dawn . . . like some old German fairy tale of knights and beautiful princesses; we half expected it all suddenly to vanish.* She writes of her pleasure about getting away from the war on the Isle of Mull: *it seems exactly like peacetime again . . . the smell and the noise of the sea outside one's bedroom window at night are heaven.* But she goes on: *at present I am not at peace with myself . . . herewith hangs a tale, a sordid enough little tale . . . last Sunday when Angela and I went out to lunch . . . she told me . . . that she was addicted to sexual relations with women.*

The seductress was her colleague from the Leighton Buzzard office. The diary tells of how, apart from seeing Angela at work, Anne had also noticed her on the local train accompanying a certain girl. Soon, though, Angela began carrying Anne's suitcases for her: *Like some rare poison, I was fascinated by the unknown . . . And I do not even know what such people do!*

There is, frustratingly, no physical description of Angela, nothing like those sketches of Lady Ann Cole or American Mary, and nothing even to indicate whether my mother considered Angela good-looking.

152

The older woman, though, had other qualities that hypnotised Anne.

Angela's proposition, when it came, was low key. She said that *some people could not live without affection* and that she had found her *way of life* was the only way of getting it, but that she valued Anne's friendship so much that she would rather not risk losing this and have her do something that she would regret. *All together it was put in a very subtle way and the supposed viciousness of it all was masked.*

Angela comes across in the diary as powerful, possibly unstable, and intent on following her own wishes. In her dealings with Anne, she used flattery, something to which my mother was always susceptible – *ever since Angela first met me, she thought that I had so much charm and personality*. At twenty-seven, Anne, despite all her foreign travel, was still in many ways vulnerable and innocent. She was also curious about people and about new experiences. Angela, no doubt genuinely attracted by the younger woman, must have hoped to take advantage.

Anne wanted to disapprove but, probably in recognition of her own feelings, couldn't ultimately bring herself to. Despite her judgemental word – *viciousness* – had Anne been as repulsed as she later pretended, she would surely have ended the association then.

She was ambivalent – *Like some rare poison, I was fascinated by the unknown.* She *was* fascinated, but also scared, and she would experience this dichotomy much of her life, in other areas also. As the war went on, she was expressing increasing impatience with the narrow life that she was expected to lead at Knowle, and ultimately marry into. While loving her home's physical beauty and security, the old-fashioned existence led there by her mother and stepfather also proved to be a sort of cage for her spirit. Making friends with Angela was another way for Anne's adventurous nature to break loose. For, despite her reservations, she went on seeing Angela, even several months after Anne's starting her new job at Bletchley, and well after Angela had left the Leighton Buzzard office nearby.

November 3rd 1941.
Dined with Angela at the 5 Bells. We had a great discussion on

psychology. They are all talking about putting her on a court martial at the station on an absence without leave charge. She told me that she had only come back because I had said that I didn't think it was a good way to do things and that she felt she could have let me down if she had stayed away. She also asked me if I would care to be seen about with someone 'whose reputation stinks'. She asked me, too, if I ever did anything that I wanted, as she didn't believe that I did, and said that I didn't give anything out and was the most nervous person she had ever come across 'Full of nervous habits', that I was 'wild by nature' and unstable. She told me that she was possessive and jealous by nature.

My mother always liked being described as 'nervous' and 'sensitive'. She seemed to think that she was different, and superior, in this respect to my father and me. As for **wild by nature**, she would have liked that too.

When I was a child my grandmother used to sing the song 'I Do Like to Be Beside the Seaside', changing some of the words:

Oh look at Mum with her legs all bare!
Dancing in the fountains at Trafalgar Square!

There was something defiant about this image of my mother, dancing alone in the fountains in a public place, breaking the rules. That idea of her as a dashing wilful tomboy stayed with me as something to be emulated. It also showed her capacity for enjoyment and for adventure, something that I admired and later, because of her alcoholism and general decline, I often forgot. I suppose it was partly this adventurousness that made her go on seeing Angela Griffiths. Also, with a stepfather whom she found restricting, perhaps the idea of women being able to enjoy a life without men was inspiring.

On 12 November, she and Angela stayed up talking together until 4 a.m. Anne then decided that Angela had given her the best analysis of her character and capabilities, ever. Anne proceeded to set down in the diary Angela's 'analysis' of her – that Anne's conscious was *completely at war* with her subconscious, and that she presented herself as the person her mother wanted her to be, while suppressing her real nature. More alarmingly, Angela also accused Anne of being sadistic – and an even greater masochist. *My face is sadistic too, and this is what intrigues A. about me to a great extent, I believe.*

Angela told her that she was like a lump of clay, to be moulded into something worthwhile. She emphasised that Anne would *always need a person, though, to do that moulding and cannot stand alone.* Presumably Angela hoped to be the one to do the 'moulding'. *In all the talks we have had, A. says she has never been bored for a moment and I can say the same about her, although she shakes me up and disturbs my mental equilibrium in an annoying way at times.*

How different that admission is from my mother's dismissive references to Angela years later – the 'official' version that she gave to me.

Angela Griffiths *was* a bit sinister, I thought. She was hoping to seduce Anne, and being so understanding was one way to achieve this. At the same time, I felt that her analysis of Anne and her relationship with her mother was correct.

My grandmother was quick, witty, interested in politics and current affairs, but basically non-intellectual, occupying herself mainly with her garden and dogs. Like many leisured women of her generation, she painted watercolours. But she could not understand why her daughter was learning Russian or why I wanted to write a book. She certainly was not sympathetic about her daughter's other 'passions' either. I recall her saying to me when I was in my teens, disappointment and bafflement in her voice: 'Your mother has always had these crazes for women!'

Perhaps it was her own lack of maternal instinct that had nourished her daughter's longing for these 'women' who kept cropping up throughout Anne's life. Many of them took on a quasi-maternal role – I recall my mother's pleasure when she told me that Posy, an older friend from Majorca, had repacked her suitcase for her during a group holiday in Peru. Then there were Anne's other mother substitutes – Mrs

Welsh, Nah, Gig and Aunt Dita. Perhaps Mrs Hunt, her landlady, also performed such a role, as did her Peruvian godmother, Kata.

Anne was somewhat unworldly and, indeed, in many ways remained so for the rest of her life. She had no father, brothers or sisters, and her mother, who was lacking her daughter's intellectual curiosity, could not be her soulmate.

Before he died, Anne's father had published a short book, *Finance and War*, and his sister, Anne's Aunt K, had managed, with perseverance, to get the diaries of the Empress Marie Louise, Napoleon's second wife, translated from French into English by Frédéric Masson and published by John Murray in 1922 – this I learned from a box containing her letters to and from various publishers and literary agents. It was presumably from her father and his sister that Anne had inherited her intellectual leanings.

My grandmother, I knew, would have been horrified by any whiff of the illicit in her daughter's friendships. I remember her dismissal of Nigel Nicolson's *Portrait of a Marriage* – his account of the extramarital affairs of his two homosexual parents, Nigel Nicolson and Vita Sackville-West – as 'that dirty book'. She preferred her close relations to be respectable. However, perhaps it was a different matter concerning admirers or friends, for one of my grandmother's beaux, Colonel Malone – Cecil l'Estrange Malone – had made a fiery speech in the Albert Hall on 7 November 1920, been charged with sedition under Section 42 of the Defence of the Realm Act and jailed for six months. 'What are a few Churchills or a few Curzons on lamp posts compared to the massacre of thousands of human beings?' was the line that had landed him in prison. He had also been the first Communist Party member in the House of Commons. My mother had told me that Malone had taken my grandmother pub-crawling round the East End, which she had enjoyed. I remember him and his second wife in a bubble car in Belgrave Square, he driving, she in the sidecar. And Dita recalled that when Malone had complained about the discrepancy between his and my grandmother's incomes – she had just bought a racehorse – instead of being discomfited, my grandmother had simply replied:

'Cecil, why not get a greyhound?' But I suppose her flirtation with the outré Malone was different from having a daughter who was a lesbian.

My mother did not see Angela Griffiths for six months. Then she visited her in Eccleston Street, not far from Belgrave Square, where Angela was sharing a flat with *her present girlfriend, a Mrs Mandeville – one of the most depraved looking women I've ever set eyes upon.* I was excited when I read this. My mother's attitude to lesbians was a peculiar mixture of fascination and fear, and here it was manifested again. She added: *I suppose I should have been ashamed to have been with such people, but I just am not and don't feel that way, so there is nothing to be done about it.*

This shame was surely connected with her awareness of my grand-mother's notions of 'how to behave'. Anne, while fighting against her own impulses, was clearly fascinated to meet women who had openly chosen that path. She wrote at some length in the diary about this encounter, trying to be honest, but not fully understanding her own reactions. She was shocked, yet intrigued, by the two women sharing a bedroom, but added primly: *there was no feeling of vice about the place, which I can usually sense at once.* This surely implies that, with some part of her, she already felt that romantic friendship and even sex between women were natural. Yet she was clearly very conflicted, since earlier she had described Mrs Mandeville as *one of the most depraved looking women I've ever set eyes upon.*

Three days later, Anne recorded more about her reaction to that visit. *These crazes for people are a part of my nature that I can't do without. I have had them ever since I remember. I suppose it is an adolescence that I have never grown out of or a result of sexual repression. Feeling is all that really matters, I'm convinced, to a nature like mine, which is highly emotional. Angela disturbs me more than any-one I've ever known.*

She had written *people* rather than *women*, though all the time I knew my mother, it was only for women that she had these *crazes.*

*

Anne was to be proved wrong about the apparently harmless nature of the relationship between Angela and Mrs Mandeville. On 25 September 1942, my grandmother wrote to my mother at the Hunts' saying she had read in a newspaper that Angela Griffiths had just given evidence at an inquest; a woman had fallen down a lift shaft at a block of flats and died. Neighbours had reported hearing sounds of a quarrel, but Angela had denied this, merely stating that she hadn't realised that the lift wasn't there. Anne, who had not yet seen the newspaper article, summarised her reaction: *I must say they are a pretty rotten crowd. Out on my autocycle, which I adore!*

I read this more than once, noting how, after absorbing that shocking news, Anne had retreated, taking her mother's cue and dismissing her former friend, and the deceased, as that *rotten crowd.*

Perhaps there was something deeply escapist in my mother's nature which rendered her inadequate in dealing with upsetting events and the implications that they held about past relationships. For, instead of exploring the matter in her diary, her secret place, she had backed off, ultimately dismissing her intense friendship in one paragraph that ended with that peculiarly frivolous – and, in the circumstances, chilling – sentence, the last time she would ever mention the incident in her diary: *Out on my autocycle, which I adore!*

I was tantalised and, after trawling through *The Times* index and finding nothing, I obtained help from the librarian in my local library's reference section, who helpfully sent me to the *Westminster and Pimlico News*, off Victoria Street. Within ten minutes, I had found in its archives the newspaper report of 18 September 1942:

FELL DOWN LIFT SHAFT
Pimlico Woman Killed.

At Westminster Coroner's Court, on Saturday, Mr Bentley Purchase held an inquest on Mrs Florence Ethel Mandeville (48), 19 Chantrey House, Eccleston Street, Pimlico. On September 8, Mrs Mandeville was killed in falling 50 feet down the lift shaft at Chantrey House.

Miss Angela Griffiths, 19 Chantrey House, said she had known deceased since February.

The inquest report went on for three pages. Had Mrs Mandeville ever shown suicidal tendencies? No, was the answer. Angela Griffiths was quoted as saying that she had found the 'deceased' on top of the lift, but then denied that there had been 'any kind of a row' in the flat. It emerged, in further questioning, that the porter of the block – this was the building that my mother had visited, in which the two women had shared a bedroom – had heard raised voices. Angela Griffiths ended up with a black eye, acquired, she told the court, while getting the 'deceased' off the top of the lift.

Angela Griffiths was also asked if she had struck her own visiting mother that night. She did not answer that question directly but admitted to having been angered by her mother's dismissive remark about the 'deceased', more or less stating that her demise did not matter as long as Angela was all right. There were also queries about the lift's mechanism.

'Apparently there is no reason to think there is anything behind this matter,' said the coroner. 'The assumption is that deceased went to the lift to go downstairs and not realising the lift was not there, fell down the shaft. I am quite satisfied that the gates were in ordinary mechanical repair.'

A verdict of 'Accidental Death' was recorded.

I felt strange when I read of these events connected with my mother's past. They reminded me of a scene from a Terence Rattigan play. I recalled my grandmother telling me about the incident (without giving Griffiths's name, which she had probably forgotten), as if to illustrate how dangerous it was to associate with such types. Indeed, my grandmother had given me the sinister impression that, at any moment, a lesbian could turn herself into a murderess.

And Angela had confessed to my mother that she was *very jealous and possessive*. It could have been Anne in that lift shaft.

Chapter 14

Anne's first day at Bletchley Park, 12 August 1941, sounds grim. *It is the most peculiar place, masses of odd-looking civil servants and men with orange shirts and long hair about.* Adding that she feared she would never be the kind of person who could be unaffected by their environment, Anne also found herself fazed by Bletchley's laissez-faire atmosphere. Unlike most of the others there, she insisted on always carrying her gas mask and wearing a hat and gloves when going out. At once she began to worry about being so cut off from the RAF, and wondered whether she had made the right decision in coming.

Bletchley Park was situated midway between Oxford and Cambridge and a forty-minute train ride from London. By the time Anne arrived, it was already playing a crucial part in the war, as a secret Intelligence Centre. It was here that, famously, the code used by the German armed forces to transmit information was broken by the Enigma encryption and decryption machine. Dotted around the grounds a number of temporary buildings had been erected which were called huts and given numbers. It was in these huts that the bulk of the work was done. Each hut had its own function. Anne had been allocated the job of an indexer in Hut 3, where about seventy-five people worked on a three-shift system. Its main purpose was to translate, interpret and act upon intelligence that had been received and decrypted in another hut. It was a complex operation that was organised using a hub and spoke system. In other words there was a central operations room, called the Central Watch Room, where intelligence was first handled.

Here, representatives from the three sections, Naval, Military and Air, worked, unusually, together. The spokes of the operation were the divisions of each of these three sections within the hut, and information would be passed backwards and forwards from the Central Watch Room down through the chain of command.

One of the most important tasks was to maintain a minutely detailed indexing system so that whenever a new piece of information came in, it would be broken down into its component parts and each piece of information recorded in a separate file. The idea was to create a database so that if you needed to find out about a particular ship, officer or place, all previous intelligence on it could be instantly accessed.

Anne's job was to work on this indexing system – on the face of it a menial task, but essential to the smooth running of the hut. It was in fact a very complex task, because of the volume of information coming in and because there were code names in use within the messages which had to be puzzled over. There were service abbreviations, service jargon, acronyms and slang used within the messages from unit to unit. Plunged into this new and daunting job, Anne did not write her diary for a fortnight. Then, on 6 September 1941, she was cheered by an unexpected visitor to Hut 3. *In came the PM himself, smoking the proverbial cigar and looking very well and pleased with life.* Churchill, after sitting down at the desk of Anne's boss, Group Captain Robert Humphreys, and reading some reports, declared: *'Well, if we don't win the war with information like that I don't know how we shall win it!'*

Anne was thrilled. She wrote more of Churchill's visit:

We are rather pleased with ourselves . . . as thanks to some of our information we have sunk a huge convoy in the Mediterranean. He only went into Hut 6 and our Hut, in fact the whole thing was rather thrilling. He went out and made a speech at the main building but we missed hearing it. It appears however to have pleased everyone very much indeed and he said how important the place was and that it might easily shorten the war and that he thanked all the personnel working there on behalf of the government . . . it really was rather a

thrill to see him, in our office, sitting at Humphreys' desk and look-
ing at our Middle East reports! Later Humphreys circulated a letter
thanking us all for our work and help, which was very nicely worded
and made us all feel pretty good. The P.M. at his speech outside the
main building said: 'It is amazing that a place that looks so simple
can really be so sinister.'

De Haan has told me that B.P. is one of the most amazing places
of this war, so I suppose it should console me for a lot of other things.

Flight Lieutenant De Haan, another of Anne's superiors, was right.
In July 1941, a month before Anne arrived, the Italian cipher, C38m,
had been broken by Bletchley. Edward Thomas, in his essay 'A Naval
Officer in Hut 3' in *Codebreakers: The Inside Story of Bletchley Park*,
edited by F.H. Hinsley and Alan Stripp, explains the significance of
this:

this yielded, among other things, advance warning of the sailing dates,
routes and composition of virtually all trans Mediterranean supply
convoys and it also threw occasional light on Italian main-fleet move-
ments. During 1941 the gist of the relevant Enigma decrypts had been
signalled by Hut 3 to the Mediterranean authorities by the SCU/SLU
[the special communications unit and special liaisons unit] channel,
while that of the C38m decrypts had been sent by a part-naval, part-
civilian processing watch in Hut 4 separately to Malta and elsewhere.
An outstanding result of these messages would be a spate of sinkings
in late 1941, which played a big part in Rommel's retreat to El Agheila
at that time.

Despite the work being interesting, Anne was unhappy, stating in
the diary that she was so miserable that she scarcely knew how to
get through the day and that she could not bear to go on like this,
wasting the best time of her life, that she had a mad longing to do
something desperate – *something that will gratify the senses. An affair*
with someone in London would be the answer to all problems.

My mother's self-pitying side shows itself more in these Bletchley diaries than in any other of the war diaries. She found the life there colourless and, although not sybaritic by nature, she yearned for material comforts – *lovely furniture, flowers, chintzes and plenty of everything. Just for 24 hours.*

She was not the only one at Bletchley who reacted like this. The naval officer Edward Thomas wrote of the 'grimness of its barbed wire defences and the cold and dinginess of its hutted accommodation', and Diana Payne, a Wren, later described her first sight of it: 'a hideous Victorian mansion standing in grounds with several large huts . . . a strange assortment of civilians going in and out of the building'.

Supporting Anne during this early Bletchley period was Mrs Hunt. Since Leighton Buzzard and Bletchley were so close, Anne was able to continue as the Hunts' lodger and remained friends with them. When I was about ten, Mrs Hunt stayed with us in Sussex, accompanying me to a village fete, where my dog Buzzy uncharacteristically lifted his leg on my sandal, probably out of excitement at the little dog show. A man made a lewd remark which Mrs Hunt chose to ignore; I remember her as a protective and benign presence. Each year, she would send me a Christmas card with a handkerchief inside.

Now I read about all her kindnesses to my mother, how she put *apricot cream roses* in the younger woman's room, saying she had picked them because they reminded her of Anne's *lovely complexion,* and how she managed to acquire three bottles of gin for Anne 'under the counter'. I hope she never knew that my mother became a serious drinker.

Anne's moods fluctuated wildly in these weeks of early autumn 1941. Sometimes she loathed Bletchley, then she would change her mind and decide that she had been right after all to get out of Code and Cipher work, where she really had just been a clerk, and into Intelligence, where there were definitely *some openings,* and which in reality suited her better. She added that her ambition was to become a flight officer, the next rank up in the WAAF: *I should get a terrific kick out of it.*

In October 1941, her close friend Cynthia, who had been at Knowle when Alan threatened to shoot himself, became engaged and Anne again turned down poor John M – *I suddenly knew that I couldn't <u>bear</u> to marry him even if it meant my remaining an old maid all my life.* She would contemplate marrying him several times after that.

Meanwhile she had made a new lifelong friend, Lettice Ashley-Cooper, first mentioned in Anne's diary on the day of Churchill's visit that September. Lettice was urging Anne to share a cottage, saying that this would make their life at Bletchley more bearable.

Lettice was very loyal. However, they seem to have fuelled one another's discontent. Lettice, more robust and self-assured, had many friends and relations in high places and was always scheming for ways for them both to leave Bletchley. And Anne, while admitting that *the work is fascinating*, still yearned to be back with the RAF and for *life with a capital L.*

The first war diaries had shown my mother doing her best, and had thus been a pleasant surprise, but suddenly this changed. I was shocked when I read the first page of her next diary.

December 1st 1941. Knowle.
I am still in bed eating masses of oranges, which seems incredible, as they are reserved for children under six. They are just what I like these days and seem to do me good too. Dr Moncrieff says that my heart is tired and that I am to stay here until Thursday.

Apart from eating oranges reserved for children as part of rationing, my mother was skiving off from Bletchley after less than four months. I was suspicious of her quoting her doctor, as I had known her often to exaggerate an illness when she wanted to get out of something. Due to a cold, she had been very late at the party to celebrate my own wedding and would not have shown up at all if Molly had not stepped in at the last moment and driven her to London. Guests, particularly her own friends, kept asking me: 'Where's your mother?' She would do the same two and a half years later at my son's christening, getting lost and simply not turning up at all.

Knowle, the Sussex house where my mother Anne grew up.

My maternal grandparents, Raymond and Gladys Hamilton-Grace, outside the old front door at Knowle (then called Knole), 1914.

My grandmother with her two children, Anne and Raymond, in the field at Knole, June 1916.

Gladys's second marriage, to 'Chow', with my mother as bridesmaid, 4 July, 1919.

Anne as a teenager with her nanny, Nah, on the verandah at Knowle, late 1920s.

Anne and her mother at a meet at Eridge, nr Tunbridge Wells, Kent, 1938.

Bathers at Knowle swimming pool, 1930s.
My mother was very proud of her legs.
Hers are nearest.

An athletic Anne practises her swing,
1930s.

Anne's WAAF mugshots, 1939.

Anne and Alan Judson, off-duty during their time at
Bomber Command, Bicester, 1940.

The Code and Cipher course, Bulstrode Park, Gerrards Cross,
1940. Anne end of bottom row, left.

Millie Swettenham, on holiday with Anne in
Cornwall, September 1944, both on leave from
their jobs at Bomber Command Headquarters,
High Wycombe.

Anne, far right, on leave in Belgium at Château
de Fontaine with friends after VE Day.

Anne's temporary duty pass to visit
Joe Darling in Paris, May 1945.

REAR HEADQUARTERS
2ND TACTICAL AIR FORCE

VICTORY IN EUROPE
CELEBRATION DANCE

THE CASERNE BAUDOUIN
BRUSSELS

SATURDAY 12TH MAY 1945
8 P.M. - 2 A.M.

SOUVENIR PROGRAMME

An invitation to a dance to celebrate
VE Day in Brussels.

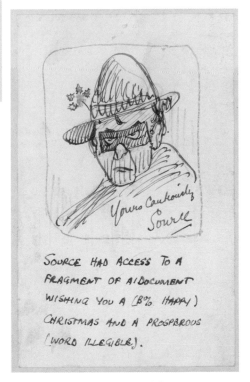

Christmas at Bletchley Park.

My mother and father on their wedding day, 1 June, 1948.

Dita and Meg, my mother's cousins, as bridesmaids.

Joe Darling and his wife at my parents' wedding at St James' Spanish Place, London.

Nah with me as a baby, late 1949.

My mother and me in Madrid, 1951.

Me and Raymond at San Vicente de la
Barquera beach, near Comillas, Spain, 1953.

Me and Raymond at Hope Cove, Devon, 1954.

Me with Raymond and Nicky (Raymond on Captain) at North Heath House,
Chieveley, Berks, September 1955.

My Braunston terrier Buzzy and me, 1961.

My mother with my then husband and
her first grandchild, in 1981, at her house
in Sussex.

She had also cancelled going to Majorca with a Sussex friend, Susan S, at two days' notice, announcing importantly: 'My doctor *strongly* advises me not to go!' Susan could not recover her air fare but my mother was seen lunching out near Susan's house the next day, and shortly afterwards went to Russia, a place where she *did* want to go.

In early December 1941, Dr Moncrieff sent her to Knowle for a week to recover, then told her not to return to the office until Boxing Day. *It is a marvellous prospect and I don't intend to let myself feel guilty, because I have needed a rest for ages and have had no leave for a long time either, so if possible, I intend to return feeling really well for once.*

Her defiance about lack of guilt – she obviously *did* feel a bit bad about not going back earlier to Bletchley – was also familiar to me. She would employ a similar tone when declaring: 'I've decided to buy myself a present!' Perhaps the most ludicrous example of this was in the early 1990s, when Molly, a busy woman, drove her from Sussex to Sloane Square, a two-hour journey, to buy at Peter Jones a large china rabbit, of which she already had several, and back again.

Perhaps my mother's charm had also worked on Dr Moncrieff. Her sick leave from Bletchley would end up lasting two and a half months.

Anne does not seem to have paid much attention to the doctor's advice to rest. Her convalescent lifestyle sounds far more hectic than the job. She went out dancing with Terence O'Neill (who later married Jean, my mother's companion in the Balkans) at the Mirabelle, motored to Epping with him and his brother-in-law, then, back in London, shopped, lunched with Terence at the Berkeley, where she saw her friend Babe, and dined with her friend Diana at Le Cigale.

December 16th 1941.
This holiday came in the nick of time and has been such a mental and physical rest; it has made the whole difference to life. Still don't feel too good and have a fever each night.

Jean suggested to me that Anne as a young woman could have suffered from glandular fever, not diagnosed then, and which I had had myself in my early twenties – I went to Knowle to recuperate. It would have accounted for Anne's high temperatures and bouts of depression. Was I being too hard on her?

December 30th 1941. Knowle.
I feel so depressed about 6 each evening and could burst into tears. It is the queerest feeling, not exactly depression, but I would like to cry my eyes out and it comes on every night about the same hour and has done for the last 3 evenings.

On 7 December, Japan had attacked Pearl Harbor – *So at last, America is with us . . . it is a pleasant feeling, now that we are all together at last.*
Anne would spend Christmas that year at Knowle.

December 21st 1941.
Heavenly day, like Switzerland. We picked some holly. The berries are simply superb this winter, masses of them.
The Russians have re-taken another largish town and Hitler has taken over supreme command of the German army.

The next day she was in London again, shopping for hats, noting the poor quality of their felt, due to the war. Books, she added, were now printed on coarse paper, had pages missing, and often the same letter was repeated two or three times in one word.

In London another doctor, Sir John Weir, and Dr Moncrieff suggested that she might have jaundice. (I wondered, perhaps ignobly, if she had found 'tame' doctors in these two, who would be inclined to recommend long rests. But the 'rests' only resulted in more frantic socialising. No wonder she went on having temperatures!)

On 1 January 1942, she visited Babe's sister in Lincolnshire, where she rode a grey horse and enjoyed herself. She returned via King's

Cross, where, shamed by a woman porter *half my size*, she explained that she had just got out of her *sickbed*. That evening she was out again with Terence at the Mirabelle, the 400 and the Embassy, and the following day, to lunch and a movie.

I have no vitality, she wrote that evening, with astonishing lack of self-awareness. Meanwhile 40 Belgrave Square was *like an ice-house*. There had been no glass in the windows of her bedroom since the Blitz.

A fortnight later, she was still on sick leave.

January 13th 1942. 40 Belgrave Square.
Snow on the ground and the trees in the square looked so pretty covered in snow. Shopping and lunch with Kata and Patrick [Kata's son] *and a movie. In the evening, Margaret and I went to see 'Blithe Spirit' and ate later at the 'Cigale'. Saw Moncrieff. I am not to go back until the 30th now.*

Anne walked miles in the snow, from Belgrave Square to Selfridges, then down Bond Street and across Piccadilly, ending with the war artists' exhibition in Trafalgar Square. She tried to understand the *fanciful* work of Paul Nash, described his planes looking like *various animals*, and returned to scrutinise the paintings a second time.

Still nostalgic for *the old jokes of Bicester days*, she then strolled through Grosvenor Square, hoping to see the WAAFs manning the balloons, but none were to be seen, *not surprising as it was bitterly cold and the one balloon snow coated.*

January 15th 1942.
Down to Knowle. Nice and quiet, it is terribly cold and the sky all overcast as though it was going to snow some more, but it never does; though the snow is still lying on the ground. We are cutting trees in the woods and getting £1 per tree for them from the lumber kings.

January 16th. 40 Belgrave Square.
I had a temperature again of 99.8 before I went out, 40 is like an ice cube and I sleep in my dressing gown and when I lay in bed in the morning the air is so cold that I can see my breath.

Despite her temperature, she was out late that night at the Berkeley. Next day it was Pimm's at the Dorchester, followed by golden plover. *I love those birds so much but it was v. good.*

Over Christmas, thousands of people had died of starvation in Leningrad as a result of the German siege that had started in September. My mother does not mention the siege but was keeping track of other events in the Soviet Union: *The Russians are reported to be fighting in the streets of Orel and are only 60 miles from Smolensk, which is Hitler's HQ.*

The weather in England that winter sounds almost Russian, certainly at Knowle, where the snow hung around without falling, where there was no sun for days and at midday it was almost as dark as in the evening.

In late January, she heard some upsetting news. Alan was engaged, to *some girl in Windsor. It gave me an awful shock somehow and yet I couldn't have married him myself, although I was in love with him for a long time.* Alan had not answered her last two letters, the first of which, she said, had evidently given him the impression that all was finished between them. She had then written to congratulate him on his DFC, but he had not replied to that either. She had not written again, having realised that she was no longer in love with him. However, this news of his engagement sent her into the depths of despair: *sometimes I feel as though I shall run out in the street and marry the first man who comes along, because this is just a series of being left out in the cold and at times the nostalgia of the whole thing drives me into the very depths of depression and yet I'm made so that I must have these affairs or go crazy. I suppose I'm much too serious about the whole thing.*

She had rejected *him* but still couldn't help feeling unwanted. Her friend Cynthia had married the previous month, and now, two days after that news about Alan, Anne's other close friend Diana decided to marry a brigadier over twenty years older than her and with a son aged twelve. Juliet was about to marry Trevor, her New Zealand pilot, and a colleague at Bletchley – another Anne – got engaged to a soldier in the Scots Guards. Then, three weeks after the news about Alan, her former fiancé David wrote to tell Anne that he was engaged to an Irish girl.

There were compensations.

January 22nd 1942. Knowle.
One, if not the loveliest morning I've spent since the war. Just ski-ing by myself and breaking new snow in yet untrodden fields whilst the sun shone and the snow glistened. The wax gave out that glorious smell when it melts in the sun and my skis slid through the powder snow with no effort at all. Overhead, the sky was a brilliant blue and for once I did not envy the fighter pilot who whined over me quite low and I wondered if he could see a lone skier in the fields and what he thought about it if he did.

Skiing, tennis, rock-climbing, flying: the pure pleasure of these physical activities enabled her to forget the war and her personal problems. I loved to read about Knowle in the snow, and of her joy in skiing. For once, all too rarely, my mother was happy.

Anne at last returned to her work at Bletchley in mid-February 1942. In the following months, she did not have time to be bored. By May, she had really got into her stride with her work.

May 1st 1942.
Capt. Bennett on and v. helpful. Nicest of the duty officers I've struck yet. The way in which it is assumed that I can check Hut 4 and see the D.O.s [duty officers] make no mistake on so short a training is past belief. The job is terrifying really, there are so many things I can slip on.

She seemed, in this situation, to come out better than some of her colleagues – one girl, Elizabeth, had been given special permission not to work nights as she

couldn't take it. When Elizabeth came in this morning, grumbling and saying, 'I must be taken off this — job at once' I could have killed her, as we are doing this 3 weekly business for her sake alone and I think, as it will be 8 weeks since she went on sick leave last, that she might make the effort to try again, as she knows the job is going to end in any case, instead, she almost brags about having burst into tears in the middle of the night.

Anne seemed to have conveniently forgotten about her own two and a half months' absence. She added robustly – her long sick leave had no doubt done her good – that she was hoping to give a dinner party the following evening: *after this war, we should all be wonderful organizers.*

This new-found confidence was so unlike the mother I knew. She was rewarded, for on 2 May she received a letter from De Haan, stating that she been granted **Acting Paid Rank of Fl.Off. WEF 14th Feb 1942. Authority Air Min Acting list 112/42 dated 28.3.42. Of course I was thrilled to bits.**

The next day was a **terrific party with John, Terence and Lettice and then to the Trout.** Soon, however, Anne was back to her almost obsessive dislike of those she worked with, this time as observed in the Bletchley cafeteria – **all these filthy civilians with their greasy hair and dirty trousers. How I hate the men too, except dear little Captain Bennett.** She added perversely:

Were I a man I should go mad working in the Hut service . . . I long for the dullest job, provided it is to do with operations of some kind, which is the nearest to doing the ops. oneself. It is in action and in risking one's life and in the achievement of the perfect harmony of mind and body that is needed for success in action that one rises to supreme heights, not over papers at a desk.

Harking back again to Bomber Command, she noted that the RAF were *bombing German towns constantly – Lübeck, Hamburg and other ports*. Her longing for action was perhaps unsurprising. After all, she was the daughter of a soldier. Her father had already served in South Africa and India before being sent to France with his regiment in August 1914. But he was not just a man of action. He had published that book, *Finance and War*, and, from a folder of letters of condolence to my grandmother (labelled, in her writing, *To be kept for Anne*), I read that, shortly before his fatal accident, he had just been transferred from the front and put into an Intelligence job, which was why he was on his way to Dunkirk.

My mother, as I would see from her RAF record, had, by the end of the war, clocked up *six* jobs in Intelligence between 1941 and 1945. Surely she could see that it was possible to perform daredevil feats like those of the fighter pilots – her father had obtained his pilot's certificate for aviation at the Cavalry School in Netheravon before the First World War – *and* to use one's intellect?

But in her diary, in reaction to those whom she perceived as conceited male intellectuals, she kept insisting that she had *no admiration for the brain*.

One interesting aspect of Bletchley was the synergy between the three services. Anne had been working under F.L. Lucas, a writer and lecturer from King's College, Cambridge, in a research section called 3R. But now, with the arrival of three naval officers sent by the Admiralty, 3R became 3N, a Naval Section, and on 4 May 1942, Hut 3 was taken over by the navy. A Lieutenant Commander Lavers became Anne's boss, and Lucas was relieved, to develop the research section of Hut 3, which became 3G. From now on, Anne, though still a WAAF, would work at Bletchley with the navy.

A Paymaster Lt. Haslam, who has just come back from the Mediterranean, came over to learn our stuff and Lt. Cdr. Lavers was also there this evening. He is to replace Mr Lucas and there are to be 3 naval officers under him to work watches, so I suppose we shall gradually all go.

The reorganisation of Hut 3 had come about because of the increasingly significant part the work of the hut had been playing in operations abroad. Hut 3 staff had become more experienced at identifying what information they had gleaned from Enigma would be of use and at dispatching it in an intelligible way. One of the code breakers' finest moments had been the previous year, when Hitler sent Rommel to help the struggling Italian army push back the Allies in North Africa. They managed to break the key used between army and air forces in Libya within days of Rommel landing at Tripoli, so were quickly able to provide information on his plans and movements. For the first time, a direct line of communication was set up between Hut 3 and the intelligence services stationed in Cairo, cutting out the conventional chain of command via the War Office and Air Ministry.

Previously all naval intelligence would have come from the Admiralty, which as well as being a Whitehall department was an operational headquarters. With Hut 3 now operating as a second, independent hub of intelligence, it was deemed necessary to boost the navy's presence in the hut, and the Admiralty reluctantly sent a party of three naval officers.

Involved in the practicalities of this naval takeover of her hut, Anne grumbled, with secret pride, *I get nothing done and have to keep showing Haslam things.* She had liked working under Lucas and was sorry that this had ended. However almost at once, Lieutenant Haslam, one of the three naval duty officers, instituted a Watch Book – *everything is tidied up to an incredible extent, which I must admit does appeal to me!* She also found that she liked Lavers. However, typically, just as the new efficient system in the hut was in place, Anne, having gone to London on 7 May, discovered there that she had *another* temperature, this time of 102, and Dr Moncrieff ordered a week's sick leave.

As usual, she disobeyed the doctor's orders to stay in bed – *when I have these temperatures, I get so depressed when I'm alone.* This reminded me of when I had undergone chemotherapy. Despite being advised to rest after each treatment, I too had then hated being alone, and although physically exhausted and feeling sick, would often attend book launches or parties. Similarly, my mother ill-advisedly went shopping with Lettice, and the following day was out again, when she glimpsed her former fiancé David (now about to marry) in a London bookshop. *I didn't feel equal to talking to him as I felt so ill.*

I found myself becoming exasperated; after all, she had just been furious with Elizabeth for having got off night duty due to nervous exhaustion, and had even written in the diary that if Elizabeth gave up the Bletchley job, Anne would have *no respect for her at all.* Now Anne's sick leave was extended to three weeks.

During that time she visited women friends around the country. She and Jean walked on the shore at Lymington, and Anne felt

that glorious exhilaration that I always get from the sight and sound of the sea, a kind of wildness and sense of adventure. It is only now when I see the sea, as I do so seldom, that I get the feeling of being cooped up here in this island and long to be free once again to roam the world at will . . . I tasted the sea and could have cried for the sheer joy of living.

I was right to have associated my mother with the sea – it was her life-blood.

On Anne's return to Bletchley, she recorded that Mrs Hunt had discovered her other lodger drinking gin before breakfast – the girl had even been down to the local grocer and ordered a bottle in Mrs Hunt's name.

I was often to experience this censorious, 'goody-goody' aspect of hers with regard to others' drinking. Eva, the cook at Belgrave Square, sometimes got very drunk. I recall my mother describing to me in shocked tones how she had had to help Eva up off the floor. Never did she admit to me that she drank too much herself. This perpetual denial, despite her often frightening behaviour and the physical evidence of her broken limbs, gave me a feeling of vertigo, as though I had imagined the whole thing.

On 17 June, Anne met Edward Thomas, who was then new in that hut. He would become a lifelong friend. Years later, he would publish that excellent essay 'A Naval Officer in Hut 3' about his time at Bletchley, and he would assist Harry Hinsley, a key Bletchley figure, in writing the official history of MI6.

When I was an adolescent, Edward had visited us in Sussex with his twins, a boy and girl, and his stepdaughter, all close to me in age. His stepdaughter had sworn loudly at him while he was helping her climb a tree and I remember my surprise that he did not retaliate, as my explosive father would have done.

Edward's manner towards my mother was also very unlike my father's patronising, teasing way with her. Indeed, I sometimes found Edward almost too reverential. He spoke as if my mother had never been given her due. When I was about twenty-five, I suddenly recalled, he had told me in front of her that she had written some very interesting diaries. I had not wanted then to take this in, as I had felt he was implying that I, like others, did not rate my mother. This made me inwardly bristle; how could I respect someone who, much of the time that I knew her, was a self-pitying escapist alcoholic?

On 28 June 1942, Anne went again to stay with Lettice, Lettice's sister Dot and their parents, Lord and Lady Shaftesbury. They all sang songs together after supper. *They are all so fond of each other and it is such fun that the atmosphere is nice just being there and reminded me of us all being together at Palm Beach and Westbury* [Aunt Dita's house on Long Island] *which is the only family life I've ever known and I adore.*

I felt sorry for my mother, an only child, when I read this. Perhaps these brief experiences of families enjoying themselves inspired her to have four children.

My brother Nicky had commented to me in his early twenties that it must have been difficult for her being brought up by our grandmother and Chow. At the time I had not understood, but I was reminded of his remark when I read her next sentence: *It made me realise just how much I have missed never having any brothers and sisters and always being so alien to Chow, who is always 'just wrong' and his whole mentality and of whom I'm always secretly ashamed, as he simply does not belong to our world or to our way of thought at all.*

Besides finding him difficult, she seemed to have regarded her step-father as socially inferior, something which would not have bothered her in her friends but which in poor Chow gave her yet another excuse to dislike him.

In July 1942, Anne found herself in the thick of the 'brainpower' action at Bletchley. Wing Commander Eric Jones had just taken command of her hut:

No one knows where they are. Chaos prevails . . . Bright missed transport last night, so Guy Haslam and I stayed on till one am. There was masses to do and I found a whole lot of inaccuracies, which drives me frantic, as it is so dangerous now not to be dead right. As every little thing matters enormously and the whole of the German position in N. Africa is dependent on supplies.

For some time the Americans had wished to land on the coast of German-occupied Europe, but had been held back by the British, who, based on their experience of Hitler's might, cautioned against it, fearing that such a move would almost certainly be defeated. A compromise was reached towards the end of July 1942, when the Allies decided to invade French North Africa, in what would be called Operation Torch. It was a huge undertaking, the biggest movement of ships so far, and much planning was needed for these landings, scheduled for 8 November. Troops were to land at Casablanca in Morocco, and at Oran and Algiers in Algeria. This would enable the Allies to advance on the German- and Italian-occupied territory of Libya, attacking from the west, as well as from Egypt in the east. It was vital that the Germans should have no idea of the planned attacks, and one of the successes of the operation depended on misleading the enemy into believing that preparations were being made for quite a different venture. Rumours were circulated that the objective was Sicily, Crete, the Balkans or the bolstering of British troops at Malta. Through Allied interception of German signals, it became apparent that they had been successfully duped into believing that a resupply of Malta was the explanation for the increase in ships and planes congregating at Gibraltar.

The main problem for both the Allies and the enemy during the war in North Africa was the lack of supplies and the difficulty of getting them. The British forces in Egypt were supplied by ships which had to sail all the way round the horn of Africa, meaning weeks of delay, but at least the passage was safe. Conversely, the enemy could have supplies shipped across from Italy within twenty-four hours, but thanks to the work of code breakers at Bletchley, their passage was by no means safe. The Italian convoys were escorted by the German air force, whose signals were being intercepted and decrypted in Hut 3. The Italian C 38m machine cipher which carried shipping information had been broken in summer 1941, so now, between Hut 4 and Hut 3N, news of the convoys' routes and their estimated times of departure and arrival at designated ports could be pieced together.

Between July and November 1942, during preparations for this Anglo-American invasion of North Africa, Anne was repeatedly praised for her good work. She felt encouraged, and even admitted in the diary, on 22 July at 00.50 while working alone with Haslam: *I love these evening shifts, though there is masses to do as a rule on them . . . I just live for the work at the moment.*

Two days later she was complimented by Lieutenant Commander Lavers.

July 24th 1942.
Lavers couldn't have been nicer and complimented me tremendously in the work I have done here and said that he would write me a chit to be forwarded to Air Ministry recommending me for as good a job

as I could be given, as the responsibility we had here before the Navy took over was so great that now we were wasted in this job. Very decent of him. [She was still hankering to leave.] *I said that I was quite untrained for a job and I didn't think I would get one, but he said that I was well fitted for a job where I could say 'yes or no' and supervise other people and that I was fitted for a better job than he could offer me now, though he would be pleased to have me as an additional to the D.O. I really felt very honoured as he sets a pretty high standard for efficiency and quickness of thought and decision, also for making decisions and acting on one's own responsibility . . . I was so worried I wouldn't sleep all night as I had been on from 4 to 12 acting as NDO* [naval duty officer] *quite on my own and had a great deal to do. I have got such confidence in myself now in this job and really feel I am worth something and on equal terms with those from the FO and other jobs, who have worked all their lives!*

My mother emerges well here. Her modesty was pleasing. She had a tendency to self-doubt and, except for her prowess in tennis, skiing and water skiing, had not, until now at Bletchley, had the opportunity to prove herself. She was particularly pleased to be praised by Connie Webb, *whose standard is 100 per cent and not the smallest slip tolerated.* Anne was thrilled that Connie had told her *how magnificent I had been, taking over such responsibility at such short notice.*

For almost the only time in my life, I could perceive my mother as someone who could take over, as someone steady who would not collapse under pressure.

At the end of the month, she had two lovely summer days at Knowle.

August 1st 1942 Knowle.
Perfect day. I am lying in a sunbathing suit on the tennis lawn, or rather, what was once the tennis lawn, near the new vegetable, once herbaceous, border and revelling in the sun.

These were temporary changes brought about by the war. Years later, after Knowle was divided and sold, I would experience other changes when I occasionally visited – a new swimming pool (part of a health club) on the old croquet lawn, a gravel path where my grandmother's rose trees 'The Bridesmaids' had stood, and a blank stretch of earth in the sunken garden instead of my grandmother's favourite bed of yellow and white flowers. The changes brought about by the war were temporary; after the war was over the Knowle garden was restored to its former beauty. But when it was sold in 1980 I would never see again the Knowle that existed while my grandmother was alive.

Chapter 15

Anne's performance so impressed her seniors that she and Lettice were allowed to go on an intelligence course at Stanmore on 2 August. They were there for three weeks, during which time Anne did not write her diary. At the end of September, she was dealt a disappointment. Lettice, with whom she was still hoping to share a cottage, had found a new job, in Horseferry Road, London. This would leave Anne without a real friend at Bletchley.

For the next couple of months, while still often complaining, Anne concentrated almost wholly on her work, as preparations for Operation Torch were set in motion: *Lavers has made me 4th NDO, which is as good a job as I could possibly get, except that now I want to get back to the Air Side and away from this kind of killing life . . .*

As a naval duty officer Anne's responsibilities were many. She was expected to check and forward signals drafted by the Naval Section. She also had to draft signals from scratch based on new information coming in from elsewhere in the hut – intelligence gathered from Enigma decrypts – and send them directly to commands in the Mediterranean. She was expected to act as a naval adviser to other sections of the hut, and to study all Hut 3 material to ensure that any necessary annotation from the naval angle was made and that the Naval Section and even the Admiralty were kept informed, when necessary.

All signals sent to the Mediterranean had to be logged and indexes maintained. The movement of enemy ships had also to be plotted on a wall chart and all data garnered from enemy decrypts had to be checked against Admiralty charts before sending a signal to check whether the enemy had made mistakes, either in their facts or in their signalling.

October 8th, 9th, 10th, 11th 1942.
The responsibility in a way is so great. I am on the watch, the sole woman on it. Connie said to me 'and you're the best representative we could have too', which was high praise.

. . . I have got the best job of any woman in the Hut now, I consider, and the one with the most responsibility and Hut 3 is the most important Hut there. I suppose, in a way, it is a big tribute to me, but I am so strung up emotionally just now, it doesn't mean a lot to me . . .

She was wrong about this; it would come to mean a great deal to her. In later life, despite my father's mockery, she clung on proudly to what she had done at Bletchley.

I too was proud, indeed triumphant, when I read: *I have got the best job of any woman in the Hut . . .*

October 12th 1942.
A typical day on the 4 to 12 shift, as I am at present, so that the sheer agony of it may be placed on record for me to look back on, perhaps one day in the far distant future when this period may be seen like a nightmare and be mercifully semi-observed in oblivion so that I shall remember only the glory of my position as the first and only woman on the watch and holding the most responsible position of any woman in the Hut, 'the thin end of the wedge' as Connie describes it.

I do not know why it does not pacify me more than it does as in a way it is a great tribute to me and more especially so, as it is through Lavers, whose standard of efficiency is 100 per cent, that I am there, but there the matter stands, it gives me no pleasure and I am miserable. And so to a description of one of countless days of misery: I wake at 10.30 and Mrs Hunt brings me my breakfast on a tray, it is delicious and typically consists of a boiled egg, often a half slice of orange, which of course is almost unprocurable these days, some Vitawheat and marmalade which I adore and a cup of tea, often accompanied by some cereal if I have any and which I eat out of pure greed. After this I stay in bed reading and sometimes writing until about 11.30 or 12 and this is rather bliss, after this I get up (I have a regular routine of doing this) first of all cleaning my buttons and then dressing slowly. Just before lunch I often have a drink from my gin bottle and orange, which I keep in a queer kind of store in my bedroom which acts as a kind of wine cellar and helps cheer me up at times. After lunch, during which we discuss mainly food and the wireless, also doings in L. Buzzard, I help Mrs Hunt wash up and listen to long rigmaroles about her family and who married who in L.B., then I retire to my room and lie on my divan by the window, which has a lovely view over the garden, down to the river and canal, and beyond and read or write again. Mrs H. brings me up a cup of tea about 3 and I leave here about 3.30, usually bumping along Hillside Road and up the Heath Rd, to pick up people either at the post office or at the Duncan Arms in Great Brickhill. Even now, turning in at the gates of B.P depresses me quite unaccountably, all along the road from the station are streams of weedy looking men who somehow look as though they had put on their uniforms for a joke and didn't know how to wear them and greasy haired women with ugly shoes. At four o clock one has to leave the car at the end of a long row in the car park and walk up to the huts, passing WAAFs who never think of saluting and so into the hut, a narrow passage with coat hangers down it and rows of civilian tin hats, of a queer high topee-like shape on a shelf at the top. The passage is so narrow that everyone knocks into you as you try to hang up your coat and the cloakroom is literally 2 ft by 2 and you can scarcely get the door open, let alone get inside if you so much as want to comb your hair in front of a glass at 4 o clock. The whole proceedings is the essence of discomfort and sordidity. Having gone through these agonies I have to take over from the NDO on the watch, where I sit under a brilliant light and often have so much to do that I think I am going mad. It necessitates continuous running between the watch and our room to check up on maps and cards and the usual

181

inevitable conversations with Hut 4 over the direct line. Last night I had Frost and a mass of stuff, which was a bit too much. BHJ (Brooke Holding Jones) is infinitely preferable but Putt and Ramsbottom are the best. For dinner one has to walk right over to the cafeteria, usually in the dark now and more often than not stand in a queue, unless you go very late. I have got such a phobia about the whole place now that I can hardly smile and am usually so worried about the work that I can think of nothing else outside it.

I like Faure best on the watch, he is rather sweet. At twelve, we hand over, sally forth into the night and pick up one's passengers in the hall, walk with them to the car and then struggle to get out of the car park and drive home. If it is foggy, it is rather hell, especially if one is tired. And I usually get home about a quarter to two, eat a small meal that Mrs Hunt puts in my room, read a bit and then sleep, dreaming usually about my job. It is a queer life! It is the atmosphere of intellectuality, of abnormality at the Park that is so depressing. I loathe every moment of it. The WAAFs in the hut are rather sweet. I believe they are miserable too and don't have much fun.

I worried about my mother's midday intake of gin and orange – she had obviously already begun the habit of solitary drinking, using the alcoholic's classic excuse, *to cheer me up.* Despite her job's prestige, she still seemed to hate Bletchley, and recorded with envy: *Lettice went to the Air Ministry today and loves it there . . . there is no one to talk to now.* She missed Lettice.

On 15 October, Lavers *bade us a fond farewell in the watch book . . . and we are to be the operation control of W/Cdr Jones, and the NDO, in spite of our reports, is to remain on the watch. I knew it was inevitable.* So Anne still had to fill in on the watch, the position of which she was so proud, yet which also caused her such anxiety.

In her diary then she shows some self-awareness: *spoilt all my life . . . wanting to be first in everything and be the most important person.* But then she exhorts herself: *do not be interested in yourself but rather see yourself as a unit in something bigger, it is the way one looks at things and faces up to difficulties that matters, not the things themselves.*

She ends that passage on a more positive note: *there is a kind of exaltation in the fact that now you have the chance to prove yourself, to give back to England a little of what you have taken from her and taken for granted all your life. For the first time you're to be judged on your own merits and are given the chance to show what you are worth and it is glorious in a way.*

What a pity I had never heard her say this out loud. It was my grandmother's words to me, 'You must take life with both hands and fight it!' which I remembered.

As I read my mother's Bletchley diaries of autumn 1942, two things became apparent. One was that, despite what I had seen of her as her daughter, she clearly was capable of applying herself to a supremely difficult and exacting task, but, disappointingly, at the same time her trait of 'I can't struggle any more' was still there. All the time she was working as NDO, she was also taking steps to leave.

It has the most most awful effect on me in the world, this place . . . When one meets someone from outside, one breathes a new atmosphere of common sense, gaiety and the things that matter in life . . . One feels ashamed of being part of the Park . . . Anyway, I have the king job, better than Kay's, Connie's or Elizabeth's, and so whatsoever they think of me, they must have respect for my work! Small comfort compared with other things, but at any rate I have proved that in fair and square competition with really intelligent people – and they are 100 per cent – that I can more than hold my own and get to the top.

Towards the end of October, Lavers left Bletchley to go back to sea and Guy Haslam took over his job. Now Anne's mood changed again and she found her job both challenging and exciting.

October 23rd 1942.
Was Duty Officer for the evening. I loved it. I adore the job and last
night was v. exciting. I am getting much more self-confidence and feel
I really am beginning to know it.

The next day saw the start of the Second Battle of Alamein:

The balloon has gone up at last and we have attacked in Egypt. Am
thrilled to bits over it and wish we could drive them out altogether.
Mrs Roosevelt arrived last night and is staying at Buckingham Palace.
The 'Alfredo', 'Prosperina', and 'Tempestea' are in the news as far as
I'm concerned. If we do not get the 'Alfredo' it will not be our fault!'

Here she seems to be dangerously close to revealing confidential
information concerning enemy Italian ships, the sinking of which was
an essential part of the Allied operation.

On 26 October she reported having being told by Wing Commander
Jones:

'I am prepared to go to any lengths to get you any job you want and a
really good one'. He said that the new NDO should be here in about a
fortnight and then he wanted a suitable overlap before he was willing
to release me. He asked if there were no other job I wanted at B.P.
I said I wanted a change, he said 'to get away from all these queer
people?' and I said 'yes'. The outcome was that he is going to make
some enquiries, but no one could have been kinder or more helpful
and they all do seem to think I have done a pretty good job of work
here, which is of value to me, as the standard is absolutely tip top and
if you are inefficient in any way, out you go.

I was delighted to find Anne again displaying qualities I personally had
never known in her – decisiveness and resolve.

When my father was diagnosed with cirrhosis in autumn 1974, she
had gone to pieces. Luckily her women friends rallied round, helpfully

ringing nursing agencies so that my father could come home from hospital to die. Was I being unfair in thinking that the strength that my mother had shown that autumn thirty-two years earlier would never quite surface again?

On 8 November 1942, the Allies landed in North Africa.

0110 hrs. Target is Day 1 + 2. I was terrified in a way of being NDO at such a moment and yet in a way honoured too, at being chosen as responsible enough to hold that position. Life at the moment is like a queer nightmare . . . The outside world does not seem to exist for us. It is a tremendous strain as well and sometimes I long for rest and yet when I am not NDO I can't bear to do anything else. All the ships got through to Gib. without one being damaged and practically unsighted, Axis sources believed this to be a convoy breaking through to Malta, a/c from Elmas attacked repeatedly. The first stage of 'Operation Torch' has been successful.

0130.9.11
We landed airborne troops and seized several a/dromes. There are about ¼ of a million troops involved, a number of them being British, dressed in American uniforms . . . The Daily Mirror *says that Admiral Cunningham is in command of the British naval forces and it is the biggest naval force that has ever sailed. There are reports that the French fleet has left Toulon to attack us, if so, surely the Italian fleet must sail as well. Operation Torch is the biggest thing since the Battle of Britain in this war and befits its name.*

0120.10.11
We have landed almost on the Tunisian frontier. Everything has gone far better and quicker than expected but there is French resistance and the GAF [German Air Force] *are expected to aid them against us in Tunisia . . . All our a/c had American markings and the pilots, lots of whom were RAF were dressed in American uniforms. So far it seems this has not been discovered and when it is, what a coup for German propaganda. The French fleet has not left Toulon, probably due to*

lack of a/c carriers, if they do they will meet with a hot reception from submarines.

'Torch' is absolutely the top. Everything seems to have been thought of.

0115. Armistice Day
'At the going down of the sun and in the morning, we will remember them.' I wonder how different my life would have been if my father had not been killed. Uncle Matthew thinks I have much the same approach in life that he had and the same will that nothing can stop. I wonder?

This statement of my mother's made me sad. Perhaps it was true that she had inherited her father's strong will, but if so, she had so often used it to shirk responsibility and to get her own way. But he would certainly have been pleased with her work at Bletchley. And Edward Thomas, whom she looked up to, congratulated her:

for the first time Edward has felt unnerved by this job, and the amount of directives we now have to deal with. He said he thought I had stood up to it v. well indeed, because the strain must have been terrific for me and this praise from Edward means a lot . . . This week has been the most important week for us of the whole war and the 4 to midnight shift is usually the busiest and most difficult to cope with . . . Friday the 13th again and so ends my week of being NDO, perhaps the most momentous week in the history of the Navy yet in this war. Certainly the most responsible position I am ever likely to hold in my whole life again and as such, I pay a tribute to myself, as it is a colossal strain really.

I realised now why Edward had held her in high esteem – he, perhaps more than anyone, had seen her at her best. When I later showed Tony Sale, the genius who had rebuilt the Colossus computer after it was destroyed after the war – on Churchill's orders, with other secret material at Bletchley Park – my mother's diaries about her work at

Bletchley, he pointed out that it was almost certainly she who was highlighted at the end of Edward Thomas's essay in *Codebreakers*:

But of all the girls at Bletchley the palm must go to the 3N indexers – an ugly word for a talented group of loyal and lovely ladies. Mostly Wrens and WAAFs, they were always on duty, keeping a record of every detail that might be needed for reference in solving some future conundrum. Often, with a gentle word, they would guide the harassed watchkeeper to the solution that had been eluding him. One of them, a senior and impressive WAAF officer, introduced the Park to the Moped and to Nescafe – both then new to British life. She would 'take the watch' when one of the regulars was sick. They also lightened the burden of the main Hut 3 Index.

The 'Moped' must have been what my mother called her 'autocycle'. Probably her cousin Mike, Peggie's brother, had given her some Nescafé, as it was the staple drink of the American troops then.

That week leading up to Operation Torch really had been my mother's finest hour and I found myself silently applauding.

One consequence of Anne's intense experiences during Operation Torch was that, for the first time, she really felt like an independent woman. She began, every so often, to feel detached from Knowle, and to question the life lived there by her mother and stepfather:

Mum is still living in the pre-war atmosphere and expects me to be the same and of course I can't be. These things don't mean the same to me as they did before and our outlooks are quite different. We no longer have the same aims and ideas, formerly I had my life as well and so I didn't mind. Now I have no life at home and no life here either, and it isn't much fun!

Bletchley seems to have given her a kickstart in helping her to separate from her mother. This is the first time in the diaries that Anne states that they no longer have much in common. Her confidence had clearly grown, and it must have been especially rewarding when, in early December 1942, Mountbatten came down to Bletchley.

Travis explained to the Chief that I was the Naval Adviser and he asked me whether my family had anything to do with the Navy, to which I replied that I had no excuse for being there at all! . . . Mountbatten was v. bored and annoyed Block A considerably by spending most of his visit talking to one of the more glamorous girls in the Index!

My father always claimed that Mountbatten, whom he had met in the navy, was 'a most frightful shit and probably a bugger boy!' Perhaps he had been mistaken in the second instance.

Anne was now brimming with confidence and even dared to announce to her colleagues that she had supported saluting Admiral Somerville when he had visited the Park – Somerville was one of the most able British admirals of the Second World War who had fought at Dunkirk and played a major role in the sinking of the *Bismarck* in May 1941. A common thread among those who wrote about Bletchley many years later was how much they had liked its informality; many wore civilian clothes and saluting was not enforced. *I replied that if people would dress up in uniform, the least they could do was to conform to the rules of the service, if only out of common courtesy to the King. This was not received with much applause.*

Anne missed the rigour and discipline of the RAF, which is ironic, given how she let herself go in later life. She was, despite her criticisms of Bletchley, very proud of her job there and even boasted about it in the diary, when writing about the others' casual attitude to saluting:

I might have pointed out that my job was more important in any case than that of the whole of the rest of the watch! They are obliged now to give me the respect due to my position as NDO and bit by bit are coming round to a more reasonable attitude . . . I am now used to being considered a person of intelligence and ability. I wish to prove to myself and them, but more to myself, that a non-intellectual can compete in every way with those who think that brain is the one thing that matters in life and despise all those they consider to be their mental inferiors and I have done this, to my intense satisfaction! I consider that both Lettice and I have proved that, with the education and life we have had, we are capable in all ways of competing with the so-called workers and are therefore not degenerate or incompetent. All my life, I have had this urge to strike out for myself, to prove that from my own merits alone and not through the position and chances I have been given I can meet life and cope with it and this war has given us the chance to show what we can do.

But she was still yearning to leave, even writing dramatically that it was *like a concentration camp one can never get out of.* (She would not be aware of the horrors of the real concentration camps for another two and a half years.) She set out possibilities for her future.

The alternatives are as follows: To remain where I am, probably for the rest of the war, in a job I like. Dead, from every other point of view, lonely and more introspective every day. Living for the work alone, in an atmosphere that nearly drives me mad at times and getting worse the whole time. To remain in Int. and go to Air Min., there is nowhere else I could go with my rank. No life outside, awful hours and pretty awful people again. Make a big attempt to get onto a station, which means throwing up everything I have ever done, and all my training, even if I were allowed to do this. Go abroad, as perhaps Code and Cipher again.

On 13 December, she wrote ruefully: *This is a man's world all right; they have all the plum jobs.*

Now, because she had done so well and shown such dedication, I began to consider my mother more seriously and feel more sympathy for her. I started to understand what it must have been like for her, when war started, to get to grips with office life, to 'muck in'.

189

All night I dreamt about before the war, when there was not this per-petual struggle and one was surrounded by congenial people and we had nice things without feeling guilty at having them. I suppose, really, we are not all democratic by nature . . . In my dreams, which are really the only part of my life that I enjoy now, I realise in a queer kind of way that I no longer belong to the old life any more and I seem to be peering at it for a brief glimpse out of another century, occasionally people wander into these dreams from this present life and I feel vaguely surprised to see them and then I cling more than ever to what I know is going to vanish with the dawn. It is the lack of love and affection, or some bright light to look forward to, to some ray of hope, that is so awful and what nearly drives me to distraction at times is the feeling that life is racing past and is going to leave us out worn out and spinsters good for nothing. Rather than that, I believe I would kill myself.

This was melodramatic, but she seems then to have been genu-inely low. I even found myself in sympathy with her feelings about the old life disappearing and her confusion over the social changes brought about by the war. She was right about the old 'feudal' ways dying: soon she would note: **the government are fighting over the Beveridge report** – this would lay the foundations of the National Health Service.

One part of her was reluctant to let the old order go.

I feel overwhelmed with a terrible sadness, at these times, I feel in a strange kind of way that my life is at an end and I cannot strug-gle along any more alone . . . I can vaguely understand what it must have felt like for the White Russians to be cast out with their world smashed for ever, their country gone, to face a world, cold and hard, for which they had never been trained to compete. Who can blame them for taking a few minutes enjoyment, on a year's savings perhaps, of a glimpse into that lost world?

She follows with a now-dated quote from Lettice, referring to Lettice's current boyfriend, seemingly not of her class: *Do you think I can cure Gil of saying pardon?*

Despite her new feelings of independence, Anne missed being at Knowle for the holiday. *I feel ridiculously disappointed at not being able to be home for Christmas, though illogical.*

On Christmas morning she was at 40 Belgrave Square on her own, Eva, the cook, having taken a train down to Knowle to celebrate. Anne attended a service at St Peter's, Eaton Square, where her parents had got married, but *only the choir sang and the congregation looked like stuffed dummies . . . I didn't belong anyhow in that atmosphere.* She drove back to Bletchley, had Christmas lunch of goose with Mr and Mrs Hunt, then at 3 p.m. went to work in the hut.

On 30 December, she was NDO again, and again on New Year's Eve, *and quite enjoyed it. I am lulled into a kind of resignation now, so that I don't think or feel anymore except just the work.*

In keeping with her new independence, Anne had made a new friend at Bletchley, Rita Davies, a Jewish woman from Glasgow. Rita pressed upon her a copy of the *Daily Worker* (the newspaper of the Communist Party of Great Britain) and offered to show Anne the Glasgow slums. It may have been Rita who, on finding out that Anne's family had a house in Belgrave Square, declared that she would never have made friends with her if she'd known. My mother told me that, in response, she had recited the following lines from Gilbert and Sullivan's opera *Iolanthe*: 'Hearts just as pure and fair/May beat in Belgrave Square/As in the lowly air of Seven Dials.'

Probably it was this friendship with Rita that gave rise to Anne's musings on 14 February 1943, the day she completed her first year as a flight officer:

I realise now how impossible, or at least difficult, it is to get away from one's upbringing, certain ideas are drummed into one's head as a child and absorbed so that eventually they become a part of the subconscious and they often prove stronger than the adult logical reasoning of later years. After years of struggle, I have at length realised that one's friends must have at least some common background, the same values, the same sense of humour up to a point. With the others, one is never quite at one's ease, there are jarring notes. In this case, why do I feel more at home with someone like Rita Davies than I do with Mary Cochrane for instance? It is difficult for me to have been brought up still with feudal ideas, drummed into us since we can first remember such things as pride in our family, setting an example always to 'our people'. Taught always that we are better than the rest and coming to believe it, against all reasoned judgement.

She was still struggling with her new working-woman identity and wondering about the values with which she had been brought up.

March 18th 1943.
I have had just about enough of this war and sometimes I think I can't bear it any more. I must either take a lover or marry someone, this life with no affection and no colour is killing me, it is cumulative and now that I'm going away from it and feel better in health, I feel I just can't bear it . . . suddenly I get a glimpse of what life might be and it was as though I suddenly received a mortal blow and I recoil from it and want to return to Bletchley to the only life I know now, that of soul annihilation. I feel a strange kind of peace again when I get back, it is as though I no longer exist any more and am just a shadow with no thoughts and no feelings, safe from this terrible mental torment that overwhelms me like a cloud. How people can live their whole lives like this passes my understanding.

I was torn between finding these sentiments melodramatic and feeling sympathy. When I was nineteen, as a junior secretary in New York, I also had felt stifling boredom, almost despair. Each morning I had strap-hung on the subway ten or more stations downtown to beyond Wall Street, pressed so tightly to the other office workers that once I didn't even notice a man masturbating on my coat till I got on to the escalator and saw the result. To try to detach myself, I would memorise passages from T.S. Eliot's *The Waste Land*, a strangely cheerless choice. I had wanted to go to America and experience the protest movement but probably hadn't really taken in what it would be like in the Public Relations and Communications department in a multinational company's office below Wall Street, for which I was supremely unsuited, despite having done a Sight and Sound typing course in Oxford Street before I went.

I never confided to my mother my loneliness and my dislike of that deadly job, partly perhaps because I had begged to go to America in the first place and she had found work for me in what had once been her grandfather and great-uncle's firm. If I had told her how I'd hated it, and longed to be free at once to travel round America, would she have sympathised, thinking of her own stultifying hours in certain offices in the WAAF?

Despite her own frequent complaints in the diary about her work, Anne, who at the start of the war did not know how to make a cup of tea, had risen to do an important job. But in many ways she was still emotionally like a child. When she finally learned that she could leave Bletchley after all – there is nothing in her diary to explain why this was now possible – she became confused and indecisive, and on top of that came a blow – Zost, her beloved Pyrenean mountain dog, had to be put to sleep due to creeping paralysis. Shortly before, although he could hardly walk, Zost miraculously followed my mother to the top of the Knowle garden, where she saw him *standing in the daffodils in the orchard, wagging his tail and looking so happy and pleased with himself. It was such a flashback to the old happier days that for a moment or two, I couldn't believe there was anything the matter.*

My mother found it difficult to express affection directly to human beings but was able to do it to her dogs. In that diary she recalled how she used to stroke Zost's head, calling him, *'My Lion . . . Sweet*

Thing!' I remembered her with one of her bassets – perhaps it was Mr Plod – smoothing the top of his head again and again, murmuring endearments like that. I was sitting beside her on the sofa. I had had the sudden feeling that she would have liked to stroke *me* and address *me* with such endearments, but didn't know how.

The passage about Zost's death also made me remember something else. When I was about eleven, my own dog Buzzy had acquired a potentially fatal viral disease: hard pad, a form of distemper. My mother cancelled going skiing with us to nurse him and asked her friend Knotty to accompany me and my father and brothers to Switzerland instead of her. (My father joked that he'd had to explain to the travel agent: 'My wife has a disease called Dogoratory . . .') For two weeks my mother had slept downstairs beside my dog, waking every two hours to spoon glucose and water into his mouth. She had saved his life.

Now I felt sorry for Anne when I read how she had cried all evening at Knowle, spending Zost's last night with him downstairs, but then *couldn't face* being there when the vet came to do the deed. For months after that, being at Knowle without Zost made her sad.

Chapter 16

Bletchley Park now behind her, the second half of the war saw Anne first posted, in April 1943, at the Headquarters of 5 Group – one of the main Bomber Command stations – at Castlegate House, Grantham, where she was a supernumerary in Intelligence. She was pleasantly surprised by the mess, which, though in the middle of Grantham, had an attractive garden of fruit trees leading down to the river, but was shocked at having so little to do in the office – *what they call a flap here seems like child's play to me and of no importance at all, such is the influence of B.P.*

Lettice was yet again trying to help Anne get *another* posting, with the Air Ministry. Anne had only just changed jobs, I thought, with irritation, and again wondered whether, in trying to be helpful, Lettice was not actually a disruptive influence on her so easily discontented friend.

Despite Anne's sporadic laments that she was still unmarried, she was now having a good time socially when on leave, and, in fact, she saw that recent marriages of her women friends were already not going well – Diana's, to the Brigadier, was to be annulled, and Anne wrote in the diary that Cynthia and *her* husband seemed bored to death with each other.

In early May, a cousin of my grandmother, Alice, and her daughter Maureen visited 40 Belgrave Square, having returned from America, where Alice, a widow, had taken her two teenage sons and Maureen early on in the war. Anne described the two women – Maureen a few years younger than her – looking *shamefaced and not quite sure of themselves or how people would receive them.* (They were certainly looked at askance for a long time by their friends and relatives involved with the war effort. I was relieved that my mother, despite her frequent complaints in the diary about her various jobs, had never once entertained the idea of fleeing to America. Nor indeed had my grandmother, who was a great friend of Alice's, as well as being her cousin.)

Now Anne declared herself bored with her work at Grantham, finding the office slow and inefficient compared with her hut at Bletchley – nothing, it seemed, would please her! On a positive note, she thought of ways in which her workplace could be improved, such as cutting the numbers of those working in the Intelligence Section. Bletchley had given her confidence in her own judgement.

Luckily, in early May she was sent for a few weeks to another station, this time an airfield, at Waddington, that reminded her of Bicester in 1940: *so my dream of a Bomber ops station is realised, what will it bring I wonder? . . . they work in complete liaison with ops here . . . we were given a target tonight.* She then proceeded – surely indiscreetly – to note down how the Intelligence at Waddington worked as regards bombing Germany.

On her second day there, Anne also met four Russian soldiers – *the first Communists I have ever seen I believe. They looked much like other people,* she wrote naïvely in her excitement, forgetting that she had seen those other Soviet Russians across the River Dniester from the town of Hotin in August 1938.

The Allies were, at that stage in 1943, all too grateful for Stalin's help. These four Russian visitors – members of the Russian Military Mission over in Britain – were given a speech of welcome in which Stalin and the Red Army were praised, and then shown maps and photographs in which they expressed *great interest*; also it was explained to them why the Ruhr was now the focus of a concerted, and prolonged, attack by Bomber Command.

Anne had arrived at Bomber Command at a crucial part of its operations. Since the very beginning of the war (before Bletchley became so important), Churchill had maintained that the only way that Hitler could be defeated would be by heavy aerial bombardment. 'The Navy can lose the war, but only the Air Force can win it,' he famously said in a Cabinet memo of September 1940. But despite the will, there had not been the means to achieve 'the absolutely devastating extermi-nating attack by very heavy bombers' that Churchill then considered necessary.

As described in Patrick Bishop's *Bomber Boys*, by the spring of 1943 munitions factories had been working flat out to build up a stock of Lancasters, Wellingtons and Halifaxes. With the resources now in place, Sir Arthur 'Bomber' Harris, who had been appointed Air Officer Commanding in February 1942, was given the go-ahead to proceed with a campaign of all-out destruction against Germany, specifically its industrial heart, the Ruhr valley.

My mother had arrived at Waddington six or seven days before the Dams Raid of 16 and 17 May (part of this action was the Battle of the Ruhr, made famous by the film *The Dambusters*. As Bishop writes, 'night after night, large forces of up to 800 aircraft pitched themselves against the heaviest flak defences in Germany and the most experienced and best-equipped units of the Luftwaffe to deliver ever greater weights of bombs'). The main targets were the Möhne, Eder and Sorpe dams. Anne, a few days earlier, had stood at Waddington near the runways and watched 'the Lancs' taking off and landing, feeling again as though she was back at Bicester and *part of the thing*. She was shown all over a Lancaster bomber and wrote in detail about the positioning, inside the plane, of the various crew members, the bomb aimer, the rear gunner, the pilot, the flight engineer, the navigator. She was also taken, by a Squadron Leader Rankin, to Flying Control, then to the roof to watch twelve aircraft taking off:

they taxied out slowly from dispersal and from the hangars to the take off point, slowly, one behind the other, like huge insects crawl-ing along the ground. Then, they turned and the roar of their engines could be heard across the a/drome as each moved up and the first began to move faster and faster, the dust flying up behind in a cloud of red they bumped slightly over the grass and then, suddenly as each

*became airborne, it seemed to change from a queer inanimate mon-
ster with no soul, into a thing of grace and beauty, curiously alive, as
though, for the first time, it had realised its power and had discovered
itself and its beauty as it flew away towards the sunset. The Lancaster
circled the a/drome 2 or 3 times to gain height before setting course, so
that there were Lancasters at various heights all round the sky, some,
just dots in the distance, already making for Skegness and others quite
low and others quite low still, the impression of power that they gave
was extraordinary and the roar of the engine was tremendous. And so
I saw my first take-off. Target – the Skoda works at Pilsen and a very
vital one.*

I suddenly saw this young woman as her escort must have seen her,
with her keenness, vitality and willingness to learn.

The brother of a great friend had just been killed in North Africa and,
after their first day of bombing those three major dams in Germany,
eight out of ten of 5 Group's 'Lancs' never came back. Anne wrote:
*at last we are bringing the war home to the Germans in their own
country and however awful it may seem, it is the only thing to do to
shorten the war and to give them a taste of their own medicine.*

Although she and her former colleagues did not know it then, it
was probably their work at Bletchley, rather than the bombing of cities by the RAF, that shortened the war by two years. But 'Bomber'
Harris, although later vilified, particularly for the bombing of Dresden
(unfairly, as it was not his personal decision), had been told by his
superiors that the focus of his operations should be, as Bishop writes:
'the built-up areas, not, for instance, the dockyards of aircraft factories
. . . this must be made clear'. The aim was to destroy the morale of the
German civilian population by more and more bombing.

Anne, meanwhile, was so excited by seeing operations from her end
that she wrote that she had

*forgotten what it feels like to want to go away on one's day off . . .
I haven't felt like that since Bicester days. I love this place, everyone*

is so nice, all the WAAFs, Teddy, Kay, Anne, 2 Margarets, Sheila and Yvonne. They are all sweet and the mess is divine. Every time I come back to Waddington again, I feel happy just at the sight of it, and I scarcely believe it after all this time. This place is full of the smell of hay and grass, of white campion waving in the wind and larks singing.

There were some lows, inevitably. Two days later, after a raid over Wuppertal, *Erikson, the nice boy from Rhodesia and F/O Holt, the Canadian* were lost. *Both 'sproggs' and on their third trips. These boys go straight out onto the Ruhr nowadays and don't get the gradual hardening process that they used to.*

On 1 June, she went to meet her financial advisers in London. (She hardly mentions her inheritance in the diaries, but this time wrote: *I have all this money, I am as a child in their hands at present – I must learn, but what time have I now for anything?*) The day before, she had got drunk to the point of being sick – at a *sticky RAF party, all very sordid.* She excused herself – *somehow one is so bored and depressed these days, one tries to forget for a moment. Everyone is the same …*

Most of her friends and colleagues did not drink to the point of being sick and I had noted several other instances of Anne's drunkenness – nowadays termed 'binge drinking' – earlier on. Her diary of 17 January 1943 records *my attack of drinking Hooch. We were all drinking whisky and water at the Berkeley. I was talking quite gaily and the next thing I remember is sitting in the cloakroom and a woman bending over me saying 'I'm a doctor'.*

I noted that my mother would not admit even in her private diary that she might have had too much to drink. Instead, she comforted herself by reporting: *2 other girls passed out in exactly the same way and had to be taken home.*

In early June, Anne received a *surprising* proposal of marriage, from Ralph Tymms (the first British cryptographer to read a German Enigma message at Bletchley Park), which she turned down, as she did yet another offer from John M. She returned to Waddington, but this time was not happy there. She became restless and wanted to work in the Air Ministry. *It is obvious that I shall never get any job in Intelligence in Bomber Command.*

She was proved wrong, as at Waddington, in the nick of time, she was suddenly given something different:

I am at last doing some proper work and love it. I am working with the Sgt. Watchkeepers in the Ops Room, on the telephone exchange. It is the best job going I consider on a bomber station, apart perhaps from Control. We hear everything that is going on here and can listen to any telephone calls. It is rather an ingenious little exchange and you can have eight people talking at once, two plugged in and the other two conversations on the 2 telephones. I have always wanted to work on an exchange and have realised my ambition.

She enjoyed it: *this is a picked job if ever there was one and I love it. I think I shall go mad when I go back to Group. Of course, this is entirely the Ops. side.* She wrote again cheerfully two days later of a visit by another suitor, Keith Rous, of hitchhiking with him on a lorry into Lincoln, of playing tennis with other staff at Waddington and of celebrating the fourth anniversary of the birth of the WAAF. She added: *Cologne was the target last night.*

In the small hours of 28 June, there had been an incredibly heavy attack by Bomber Command on Cologne, which, as the nearest big German city to the British bomber bases, had already been bombed fifty-eight times.

This bombing of the Ruhr is a v. big thing. Far bigger than the public I believe realises. With new methods, the accuracy is 100 per cent better than it was a year ago and although we have a few failures … most of the raids have been successful and the photographs of Dusseldorf the other day, seen through a magnifying glass, show incredible devastation with whole areas just wiped out. We bomb the Ruhr every night, except when we have a special operation to do.

She went to London for her twenty-ninth birthday. John M took her to *The Merry Widow*, then to the 400 to dance. However she complained that he treated her *as though one were his dog*.

There were three further attacks by Bomber Command on Cologne; twenty factories were hit, and the homes of their workers.

July 3rd. This is the day that all Axis sources report as the invasion date. I'll bet it is not. Was on duty all yesterday. Target was Cologne. Went on to watch the times of take-off which we chalk up on the board. 50 Squad 3 E/R's (early returns.) The last a/c was off by 0030 hrs. Went to bed and was called at 0330 again, drove to Shellingthorpe with Bernard to see the Interrogation.

Interrogation took place in the briefing room, where Intelligence officers – trying to find out more about the German defences – cross-questioned the air crew about what they had seen.

It seems to have been a good show. One was lost from 9 Sq. (Flt. Lt Wakeford) the only loss in Group. We have six photos showing the aiming point. A Halifax from Middleton landed at Shelby, for no apparent reason I can see!

As I came out of the Interrogation about 6 o'clock, the hulks of the Lancasters loomed up out of the haze looking like great insects with the black figures of men hurrying and scurrying about like ants. It is strange how alive these a/c seem and I never tire of the sight of them crouching at their dispersal points. Somehow it is difficult to realise where they have been, so cut off are we from the continent of 'Europe'. Paul Nash perhaps better than anyone else in his paintings, has caught the queer aliveness of these war machines.

Anne did seem much happier surrounded by aircraft and pilots; this was a very different life from the hothouse atmosphere at Bletchley. With typical contrariness, though, she kept using her time off to go back and see her old colleagues at 'The Park', recording, after one visit to Bletchley, having received *a real welcome . . . there is something about this secrecy business that binds one into a small band of those in the know, whom you really feel at ease with, whether you like it or not.*

Of her Bletchley friends, Anne had remained in touch with Lettice, Rita Davies and Connie, and also Edward Thomas, who, in between postings, took her to a Chinese restaurant in Soho. *Edward is off to Sicily soon in a battleship. He tells me that the Battle of the Atlantic is going better than it ever has . . .* Edward of course, besides being very clever, was also a man of action – he commanded ships, as my father was doing.

When I went through my father's modest book of cuttings – he had lamentably few papers compared with those kept by my mother – I found that in that month, July 1943, he had been in action in the North Atlantic and was awarded the Distinguished Service Cross as a result. Three German submarines were sunk within six hours and my father, who was commanding the sloop *The Kite*, was responsible for sinking one. My mother would not meet him for another five years.

The bombing of Germany continued throughout July 1943, although it was dependent on the weather; Anne's diary of that month highlights the extraordinary mixture of exhilaration, sudden death and occasional pleasures – such as a trip to Skegness, where she swam in a saltwater pool and spotted a dog like her darling Zost – and the day-to-day life in the mess.

By the end of July, the Battle of the Ruhr was over, there had been *riots and cries for peace in Milan* and Mussolini was a prisoner in his palace. The air blitz on the Italian mainland – Rome bombed in daylight by the Americans – had been called off temporarily and the Battle of Hamburg was about to begin.

On 1 August, while on leave at Knowle, Anne noted that Bomber Command had carried out *two devastating raids on Hamburg and the city is reported as reduced to ruins. The Germans are obviously in a flat spin and are talking of evacuating Berlin.*

On her return to work through London, she uncharacteristically complained of it being *full of foreigners* and wrote that she *loathed the sound of broken English*. Presumably these were refugees from war-torn Europe; Anne did not seem to appreciate this.

She made a day trip to Bardney, another Bomber Command station, and became fascinated by the Link Trainer, which taught pilots different flying techniques. She wrote about this in great detail, so excited that, back at Waddington, she had a go in their Link Trainer after dinner. Reading her thrilled yet precise account of it, I realised that in this respect she was like her father, who had learned to fly in the early days of aviation.

Indeed, she was learning new skills all the time. When the bombers returned from their raids, the photographs taken from the air would be developed, a task she enjoyed mastering. After one sortie by bombers over Italy she records:

some v. good photographs with amusing points, showing the centre of Milan . . . the best I've seen yet, as though taken in daylight with lots of ground detail and at least 3 aiming points were plotted. It amazed me how quickly you can take a point from a negative. First of all you put the negative over a special machine, place the print on top of it, close the machine and give it whatever length of time you deem necessary. You then take the print, which is still a blank piece of paper and put it into a tray containing some chemical, you then swill the water over the print and gradually the picture emerges, the longer you swill it the darker it becomes.

Once again I realised how wrong I had been in thinking that my mother had no practical skills. I now recalled her developing her own photographs in a darkroom at North Heath; before Raymond's death, she would often show us children her home movies of Spain, and of us in the countryside around North Heath House. There was one of me and Raymond jumping up and down in a cornfield full of poppies. She had not only shot those films herself, she had spliced them and put the spools on their reels, using equipment that required immense patience, a process which would nowadays seem irritatingly time-consuming. She had determinedly mastered the technique. It dawned on me that my mother, once she had set her mind to it, and if she had not become dependent on drink, could have done so many things.

A pattern was slowly establishing itself and I was reminded of those 'magic' painting books that I had been given as a child – you put a paintbrush in water and gently stroked it over a blank page. Then a picture, hitherto invisible, would slowly take shape. But here, what was transforming my mother's hidden, and later chaotic and sad, life into an emerging and colourful picture was not water, but her diaries. Because of them, I was becoming more tolerant towards my mother.

Now I, like her all those years ago, was getting caught up in the war. I had never studied that period in history at school and, apart from having watched war films, my knowledge of those events was scant. I began to read up about the war and watch documentaries on television. And among all this, my mother, in her WAAF uniform, would appear as if on stage, as someone hitherto unknown to me. I even dreamed one night that I was taking her place and it was I going through the war, not she. Was I even envious that she had had such exciting experiences?

Back at Grantham after Waddington, Anne was fed up: *August 9th 1943. I loathe it more than ever now, the atmosphere is half baked and there is nothing to do most of the time. I have got nothing now, no outside life and not even an interesting jobs I had at B.P. . . .*

She ended the month even more despondent: *My room is dark and there is damp coming all through the ceiling. Often I wake to hear the plaster falling down onto the floor. Life seems just like one long dark road and each day I wake up to think, thank goodness that is one more day gone. What will there be to show for it in the end? Nothing except a restlessness and inability to get back to normal life.*

She had spoken prophetically for all those who, after the war, never did get back to 'normal' life. Apart from refugees, orphans and other displaced persons, there were many like herself who, despite not being victims of war, had nevertheless had their futures irrevocably changed.

Besides those girls who had left jobs as maids in large houses such as Knowle to work in munitions factories, never to return to domestic service, there were plenty of young women such as my mother who, before the war, had not had a care about their material circumstances and the easy tempo of their lives. As for the men, during the war there were those daredevils who had parachuted into the Balkans, the two who had kidnapped the German general in Crete, others who had volunteered as fighter pilots, and boys such as Mr Dixon, from a small country village, who had gone into the navy at fifteen having lied about his age, then been awarded the Croix de Guerre for his services in submarines. Many of these would later find it difficult to settle back to a mundane daily life. My father admitted that he had enjoyed the war, but my godmother Meg's soldier husband said my father's nerves had been 'shot to pieces' after four years on the North Atlantic. (This was one explanation for his charging about our house shouting orders, never able to relax.)

At Grantham, Anne was given an interesting job on the watch, dealing with bomb loads and totalling them up. There were other perks in her life: Peggie's brother Mike arrived from North Africa with a present of bananas, the first she had seen for four years. The Allies invaded the toe of Italy and then, on 8 September, Italy surrendered.

Drank wine to celebrate Italy's defeat and went on to a little club round the corner to drink beer. After this I rushed home for dinner and a funny thing happened, an old man appeared at the front door with an envelope addressed to the U.S. Federal Dept at 40 Belgrave Sq. In it were about 12 sheets containing all Reuters' latest dispatches and whilst he got on the telephone to Reuter to ask for the correct address we read all these and gleaned the following: The Armistice terms were actually agreed to on Sept. 3rd, the day we landed on the Italian mainland and it was arranged that they should not be announced until the moment most opportune for the allies, which evidently is <u>now</u>. About 2,000 of our P/W (all other ranks) have been taken to Germany, the remainder are to be released. Admiral Cunningham has called up all *on the Italian Navy and Merchant Navy to sail for Malta, Gib or any of our ports, and these in the Black Sea to make for Russian ports, those that are unable to get away are to scuttle themselves.*

My mother surmised that the Italian navy coming into Allied ports must surely mean *the end of 3N* – her hut at Bletchley.

There were yet more positive diary entries:

September 19th 1943. Knowle.
A perfect day, sun and a lovely clear atmosphere. Just to be in a congenial atmosphere these days, where things do not jar and one can smell the grass and the earth is Heaven. There are still roses in the garden and the most enormous tomatoes, potatoes and onions. The biggest I have ever seen. News is that the Germans have evacuated Sardinia and the Battle of Naples is beginning. Badoglio is with the Allied Army. Mussolini has made a speech to the Italian people . . . Came up to London in the evening . . . caught the 10.15 to Grantham as it was Sunday night, it was packed to the doors and people were lying stretched out flat in the corridors, asleep. I got a seat in rather an amusing carriage with an American soldier, a Lieutenant in the Guards, 2 Scotch women, an ATS girl, a Grenadier Guardsman and another man in civilian clothes who had 'played' for the BBC. The American Frank Cox by name produced a bottle of whisky and ginger ale and Scotch ladies a bottle of lemon squash and we all had drinks. The Americans had thousands of cigarettes and packages all labelled 'U.S. Army Rations' – Breakfast, Lunch, Dinner, etc. They certainly do their troops well . . . the Scotch ladies were in cracking form, also the American who was 'the life and soul' . . . I was quite sad to get out at Grantham.

She was beginning to show signs of nostalgia for her happy times in America. Perhaps it was not surprising that she was now attracted to a Lieutenant Dubois, who, she wrote, reminded her of the character Larry Budd, who appears in a series of novels by Upton Sinclair. There were further indications that the war might eventually be over – and won – by the Allies. She was correspondingly cheerful and, instead of complaining about her circumstances as she often did, even pointed out:

Every place seems to have its advantages . . . hot buttered toast and jam for breakfast in bed, if you are lucky enough to get the morning off, not to mention quite a lot of time off and a good train service . . . The PM returned yesterday after a stay of over 6 weeks abroad. Today, he made his speech to the House. It was Bd'cast on the 9 o'clock news . . . the first really optimistic speech since the war began and full of hope and common sense.

She would still sometimes lapse into her old despondency and long for a *husband, children and a nice home . . . meanwhile the years roll on, a sea of wasted effort, like a never ending illness.*

I could not help thinking how, in one sense, she went on to 'waste' her life in the years after the war was over, in the sense that she never worked properly again and drank more and more heavily. At least in those six years of the war, despite some of her jobs being dull, she had mostly been 'in the saddle', doing her best.

Smolensk had fallen to the Russians and, on 1 October 1943, the Allies occupied Naples. After taking her mother to see the damage in the City, at Cheapside – my grandmother, unlike her daughter, had lacked the curiosity to go and see it earlier – Anne ended the month with a summary of world events:

So ends September, with the Russians crossing the Dnieper . . . miners on strike all over England and at loggerheads with the T.U.C. representatives . . . In Italy, we are in front of Naples threatening to occupy it at any moment, whilst the Germans have blown the town to smithereens. I find such things hard to believe in places that I once knew in the peaceful somnolence of the sun . . . Sardinia and Sicily are ours . . . the Italian fleet is intact in our hands. Leros (my old friend!) and Samos are also in allied hands. King Peter has established his govnt.

in Cairo and fighting rages all over Yugoslavia where nos. of Italians are fighting with the rebels, or have handed over their arms. What will October bring? It is the last month perhaps that will see much before winter sets in. How far will the Russians have advanced?

Chapter 17

Anne was now ready for another romance. In her diaries of 1943 men came and went: that autumn she had hankered after Lieutenant Dubois, the 'Lanny Budd' figure met at a dinner party given by her diplomat friends Jack and Daphne Ward; Dubois, however, proved elusive, first breaking his leg in a parachute jump, then turning out to be married. Several other men proposed, and Anne even promised the faithful John M that she would marry him after all, after the war. It was clear, though, that she had not developed any relationships as intense as those she had had with Alan Judson in 1940, or with Angela Griffiths in 1941 and 1942.

It was not until the early autumn of 1944 that a new love affair materialised. I was fascinated to read that now it was a woman eight years younger than Anne that she gave her heart to.

In November 1943, the same month that Anne's beloved Peruvian godmother Kata died – leaving her the silver stirrup of a Peruvian princess – Anne's 'outfit' moved from Grantham to Moreton Hall, Swinderby, Lincs. In April 1944, she was transferred again, to the headquarters of Bomber Command, at High Wycombe. In the diaries she makes a fuss about working underground, but one aspect of the job that she thoroughly enjoyed was the camaraderie with her female colleagues, most of them with archetypal WAAF nicknames of ambiguous gender: Andy, Paz, Bunty, Knotty, Kiwi, Ronnie, Doc, Dovey and Hammy.

May 24th 1944.

I had no idea such people existed before. Hammy said to me yester-day: 'I have never been out to dinner with a man in my life, that sort of thing doesn't interest me and I'm scared as to what might happen. I find it much easier to fall for a girl, in fact I find it v. easy to fall for a girl.'

Quite amazing to admit it, although I suppose when I went around with Angela I was 'in love' with her in a way, she certainly was with me and told me so. I was more fascinated and interested to find out what went on than anything else. I was attracted by the sensuality and exoticness of it, but disgusted by the 2nd rateness and sordidity. I was held back too by the thought that 'I' the upholder of traditions of conduct can't do this kind of thing, had I been any little street girl perhaps I should have. It is this segregation and sharing of rooms that brings about these situations. If they are only temporary presumably they do no harm.

I wonder what there is about me that attracts lesbians because I am not really one although at one time I was afraid that I might be, but discovered that I was not interested beyond a certain point, yet I am certainly attracted to them. By their hypersensitive nerves and their quick brains and intelligence. The unknown has always intrigued me and one is so bored these days that anything to relieve it is welcome. There is something in one's unconscious that is stronger than any rea-son and which leads one against one's will.

This was the first time in the diaries that Anne used the word 'les-bian', certainly as regards her own attraction towards other women. Previously she had employed euphemisms: **they** and **such people** and **that rotten crowd.** In this next part of this diary she is trying to be honest – at first.

I can't imagine why I am attracted to Andy, she is v. masculine look-ing, blunt, to the point of rudeness and <u>most</u> moody. I find myself repulsed and yet attracted as I did with Angela and at the same time

210

I look for her every time I go into the mess and am vaguely disappointed when I don't see her. At the same time when she sits next to me I avoid her almost rudely and talk to other people instead, in whom I am much less interested. I feel continuously embarrassed in her presence, there was something in the way she used to look at me that made me terribly shy and for escape I tried to talk ordinarily. Now, she avoids me and when she does talk, talks like an ordinary girl to girl. How do their minds work and what are the responses if you 'are one too'? Do they try out a certain approach if they suspect you of their own tendencies or do they try it on every woman whom they find attractive? I don't know, but Angela did not give up easily, although she told me that she thought when she told me that she was in love with me, I would be furious and never speak to her again. In point of fact, it had been obvious to me for some time but I didn't know the form for such things. Until she left L.B. I was still under her influence. I wish rather now, that I had spoken frankly with Andy, it would have been fairer as it is I don't suppose she can make me out, but supposing she had had no such ideas in her head and I had spoken. What then?

Anne then breaks into Italian in the diary, the English translation of which is: *I hope that nobody is able to read this page otherwise they would have an idea of my unpleasantness.*

She continues in English:

How strange it is that when I am depressed up to a pitch I find relief in writing, but when I am so depressed that I can't bear to think, then I cannot face putting my thoughts on paper, but prefer to deny them even to oneself.

When words are spoken or written they assume a concrete and a 'you cannot go back' capacity and it is better to leave them merely nebulous in your mind.

Anne, in escapist mode again, was, for much of the time, denying her homosexual feelings. Indeed, when, on 17 August, Knotty told Anne:

'Millie has a tremendous crush for you, not in a silly way, you can do nothing wrong in her eyes', Anne commented innocently: *I am most awfully fond of her too as a matter of fact. She is terribly sweet and sympathetic.*

Millie agreed to come with Anne on holiday to Cornwall in September. Paris had just been liberated after four years under the Nazis and this gave Anne and, presumably, the others working with her a surge of excitement over the prospect of the war ending in a now foreseeable future. The Allied D-Day landings in Normandy had taken place on 6 June when she was on leave at Knowle and all this, plus her growing affection for Millie, made her much more optimistic.

On the train down to Cornwall on 8 September Millie writes the first few pages of Anne's diary. Her forward-sloping, looping handwriting, unlike Anne's inscrutable upright scrawl, recounts the two women's train journey from Paddington. Millie's more schoolgirlish prose – indeed, she and Anne seem like two schoolgirls on that holiday – is full of slang – 'old boy', 'army clot' – and clichéd phrases – 'all's fair in love and war', 'all shapes and sizes, colours and creeds' (describing the crowd at Paddington) – but is generally good-humoured and the women seem to be having a wonderful time together.

Anne soon takes up her own diary again, from their B&B, near Portreath:

Millie has written all this up to date while sitting on the floor in her bedroom with a candle nearby and a bottle of gin and orange between us – I shall always remember these evenings sitting there discussing every subject under the sun and finding to my amazement that we agreed over most (almost all) of them and had arrived at the same conclusions about life, although 8 years divide us in age. How strange to find someone with whom one feels so at home, it is worth everything in the world and makes one smile for sheer joy of life, at last we can relax, be natural. All the thoughts and feelings that have been stopped for so long breathe once again like being reborn over again. I cannot express just how much this means to me, who has lived for so long now in an uncongenial and hostile world – so that although one is with a mass of people always, one is ever more alone and cannot feel anymore. I think this sympathy between us has its origin in our mutual love of America, of American thought and ideas, for although Millie has never been in the States, she has an American mother and was brought up in France by American grandparents and she is more American in out-look than she is English. I have long ago given up except amongst the family, who do not count in that way, trying to reconcile my American friends to my English. They do not seem able to meet or understand each other, so a part of me is always closed. To find someone then who understands this and can grasp both points of view is a joy that I never hoped to meet with and I therefore prize most highly.

Anne, like many other Englishwomen, was certainly drawn to Americans at this stage of the war; first there was Lieutenant Dubois, then her cousin Mike, Peggie's brother, then various American soldiers met on trains, and now there was Millie. Her longing for America was also manifest in her description of the army camp of black American troops outside her and Millie's B&B: *Whenever a few were together chattering ten to the dozen, their soft voices sounding kind of queer in the midst of the Cornish fields, it gave me back feelings and memories of the South that I thought I had forgotten, and I could smell the dusty roads round Baltimore and see them in their blue shirts gathering in the Indian corn in the fall.*

The few days with Millie staying on the Cornish moorland, with its disused tin mines *looking like ruined castles,* sound idyllic; the women bathed, bussed or hitchhiked to neighbouring villages, browsed in sec-ond-hand bookshops in St Ives, then drank gin and chatted into the small hours. Anne was protective, and in one long diary entry, com-ments on how difficult it must have been for a young woman to have left school without having had any fun, to go straight into the forces. Indeed, my unworldly mother perceived herself as experienced com-pared to Millie: *We were lucky indeed to have formed our opinions already of a wider world, swept though it was from under our very feet and with all its values shattered at one blow to be replaced by values and standards that are (thank God!) alien to our way of life and thought.* Millie's illusions, she writes, were *shattered* by life in the WAAF, and Anne wanted to help her become more idealistic again.

Like many of my mother's close relationships with women, there was no physical consummation of her love for Millie, but they returned to London even closer emotionally. The first V-2 rockets – the new German weapons, soundless until just before they fell – had arrived and Anne and Millie had heard one fall just after their train pulled in at Paddington; they later heard it had gone down as far away as Chiswick. Back in London, Anne was introduced to Millie's American mother, Mrs Swettenham, who had just left the WAAF after four years, having lied about her advanced age in order to enlist, which impressed Anne.

Anne's friendship with Millie became more intense. At a party in the mess she and Millie danced together to the song 'You're in My Arms and a Million Miles Away', then went to London looking for more second-hand books. In the Charing Cross Road, Anne bought Millie *A Narrow Street*, about a particular street in Paris's Latin Quarter – where, by chance, I would stay with friends in a small hotel for my twenty-first birthday. Anne quoted Millie saying: *'Bless yr. little heart, it was a sweet gesture.'* Anne added in her diary: *I can't say how much this friendship means to me, it has brought me back sanity and peace of mind and when I have been talking to Millie, I feel rested & restored again.*

No doubt keen to reassure herself that there is nothing untoward in the relationship, she does not mention the word 'lesbian' again. *It is not a disturbing friendship as so many are, just a complete understanding, love and harmony, so rare to find. M. said yesterday 'Men are not essential to my life, I can be quite happy without them, although I like them about.'*

However, Anne does seem to have been besotted by Millie, even praising her *original and good ideas*, which sound very *un*original:

Her ambition after the war is (a) to have plenty of money in order to be able to travel, see and experience everything (b) to have a house, not too big but with lovely grounds and with plenty of servants so that she needn't do any of the housework or be bothered with it, there she intends to breed all kinds of horses and exchange them for old ones that are worn out & need to spend the rest of their lives in peace and quiet. Millie loves horses and dogs too, in fact almost prefers animals to people – when she gets excited or feels strongly about something, she talks with quite an American accent, which she does not realise herself, but certain intonation and phraseology are so familiar to me such as 'figure it out' and so on.

A few days later, Anne had her fortune told by someone at work; he observed that she had a very vivid imagination and must come down to earth more, to everyday things. She was still sometimes getting her high temperatures, making her want to weep. She heard news from Knowle that made her furious; her stepfather had gone into her room and confiscated her copy of *Lady Chatterley's Lover*, saying that it would corrupt young minds. Anne was thirty and Millie and Knotty were indignant on her behalf, Knotty pronouncing that this was the sort of thing that made people leave home.

Meanwhile at work, despite the camaraderie, there was a great deal of bickering and petty jealousies, some of which sound pseudo-lesbian; perhaps this was inevitable, with so many women working together. Mrs Swettenham, Millie's mother, was also embroiled, confusingly, with a Mrs SW, who shared her flat. Mrs SW had a crush on Millie's mother and consequently was very jealous of Millie. There does sound to have been a hotbed of seething female relationships around Anne at this time.

On 28 September, Anne went to Quaglino's with two men friends, while Millie went to her mother's in Earls Court. However, the following night, Millie and Anne shared her bedroom at 40 Belgrave Square, and talked till 6.30 a.m., Millie confiding that she, like Anne, had had a broken engagement, having perceived that her fiancé was 'weak'. He

was then killed in Salerno, which still made her feel guilty for not having gone ahead with the wedding. Millie also spoke of how, in one of
her first WAAF jobs, she had been bullied by a group captain, because
she refused to go out with him. Anne was livid.

*It really is one of the most awful stories I have ever heard, that these
people should have power over people like Millie, who are terribly
sensitive and highly strung and who feel things so much. If I could
restore to her, her faith in human nature, in herself and make her see
all this in its true perspective, I would consider that I had done something really worthwhile.*

(Anne's Aunt K, who did readings of people's handwriting, had
observed from Millie's writing: 'Rides roughshod over people.' Perhaps
she was not as sensitive as Anne liked to think.)

On their various short leaves in London, she and Millie often met
in Piccadilly Circus, under the lamp post where the statue of Eros had
been. Anne, despite recording that she and Millie took photographs of
each other 'by Eros', never comments on the lover-like connotations of
this meeting place. It was clear to me that Anne was in love with Millie.
Then, in early October, came a blow.

October 6th, 7th, 8th, 9th.
*Came back to a bombshell – Millie rang me to say that she is posted
overseas with Knotty.*

*It gave such a shock that I felt quite dazed – they don't know where
they are going – I can't describe the hell of misery these last 2 days
have been. I feel as though the whole world has fallen to pieces around
me and left me standing by myself in a world of shadows who mean
nothing. I didn't know that I was capable of caring for somebody as
much as this or of feeling this way.*

*Since knowing Millie so well, I had begun to love again and to feel
and to be happy for a brief space – Is this love or what?*

If it is not love in a physical sense, what is it then that we should

care so much? Millie has been to a Scottish party to celebrate some-
body's homecoming and was asked to bring a friend 'so I said I was
going to bring "me friend"' and has asked me to go. The night after
we heard, we drank in the mess, Paz, Knotty, Millie and I. Paz was as
depressed as I and I just felt that the bottom had fallen out of the whole
world and that all I cared for had gone. I felt this before when Alan
left Bicester but I feel it even more now and I shall never forget these 2
days. It is one of the worst things I've been through in the whole war,
though I know that is an awful thing to say when other people have
suffered real loss. We got pretty tiddly and played all the records we
loved, especially 'You're in my Arms,' I wish to God that I didn't feel
things so strongly, most people and things don't mean a lot to me, but
my God when they do, it is so strong that it invades my whole life, my
every thought and feeling and I could share every one with Millie and
know that it would be understood. I have never met anybody before
with whom I was so much in tune, so that I feel now that a very part
of me has gone – and that I again move in a meaningless world . . .
We went to bed that night and none of us slept, neither Paz (who feels
I believe, as strongly as I do), Millie, Knotty nor I – we lay awake all
night and I wished I were dead and no longer had the power to feel –
every time I lay down, those tunes 'Mexican Rose', and 'You're in my
Arms' and 'San Fernando Valley' ran endlessly through my head and
I thought I was going mad. I shall never forget that evening as long as
I live, with a prospect of another which I dreaded ahead.

It is worse to keep seeing people when you know they are going and
yet you <u>must</u> see them – you want to imprint their features, their smile
and their voice on your mind forever, so that it may never fade – and
yet you want to run away and hide alone in your misery. I cried most
of the night and had no resistance or strength left to stop myself. One
is so weak now, so strung up that everything is magnified a thousand
times. It must have been obvious to all how I felt, but I was beyond
caring and that life no longer mattered . . . What is this strange love
that one has for somebody? It is inexplicable and is it perverted? No –
because you desire nothing from them, you wish on the other hand to

give them everything – there is nothing queer or odd about it. It is just something without price and beautiful as a Chinese Vase or whatever you love most in the world and it seems to lift you way up to the stars. Are we – sophisticated people, always looking for the perverted side of life and trying to explain things by sexual theories, missing something greater that cannot fit into a theory because it is so rare and elusive? It seems so. The attraction I felt for Angela Griffiths was the opposite of this, I disliked her almost and yet I was fascinated. This feeling is a v. different one – Whenever I am with Millie, whatever we are doing, I feel like smiling with happiness and I think she feels the same way with me. All the time in Cornwall, I wanted to restore her to happiness and I think I succeeded because there was such a sympathy between us.

I would like to talk to somebody with a knowledge of psychology and of the world, greater than mine, to explain it to me. Even now, I want her to have everything in life and I care more that she should be happy than I myself – If it were a choice between us, I believe I would give it to her –. I must write all this because I feel so strongly that I cannot talk about it to anyone except perhaps to Paz, who understands and feels the way I do. The world would think we were suffering from odd Freudian diseases and perhaps we are. We are certainly suffering from lack of affection and mental agony that is undescribable, so awful is it at times, in fact most of the time when I thought I was giving something to Millie, I suddenly found that she was giving it to me instead – Whether I have given as much to her as she to me I suppose I shall never know – but what has touched me more than anything else is that she came into my room last night just before dinner and brought me one of the things which I know she most values in the world – the model Lanc which she always had hanging on the light in her room and which was a real model of one of 407 Sq at Bottesford, the squadron which means the RAF to Millie, in which all her friends were and so many were killed.

I just know how much that Lanc meant to her and in giving it to me, she has given me something which I value beyond everything, it

was as if she said to me 'Au Revoir, I think you're "a bit of all right."'
She brought me too, a bunch of white heather, symbolic of what she
wished me and a small brown paper hat saying 'Wear this for me on
Christmas Day' and then turned away hurriedly as she was crying.

A week later, on leave, Anne met Millie, again by Eros, and they spent
the rest of that day and most of the evening together, first going to the
cinema, to watch *Till We Meet Again*. An American corporal put his
hand on Anne's knee, undeterred by her deliberately having placed a
wet umbrella there, and then she and Millie went to some impromptu
drinks together at the Hyde Park Hotel, where Millie 'fancied' an
officer; Anne, who knew his brother, introduced them. *After they had*
gone Millie said to me 'Annie it's amazing how things go right when
we are out together, we will have to live next to each other after the
war, this sort of thing doesn't happen to me except when I am with
you – I wish to goodness you were coming with me, we'd have such
fun!' Anne suddenly declared an urge for a sausage so she and Millie
asked a policeman, who escorted them to a café in a tiny street behind
the Scotch House. No sausage materialised, but Anne had *an ersatz*
omelette with tea, chips and tomatoes. The policeman ate with them
and told them all about his job.

When Anne returned to Bomber Command the following day, she
found that her own job was at risk – she does not explain why in the
diary. This news, coupled with the imminence of Millie's departure,
sent her into a state of grief and confusion:

I am writing this after a few drinks with Andy and Paz and bridge-
playing in the mess – these are my impressions – Millie coming down
here to say goodbye – talking only with Peggy, who appeared to be
the only person she cared about. Hitch hiking to Uxbridge, in the
pouring rain, a policeman in Wycombe stopping a lorry for me and
seeing a market stall fall just behind us, great wooden rafters, it hit
him on the head, fortunately he had his helmet on & it missed me
literally by inches – . I couldn't have cared less at that moment what

happened to me – Millie writing to say she couldn't bear to speak to any of us on the telephone, it upset her so much. A farewell letter from Knotty, to thank for the whisky, a v nice one. The complete loyalty of all the WAAF officers' mess here to me . . . Uncertainty all around. Margaret Bowman – my successor, telling me how to do my job before she had been there 5 minutes – Varcoe just giving me a type written piece of paper and saying 'Give this to the clerks with your ops pass to transfer to Flt/O Bowman, it is the only way we shall get another one for the section.' This hurt me perhaps more than anything else, he added 'the sooner it is done the better' – Wheels within wheels – not knowing what is happening, caring less – seem to have lost all powers of feeling, am just dead mentally. Must pull myself together. Marvellous loyalty of all the sergeants through this – Interview with Holmes who is v nice, interview with the Gp. Officer. Incessant uncertainty – beastly altogether – v rude to Varcoe.

One of the colleagues who helped Anne during this period was Andy, the 'masculine' WAAF whom Anne had been once attracted to, against her will, when starting at High Wycombe in the spring of 1944. Anne's job at Bomber Command now really was at an end; again, she does not explain why in her diary, though hints that its termination was partly due to her recurrent ill-health. After a farewell party for her, Andy put her to bed, then gave her breakfast next morning; Anne apparently had had a sort of breakdown – or was she just drunk?

When everyone had gone, I collapsed completely and was sick, a mixture of drink and nerves, mostly nerves. Andy coped marvellously and took me home and put me to bed, stayed with me till I went to sleep. Was completely worn out and raved in a kind of delirium, she told me, saying I could not face life etc. A Sq/Off with an Eton crop came into the mess and was v. amusing. I'm always being told 2 things 'That I am v. much alive & have a gt zest for life and that I am a v. sweet person.' Don't know why I'm writing all this, except that I am v. sad to leave all the clots at Command and the staff too.

There was no doubt that relationships during the war were volatile; even my grandmother, still married to Chow, confided that *she* had fallen for her Communist suitor: *Mum told me she is in love with Col. Malone but realises it is just the war. Have known it for some time. None of us are sane at the moment, so we can't help each other out at all – What a life!*

After Millie had departed – Knotty had been posted with her, but no one was sure where they were going – Anne began to pull herself together. She showed again her attractive modesty, as exemplified in the following tribute to her colleagues:

I shall mind leaving the mess and a lot of the people at B. Command v much. I have had nicer gestures in this mess and met nicer people than I have ever met in the WAAF . . . People who have worked all their lives and have felt misery and have risen above cynicism and despair – they are those with depth, not my world (that was) that has 'lived' in luxury, the unpleasanter sides of the world hidden away from them . . . and we are having fun with our bridge. Andy is getting <u>most</u> enthusiastic and so am I – I adore every moment. Am just so muddled up though, that I don't know whether I am coming or going – what a life!

Back in London, she rallied; she went with Gig to a play, then to visit Lettice, who, with her usual insider information, was pretty sure that Millie and Knotty were in Cairo. She met yet another 'sweet' American boy, then, with her characteristic curiosity about other lives, described with enthusiasm standing on a full bus from Hyde Park Corner at 6.30 a.m., crammed with London charladies, then on to a train via the film studios at Denham.

Hyde Park looked rather lovely in the moonlight. I have certainly seen London at all hours during this war, a city is like tuning in to all a person's moods whom one loves . . . The moment you get in a carriage you can tell who will get out at Denham. There is just something about

221

them, old broken down stage hands, threadbare clothes, occasionally a bowler hat & manners of a bygone generation – fat foreign Jews who haven't presumably got on too well – cheap little girls, determined Scotsmen with strong political and religious views, tall men with torn trouser turnups, hollow cheeks and a look of hunger.

Anne went on being cheerful and, in her last two weeks at Bomber Command, took herself on cycling tours of the countryside surrounding High Wycombe, once going to Disraeli's former house, Hughenden. On 14 November, she even knocked out some rhyming verse as a farewell to 'the clots' which included the lines:

At Bomber Command, there's a place called 'The Hole'
And it's here that Intelligence play the main role,
The atmosphere's shocking, there's often a fight –
But <u>one</u> end of the room is 'A bit of All right!'

I was rather proud of my mother's being able to knock out this doggerel with such merry insouciance.

She had her fortune told again, this time by a colleague, Doc Mackay. Anne seems gullible, interpreting Doc Mackay's forecast of how she would do better abroad as a sure sign that she would soon go to a new job in Washington, something that Lettice was trying to engineer. Anne therefore wrote that Doc Mackay's seemingly prophetic words *shook me rigid!*

Millie, meanwhile, had sent a postal address. The receipt of her letter inspired Anne to praise what she perceived as Millie's rare sensitivity, great courage and sense of humour:

She gave me all I needed, restored me to sanity and feeling again. Why can't I feel like this about John or Mervyn? . . . Someone (a man presumably!) has got to restore me to sanity, someone who understands my mental moods, who is wild and temperamental like I am, no one else can help me . . . I cannot say this to people, so I write it all but to not arrive at any answer thereby.

It is clear that she feared she would never feel for any man what she felt for certain women. Millie's mother, she noted, had said that Anne was the most 'alone' person she had met out of her generation. *How did she recognize it? . . . I am unstable as hell & yet never get the credit (or discredit!) for it, because I do not show my feelings.* I felt sorry for my mother when I read this. At the same time I wished that she had shown *more* restraint, towards us, and had concealed her instability from me, my father and my brothers.

The day after Doc Mackay's fortune-telling, much of it came true:

November 15 1944. The most amazing thing has happened. Was in the office as usual this morning when was told that John Lodge (The John of my ADIO Ode!) wanted to speak to me. He said that he had been talking to Humphreys and H asked him to find out from me whether I was 'happy in my work' – If not, he would like to have me back again to work for him. He is i/c of 'Disarmament of Germany' whatever that means. Suspect that is merely a pseudonym for something quite different as is usual with H's activities.

Would like me to do a spot of his Admin. And write up some Intelligence data as well – They are going to Brussels in six weeks and will move on as the armies advance – Lettice of course will be there too. Nearly fell over backwards was so surprised and asked him if I could possibly let him know on Saturday morning. He said he thought it would be O.K. & has promised to ring me then. It would not mean that we should be forced into the Army of Occupation but would be demobbed according to our Groups as usual. Can't collect my thoughts as yet, but it seems too good an opportunity to miss. To be right in at the start and in RAF uniform besides in Europe where it means so much. Brussels is v. uncomfortable, no heating whatsoever, being buzz bombed and rocketed besides, but to have the chance to see Europe now when it is 1st liberated and when almost no one can get over there seems worth these 5 years in the RAF.

Anne at once saw this job's potential:

It will be seeing history at first hand and perhaps may be the thing that will restore me to sanity again, besides which, Lettice being there would make all the difference in the world. Rang her up at once and she seemed thrilled to bits. Am going to London with her on Friday and will get <u>all</u> the dope I can re H's activities, conditions etc. The more I think about it, the more it seems too good to be true, perhaps I will come alive again.

I was excited by this and wished that I too had been able to witness post-war Europe. My own life seemed dull in comparison.

Chapter 18

By January 1945, Anne had had four jobs in Intelligence and received over twenty offers of marriage. Having just turned down another ex-public schoolboy, she wrote: *January 13th 1945. Can no longer get on with the people of my own world whose ideas have not changed with the war. How have they managed to stay the same and not be shaken to their very foundations with new ideas, new ways of life and a wider viewpoint?*

Earlier in the war, when Anne had been less sure of herself, she had often written of how she really only felt 'at home' with those from her own world. Now she decided that the *colonial (American, Canadian etc.)* outlook was more balanced and less prejudiced. She had always felt comfortable with Americans, finding their men warmer and more gallant. (She had observed that the serial proposer John M treated her like his dog.) American troops were now much in evidence in Britain. There was an American car park in the garden in the middle of Belgrave Square, the smoke from the bonfires there like *a Red Indian encampment*.

Most of her female friends were now wed, and Anne, at thirty, must have feared that she might never be married or have children. She did not wish to marry a man she did not love and her independent means meant that she was not under pressure to marry for long-term financial support. But she still felt confused: *Why can't I be like other people who are contented with the routine order of life without questioning everything . . . Can't I find a man with my own ideas, broad minded and poetical in spirit, gentle and with quiet charm . . . If there is such a one, he does not come my way.*

Anne was now working at Bushy Park, a GI station near Hampton Court. One American officer, of Croatian descent, invited her back to his flat and played the balalaika to her: *gypsy tunes, showing the subtle differences between Russian, Polish, Serbian, Hungarian and Croatian music.* She was intrigued, but refused to go away for a week-end with him partly for fear of appearing *cheap* and also due to *lack of sex knowledge.* At thirty, she was still a virgin.

On 21 February, Anne first mentions in her diary a Major Joe Darling, who took her to lunch at the Churchill Club, near Dean's Yard, Westminster, then on to an afternoon concert at the Albert Hall. (She had almost certainly met Joe at Bushy Park, but does not say.) They returned to 40 Belgrave Square for tea, where Joe discussed *Russia and the Polish question* with Bill Sydney, who would inherit the beautiful old house of Penshurst in Kent and his father's title of Viscount De L'Isle. (My grandmother, always on the lookout for a good county marriage for her daughter, told me that she had hoped he would marry Anne; no doubt she and Anne were also impressed by his winning the VC, for his bravery in the Battle of Anzio in January 1944 – he was in the Grenadier Guards.)

The same month, the 9th US Army Air Force had launched a huge aerial assault on Berlin, in an attempt to prevent a German counter-attack against the Russian army, which was pushing on fast to the banks of the Oder, only fifty-five miles to the east of Berlin. On 13 and 14 February 1945, Dresden had been bombed by the Allies; 25,000 people were killed and the city was in ruins. The Germans had almost certainly lost the war.

Anne now heard that the first of her units would go overseas imminently, and her whole headquarters, minus WAAFs, would follow them to Europe within a month. Some weeks later, her own unit would proceed to Germany. Typically, Anne now wrote that she *not* pleased to be going abroad, and did not look forward to being with an army of occupation. She was, however, taking compulsory German lessons, in preparation, and also learning Russian independently.

Anne's job at Bushy Park involved trying to obtain Intelligence

Publications from various places in London – this sometimes proved frustrating. Attacks from the German V-2s on Britain had increased, sometimes as many as eight or nine a night on London. In late March, during a weekend at Belgrave Square with Nah, they both heard the *terrific explosion* of a V-2 falling at Marble Arch. Anne rushed up there that evening: *2 or 3 trees and lamp posts uprooted and earth all over the place . . . 3 people killed.*

The following day, she was back at Bushy, working hard, with only ten minutes for lunch and for tea, having to issue *all* Intelligence *Material to all the newly mobilized units (8 of them).*

She was soon seeing Joe Darling regularly. In late March she lunched with him at Hampton Court. Joe had already fallen in love with her, and kept telling her so, adding that he relished her *joy of life.* (It is odd that my mother always appeared like this, given the tortured inner life that she exposes in her diary.) If he had not been married already, Joe insisted, he would have proposed to Anne immediately. He added that he would like to take her to bed with him, but only when she was ready, and he went on to describe a gentleman as 'one who knows how to wait'.

Anne must have been tempted, because, two weeks earlier, she had visited a female gynaecologist, *to get the low down on sex.* Presumably, she had gone to enquire about contraception. She then booked herself in for two more visits. On 25 March, Joe left England for France, where he was working for the Supreme Headquarters of the Allied Expeditionary Forces (SHAEF), under General Eisenhower. Anne found that she missed him, *more than I thought possible – his light touch and his enjoyment of life and way of making things rather charming. Feel deserted and terribly unhappy . . . Never knew how much I had begun to count on his company.* Bushy Park was now almost empty and Anne found she also missed the other American soldiers.

On 12 April, President Roosevelt died, giving *one a tremendous sense of personal loss in a strange way.*

The war was clearly winding down; in London the blackout was lifted for the first time in nearly six years. Andy, from Bomber

Command, was with her at Belgrave Square and in celebration they put on every light in the house, then walked round the garden: *a lovely moonlight night and it was rather beautiful to suddenly come into the house and see all the windows a blaze of light.*

Stationed in Versailles, Joe Darling wrote many letters to Anne over the following weeks. My mother kept them all and I was thus able to experience his devotion almost first hand. In one he writes of how '*the charm of your friendship greatly mellowed my outlook, softened the harsh outlines of existence, put a patina on everything associated with you. It's strange how rarely one comes upon a really congenial person . . .*'

Joe was a more subtle seducer than her younger suitors; he wooed her gently and genuinely appreciated all her qualities, not just her looks. I could not help thinking how different this was from my father, who, the first time he met his future wife, had been struck by her décolleté: 'Your mother was showing her charlies!' he told me triumphantly.

Despite the somewhat over-serious phraseology in some of Joe's love letters, I could not help liking him, and, as I read more of his correspondence, I came to appreciate his sincerity, his tenderness towards my mother and his appreciation of her intelligence. He wanted her as a companion, not just as a lover.

On 30 April 1945, Anne went with her unit to Brussels, taking off from Croydon airport in a Dakota. Sadly for Anne, Lettice was now not going. Anne recorded that she was a sport about it, and it was thanks to Lettice that Anne was given a few extra days off just before leaving, during which she had gone to the society wedding of her friend Rosemary Bowes-Lyon, attended by the Queen and *the two princesses* – the future Queen Elizabeth II and her sister, Margaret.

Anne and Joe Darling were now both in Europe – he in France with 'Ike' – though many miles apart. Anne's unit was billeted at the Residentz Palace Hotel in Brussels. On her first night she went *screaming round the streets in Lewington's jeep with Ken Hollen and Betty Wickham-Legg, first to the café, where there was a floor show, the women here wear very high hats and which look rather idiotic to us and shoes with built in high heels . . . we have become dowdy since the war.* Later she found herself in a nightclub, the Lancaster, with 'Lew' – Squadron Leader Lewington – where they danced. *One Belgian offered us some coffee and another asked us to join their party for a cognac.*

Her first impression of Brussels was that it was like peacetime; the people looked well fed and, except for the masses of British soldiers and a few Americans, it seemed extraordinary to her that there had been a German occupation there for four years. She was flabbergasted by the amount of goods in the shops: *all kinds of handbags in the best taste, watches and scent (all the best Parisian varieties), drink etc. . . . I felt like a child at a Christmas party* – she sent *millions* of presents home. She looked up the two racy Belgian women – Titi and Gigi Jacquet – that she and Chow had met on a pre-war skiing holiday and was out every evening in nightclubs: *it is a much more lighthearted and carefree atmosphere than at home and London is far more war-scarred and weary than Brussels.*

Lew drove Anne to Ghent, to 85 Group Headquarters, Disarmament, and she visited Intelligence there. She was told by a Flemish girl that in Belgium much of the food was black market; if you had money you could get almost anything but *if you are poor you can almost starve.*

She discovered that the Residentz Palace, where *we eat, sleep and eat,* had been a pre-war luxury block of flats and also a Nazi headquarters during the occupation, so there were still *a lot of German notices, desks, etc* around. A little Belgian man who owned a local restaurant, the Charbord, suddenly produced a card to show her that he was a member of 'The White Army', a Belgian Resistance Movement whose badge had the insignia of a lion, and told her that he had been in prison in Germany for eight months. She felt that she was beginning to penetrate beneath the surface and to learn more about how it had been in Belgium during the war years. This, coupled with her lively nightlife and driving round with Lew in his Jeep – '*I associated with morons till I met you!*' he declared – meant that she was enjoying herself.

On 5 May, she saw in a newspaper *awful photographs of the bodies of Mussolini, his mistress and 2 other fascists hanging in the Square in Milan, where crowds spat on them etc.* She found this sickening, observing that the Italians *were only too keen to follow him when he was a success.* Hitler was also reputed to be dead – it later emerged that he had shot himself on 30 April, after marrying his mistress, Eva Braun – and the German army had lost Berlin, but my mother wrote loyally: *When Churchill announces the end of the war, that will be the time to rejoice.*

On VE Day, 8 May 1945, she was sad not to be in London to celebrate the Allied victory in Europe with her old friends in Bomber Command. She even thought wildly of stowing away on the plane in which her boss was flying back to Britain that morning. Instead, she made do with listening to Churchill's speech on the radio, then she, Lew, Betty and a few others went to the Brussels Officers' Club, where they talked to several RAF ex-prisoners of war, all making their way home,

dressed in every kind of get up, American shirts, khaki trousers, RAF tunics etc . . . most of them look in fairly good shape. Got a lift down to the town where there were crowds of people, but not much enthusiasm. We made more noise than most of the Belgians put together – The Cathedral was illuminated and a lot of the shop windows and flags everywhere. The Grande Place, which is the most beautiful place I have seen yet in Brussels was illuminated and a band playing and there were some fireworks – we called in at some cafes and sang 'Tipperary' etc, but the best fun of all was driving through the streets standing up with our heads through the sunshine roof and then Lew, Betty and I sitting right on the roof itself and singing every song we could think of.

Thus the war in Europe ended for my mother, but, like many others in the services, she went on working. Just after VE Day, perhaps because of the feeling of anticlimax, the diary is full of complaints: about her boss, about the inefficiency of her *set-up*, about the idea of imminently being *cooped up with them in Germany*, about RAF life in general, about being cut off from home – she and her colleagues were not allowed to tell family and friends where they were until censorship relaxed on 14 May – and about many Belgians' assumption that the British had not suffered as they had. *A lot of photographs of around St Paul's, Coventry etc would have an enormous propaganda value out here, just to give them some idea*, she notes.

Anne amused herself during her time off by going alone on mini sightseeing tours, once taking a tram to the outskirts of Brussels, where she watched locals dancing in a little square to three men playing the concertina, and sipping aperitifs in cafés under the trees; another time she went to see the statue of the Manneken Pis. She wrote that she would have enjoyed these outings even more if there was *someone congenial* with her. She must have been thinking of Joe.

In May, she decided *to try my hand at my greatest ambition, to go to Paris*. This was difficult without a Movement Order and she was told by Air Movements at Tactical Air Force (Main) (TAF) that she needed a signed authorisation from the head of her section, Group Captain Walker. Certain that he would say no, she went anyway, *in fear and trembling*, having decided to tell him the truth, that she wanted to go to Paris, not on duty, but to see 'some people' *and this was the only time we should get two days off together*. Walker, telling her to keep quiet about it, said that she could go. He *couldn't have been nicer*, getting her a Movement Order typed out, signing it himself and cautioning her that she had better say she was on duty. Within a short time, she was flying to Paris in an Anson; the plane passed over a wrecked marshalling yard, which, she guessed, had recently been bombed by Bomber Command. She felt that she really knew now what it felt like to be one of those pilots, *to streak over, bomb your target and get back again*. Her plane landed at Le Bourget and by four o'clock she was in Place Vendôme, Paris.

First, she had to go to the British Army Staff HQ in the Faubourg St Honoré to arrange a return passage next day, and to get accommodation for that night. To her shock, she was told that there might be no flights back next day, due to impending bad weather, and that the third flight back to Brussels was already full, but *'as I was on duty'* *(thank God & G/Cpt Walker!) I was entitled to Air Passage.* She was then given a ticket for the Bedford Hotel, Rue de l'Arcade, behind the Madeleine, which had been requisitioned for those in the forces and cost only five francs a night. She was amazed and delighted to have a private bath, though she had forgotten to bring a towel and had to dry herself on handkerchiefs. She rang SHAEF, and Joe came at seven to take her out to dinner. They walked to the American mess in the Place St Augustin, seeing in the street two Americans she recognised from Bushy Park. Compared with Brussels, she found Paris *like a dead town.* Taxis cost a fortune and stood empty, there were no buses or private cars, very few civilians in the streets and the only means of transport was the metro – except, at the Rond Point, there were a few bicycles attached to small carriages, reminding her of *old wheelchairs in Palm Beach.* At the Arc de Triomphe, a small crowd stood around the Unknown Soldier's Tomb, its light still burning. She and Joe went in the metro to the Trocadéro, walked down the Champ de Mars, then, back at the Etoile, found themselves in a small nightclub with an American band, where they drank a bottle of red wine. Joe had missed the last train back to his base at Versailles, *so only 1 answer was possible but it was not a great success due to my inadequacy.*

From this, I deduce that my mother lost her virginity to Major Joe Darling in the Hotel Bedford, Rue de l'Arcade, Paris, on 20 May 1945, twelve days after the war in Europe ended.

I savoured my mother's descriptions of Paris then and I thought of her undermining remark to me years later, that Paris, which she knew I loved, had 'lost its soul' because of the German Occupation. As I read of how she traipsed about next morning after only one hour's sleep – Joe had had to leave early to see his boss, General Eisenhower – I was curious to see more of that post-Liberation Paris, through her eyes.

May 21st 1945. I had no coat and it was raining and it made life awkward, but was determined to go out just the same – walked past the

Madeleine (missing the way and was helped by 2 Americans) down to the Rue de Rivoli. All the shops were shut as it is Whit Monday. In the Place de la Concorde, there were a few wooden barriers stacked up and the statues representing the main cities of France were scarred and looking rather dilapidated, some of the columns at the foot of the Crillon were scarred too and some windows broken, there were also marks of m/gun fire on the walls. On the corner of the Rue de Rivoli and the Concorde were some plaques on the wall with wreaths of flowers at their feet, giving the names of various people 'Mort pour la Patrie' and the dates, one of them a French nurse shot by the Germans in Sept 1944. I walked right down the Rue de Rivoli under the colonnades and thought of the first time I came to Paris and stayed in the Meurice there with Aunt Dita and Uncle Jay.

That was in April 1930, when Anne, fifteen, had toured the South of France and Italy, first staying one night in Paris. How different the French capital had been then!

She went on:

The fountains were playing in the Tuileries Gardens – I saw v few civilians and nobody nicely dressed – practically all American soldiers and a few French. Bought some post cards as that was the only shop I found open – the statue of Jeanne d'Arc has been newly painted in gold paint. There is quite a different atmosphere in Paris as to in Brussels somehow, it seems rather apathetic and a bit hopeless, but I love it still. Came back to the Concorde and walked down to the river, a few boats were going up and down, but for the first time in my life I saw nobody fishing. I looked up the Champs Elysees to the Arc de Triomphe, then walked up there, a few people were sitting outside the cafés, practically all the traffic was military and there was not much of that – the Germans took all the taxis and buses when they left . . . Met Joe at the St Augustin Mess for lunch – he was in bad form and so was I. Phoned British Army Staff, who to my amazement told me that they were flying in spite of the rain and that there had been 2 cancellations so I could go, the lift boy at the Bedford was rather sweet and a great help. Walked to the Vendome in pouring rain and then went out to Le Bourget in the bus . . . It was the greatest luck that I ever caught up with Joe. He had planned to come up to Brussels to see me this weekend and couldn't make it as he had to see the General!

Despite Joe being *in bad form* the morning after, seeing him had done her good. She returned to Brussels in a much better mood. She continued going out with her Belgian friends – Yseult de Jonghe, who told Anne that, being half-Jewish, she felt 'international' – and Yseult's aristocratic friend Solange de Borchgrave, who, like Anne, had worked throughout the war. Then there were the Jacquets, Gigi, Titi and their brother Raymond, who flirted with Anne.

Yseult's mother had told Anne that her family had friends and relations still in the camps, but Anne seems to have been ignorant of what was going on in them. Then, on 25 May, she was shown some photographs of Buchenwald concentration camp. *I seem to have so little imagination these days, that horrors just don't seem to register and I can't believe the photos are real people somehow. Not having people we know (thank God) in these camps makes it even more difficult – the things they did though seem quite incredible and amount to sexual sadism of the worst description.* It seems odd that my mother associated the concentration camps with sexual sadism. I also wonder if, in her lack of a horrified reaction, she was displaying again her escapism. For the diary quickly moves on, to gaiety; that evening Raymond Jacquet took her to a club called L'Elysée, then to a restaurant where she had *the best dinner I have eaten since the war, there we danced until about 2, then to a night club called the Kasbah, where a Russian man sang beautifully, and lastly to the Habanera.*

Around 4 a.m., at the Habanera, Raymond told Anne that he wanted either to marry her or to sleep with her – *it was phrased in such terminology that I didn't know from Adam which he meant!* She went out again with him the following night, after dining with his family, but does not record him repeating his ardent request of the night before.

All this male admiration, from Lew, from Raymond and from Joe, and in particular the tender love letters that Joe wrote her, made Anne more cheerful. In her job – *this Air Disarmament racket* – she was also happier, writing proudly of how she had *got things straight in our little section* and she was pleased to hear that she was entitled to three medals – the 1939–45 Star, the Defence Medal and one for the British Liberation Army – *as I was here before VE Day*. She added that she was particularly pleased about this last one, as very few WAAF officers would have it and she and Betty Wickham-Legg would be the only two in Air Disarmament who would qualify.

On 2 June, Joe suddenly appeared in Brussels and stayed for three days; they went to the RAF Officers' Club, then to the Habanera, where they met Titi and Gigi Jacquet with two male escorts. The following day, Anne and Joe went to a procession in honour of St Gudule, the first time that the locals had been allowed to hold this ceremony since the Occupation. Anne delightedly described it all:

little girls in long white veils and white dresses, small choir boys in red and white singing . . . apostles, others dressed as angels with plum coloured wings . . . Christ represented with a Crown of Thorns carrying the Cross. Mass was celebrated outside . . . at one stage the whole square knelt and incense drifted round the square. The whole thing might have been in the 15th century and when an American fighter flew over quite low, it looked incongruous.

She seemed to always love these spectacles in Catholic countries; I thought of the *fiestas* she had enjoyed so much when I was an infant in Spain. Perhaps with her love of ceremony it would have suited her to have been brought up a Catholic.

After Joe had returned to his job, Anne wrote in her diary that she was enjoying Brussels so much more now she had seen it with him.

She met more Belgians who had been in the Resistance, and on 6 June – the anniversary of D-Day – when Eisenhower announced that all the troops could have the day off in commemoration – enjoyed the Marché aux Puces. Then, just before leaving Belgium for Germany, she had a wonderful trip, first with Claude Knight to the Ardennes, followed by one night at Yseult de Jonghe's parents' house, Château de Fontaine, in the village of Anthée.

I thought I was going mad with pleasure when I looked out of my window onto green woods and newly cut hay ... the chateau is medi-aeval, with turrets and a kind of drawbridge ... I sat in the hay and watched a large fox loping along ... The Germans were in the chateau twice this war, first the S.S. Panzer Divisions and Rommel himself stayed there for 3 days, and later other Germans. Last war, the Crown Prince stayed there and the Visconte showed me a signed portrait of him, of which he seemed v proud and surprised me somewhat.

My mother then lapsed into one of her rhapsodic soliloquies about *how one is more at home with people of one's own world of another nationality than with people of another class of one's own, our ideas and manners are far more akin, which is rather awful I suppose.* She seemed to have conveniently forgotten her diary of a few weeks earlier, when she had attacked those of her own class for being mired in past traditions. However, on that visit to the château, despite loving its fairy-tale aspect, Anne also noted:

Mme de Jonghe was telling me all about the concentration camps, only now do I begin to realise just how awful it has been for these people ... every day they still hear about another one who has died from the effects of torture or lack of nourishment, a great many of them too were young people, not more than about 22. She said that the Belgians cannot relax over the peace, because the horror still weighs so heavily upon them. Yseult was at a service yesterday for someone who had died of torture in a concentration camp ... another family that they know, one son died on his way home from lack of food and ill treatment and the other one is still missing. One does not realise just how ghastly it has been for them in this way until one hears personal stories from such people as the de Jonghes – my goodness England has been lucky in some ways – this was one of the loveliest weekends I have ever spent.

One virtue of her often changing her point of view – something that used to irritate my father and me – meant that she was able to be flexible after new facts she had heard, and after new experiences. I realised that my mother could be refreshingly open-minded.

Chapter 19

By mid-June, both Anne and Joe Darling were stationed in post-war Germany. She was with Tactical Air Force (Main) 2, at Bad Eilsen, near Hanover – the same outfit she had been with in Brussels – and Joe was at Höchst, just outside Frankfurt. On 8 June, in one of the many love letters that he wrote to her in two years, he describes his new quarters at the IG Farben building, the offices of the chemical company that had helped Hitler and the Nazis to power and which had held the patent for Zyklon B, the gas used to exterminate the occupants of certain concentration camps.

From his letters, it appears that he was doing Intelligence work and related information gathering. I wrote to the US State Department and found that Joe had attended the University of Berlin in the summer of 1929; he must have retained German friends and contacts from that period and would certainly have spoken the language adequately, if not fluently.

Anne arrived in Germany on 12 June 1945, in a Dakota, with twenty-one others.

We landed at B116, otherwise Wunstof. The hangars were v. well camouflaged and hidden in the trees surrounding the airfield. The first thing I saw was people haymaking with ox-carts and the fields were full of blue cornflowers. It all looked very prosperous and the crops appeared to be flourishing. We drove about 30 miles along very good roads, all the people looked well-fed and well-dressed and there were no signs whatsoever of war, except for a number of lorries and carts piled high with luggage of all descriptions and people sitting on the top. I suppose they were people returning to their houses. The fields were full of poppies in amongst the corn and the country looked very beautiful. Numbers of the women were dressed in wide scarlet long skirts with black bodices and had white scarves over their heads, most attractive it looked as they worked in the fields as their skirts exactly matched the colour of the poppies. The children were attractive too with their blond hair and lots of the little girls had pigtails.

At first she felt at sea in these unfamiliar and challenging circumstances.

H.Q. 2nd TAF (Main) RAF, B.L.A. (Bad Eilsen. Schaumberg-Lippe, Germany.)
June 13th 1945.
Am in an office of my own with rather an attractive view over to the mountains in the distance. It seems to rain incessantly here. It is difficult to imagine that these people are Germans and our enemies. I feel terribly depressed and alone just now. It is hell living in the cramped space as we are at the moment for 4 days. Have never felt so cut off as I do now. Went to an army party, the other side of Minden, the only girls were some ATS and some displaced Poles and Russians, the officers are quartered in an old schloss, rather attractive – Minden is quite quaint. This is a queer life and no mistake. I can see it driving me crazy within a week or two if not before – depends on whether we can get around and how often we get leave – we can't even unpack our things yet, due to the roof of the house falling in and are living in cramped style with half our luggage in one house and half in the other – absolute hell. We are not far from Hamelin, otherwise Hamelin of Pied Piper fame here – wd like to see it and Hannover very much. When I told McCorquodale that I was half American, she said 'I knew that before you told me, you look American'. I can think of nothing but America these days, I am so much happier with them than I am with English people, it has always been the same since I went there as

a child and received more kindness than I have ever met in any other country, except perhaps now, in Belgium.

In these post-war diaries Anne writes almost nothing about the actual details of her day-to-day work. She was not really half-American, except that her mother was born there, and her Aunt Dita had married an American and her grandfather Michael had worked and lived there after leaving South America and before moving to England. But she was certainly gravitating seriously towards her American beau, Joe. She noted that the WAAFs in TAF were not allowed to drive cars, carry revolvers, 'mess' with the men or go into the bar. Furious, she wrote that the RAF treated her and the other women as *a mixture of tart and skivvy considering that we have worked for them for six years. My God, I can't imagine how English men have been allowed to get away with this kind of behaviour for generations and I am pretty nearly resolved to go and live in America after this war, where they are courteous, kindly and even minded towards their women and treat them with respect.*

She was certainly in the right frame of mind to have a love affair with an American. During those five months in post-war Germany, when she had so much contact with Joe, her diaries are cheerful and positive. Besides building up her confidence, Joe made her feel safe.

She was also fascinated by what she saw around her:

June 15th.
Have been grumbling about never leaving this place and have got the Int. Section on my side about it. At the moment it is very quiet in Germany, as all the Luftwaffe and the Army in this part are in POW camps and the only members of the armed forces who surrendered 'entierement' and have remained with their units under their own commanders are up in Schleswig Holstein.

It is considered safe to wander over most of Germany at the moment, although there are some isolated bands of Russian Guerillas (who fought with the Germans) at large in the hills and one of these attacked a farmhouse a few miles from here with m/guns 2 nights ago and stole a lot of food. Most of the Germans look at one completely blankly when you pass them in the road, but the children sometimes wave. This place is in the province of Schaumberg-Lippe, an ancient principality and was chosen because it is one of the most undamaged parts of Germany. We went down to HQ2 Group at Detmold, the Int. Section. Driving down there was v interesting, the country being v pretty, rolling with woods. We crossed the river Weser, all the bridges have been blown up and have been replaced by wooden bridges built by the Americans, most of the displaced persons have gone home by this time, but you still see some lorries loaded with people going along the autobahnen. The Displaced Persons travel under the auspices of the Military Government and there are also some Germans returning home. All the women seem to work in the fields here and you see quite small flaxen children driving the farm carts. It all appears v quiet, but they are afraid of trouble when the men begin to return home and when the cut in the rations (which is pretty drastic) begins to be felt. It is a queer feeling to be driving through Germany as a conquering nation. One of the prettiest things here are the red tiled roofs, which are very low and a lot of the houses have wooden beams down the walls. We passed two cemeteries with some newly dug graves, with soldiers' steel helmets on the top. This part of the country was taken by the Americans and the bridges they have built are named after some of their people who were killed in action. All the Germans here appear to be completely untouched by the war and going about their harvesting. I saw someone ploughing with a donkey yesterday and you see a horse and a cow together too drawing a cart!

She still was at times volatile and moody, pondering on what the future might bring:

June 16th 1945.
One goes through terrible moods of depression here, sometimes I think I am going crazy and wonder whether I will ever be able to get

out of this racket. If I thought I should have to stay here until I was demobbed, I think I should go mad. At the same time, I like being on the continent and should hate to think I could never get back to Brussels to see my friends there. Of course I am in love with Joe a bit, I think of him all the time and want to be with him and yet at first I found him ridiculous – life is quite extraordinary.

All I want now is to marry somebody with whom I am in love and have two children, then I should be happy, but I am doomed to ruin my life it seems – Joe captivates me completely and I think of no one else.

She describes an evening excursion with her colleagues to Minden that caused her to reflect on the German national character:

We climbed up through vast beech woods (no bluebells seem to grow here) but there were huge orange coloured slugs in the ground, until we came out onto the top of the hill overlooking the Weser river and Minden and with a magnificent view right down over the valley to Bad Eilsen. The red tiled roofs were v beautiful against the green and the wooded mountains on the side were blue and pink and grey all at once in the evening light. On the top of the hill was a huge monument to Wilhelm die Grosse, the Kaiser's father, standing with arm upraised surveying the valley, the monument was built of great massive stone pillars and gave one a feeling of might and primitive passions.

For the first time I began to realise why the Germans behave as they do. This is the land of vast forests, glowering over pleasant plains, forests where the voices of the Valkyrie can be heard still if you stop to listen, it makes you understand Wagner's music. There is a tremendous feeling of primitive instincts hidden in the forests and the country is untamed.

On 17 June, Buster, an American friend, no doubt met first at Bushy Park, located Anne and took her to where he was stationed, on a hill above the town of Vlotho. The American soldiers there opened a bottle of champagne in her honour, saying that she was the first British woman in their mess for a year and a half. To her surprise, after dinner she found Joe, who had been there since lunchtime – *was terribly thrilled ... he flattered me by telling me I was very special and superior, with wider interests than most people and that he loved me very much.*

The following day, 14 June, her boss allowed her to go out for the day with Joe and his driver, Barnes from Tennessee, to Bad Oeynhausen.

We ... missed the bridge over the Weser and had to go a long way until we found another bridge. Practically all the bridges there are blown, so if you miss one you have rather had it. In the same way the bridges on the autobahn are blown and there are quite a few diversions, some of which are rather rough! ... The roads are lined mostly with apple trees round here and a lot of their branches have been broken off by passing convoys. Sometimes you see a knocked out tank or a burnt out car, but otherwise not many signs of war. There are masses of women working in the fields. Joe insisted on holding my hand all the way, they are quite unselfconscious about doing this in front of their drivers, but don't do it in a town or in front of the British!

Barnes was *half-German and half Cherokee Indian.* My mother marvelled at his informal relationship with his superiors compared with British soldiers towards theirs, later quoting Barnes hooting his horn at an officer and shouting: 'Hey Lootenant, how about my dough?'

It was not until 1 July, her thirty-first birthday, when Anne set off again with Joe Darling and Barnes, in the US Army weapon carrier, this time to Hamelin, then to Hildesheim, that she began to see signs of bomb damage:

when we reached the town, it was the most amazing sight I've ever seen as there was practically not a house left standing and this is literally true – just a mass of twisted iron girders, half-burnt timber beams and rubble, far worse than anything I've seen in London ... there was an odd scent in the air which Joe told me was due to the bodies still in the ruins . . . the blitz happened the day before VE day and just before the Americans went in there. The inhabitants were given an ultimatum to surrender. The Burgomaster was a strong Nazi and refused.

At Guslav, the next town they came to, Anne noted that, for the first time since she'd been in Germany, she saw the shops full of things and that the ex-soldier boys leaning out of the hospital windows appeared to be *14 or 15 at most. I noticed the same thing amongst members of the Wehrmacht who one sees trudging along the roads carrying bundles on their backs.*

She and Joe lunched at the Steinberg Hotel, overlooking the Harz mountains, above a building which, they were told, *was one of Hitler's baby farms, for babies born to girls by members of the S.S. and where they are still cared for.*

The Steinberg Hotel was a headquarters of 'T' Force:

They follow on right behind the combat troops and seize the important 'targets' before they are destroyed . . . Part of T Force's and Joe's job at the moment is to get hold of the people who have information that may be of use to us and either take them to England or get them out and it is a rush just now to get them out before the Russians move into that zone, as the Russians won't allow us into their zone at all . . . Apparently some of the V (ie experimental) stuff that T Force have found has staggered them in its potential destructive possibilities.

Anne was clearly interested in Joe's work and this must have been an important factor in her getting on so well with him. He was serious and dedicated. (Similarly, my parents' marriage went well when my father was naval attaché in Madrid; his job interested her. However, I believe that, for someone of my mother's temperament, a husband's job would never be enough to engage her fully. She would always be dissatisfied unless using her own mind. She was not a 'man's woman' and never could be.)

She basked, though, for some time in Joe Darling's adoration. His letters – he calls her, among other things, *dear, sweet, a haven of understanding, a sympathetic soul* – surely gave her an exalted view of herself. She would probably never feel so 'womanly' again.

Joe gets a terrific kick out of having me along I think, as they are all so surprised to see a woman so far forward and everyone in the messes is charming to me. I have never quite realised before just how much men needed us and how much we can raise morale just by being there and talking to them!

As we went along the road we saw cars (many of them with Red Cross flags) coming along loaded up with refugees, returning Wehrmacht and Luftwaffe, trudging along with their equipment. Some limping, others sitting by the roadside for a rest. Some of them asked for lifts, but we just drove straight by. The Wehrmacht are sent by train to within 20 miles of their homes, given a day's rations and some money and then they walk the rest. All these people were walking in one direction, away from the Russian zone!

A few hours later, my mother was in the Soviet zone herself, without a permit.

In the villages were knots of people evidently discussing what to do and where to go or whether to stay. I must say I began to feel v. sorry for them. The other side of the zone was guarded by some British soldiers, who told us that they had orders not to let a single civilian through as from 0300 hours this morning and there had been 'tears and that sort of thing' all day.

At Blandenburg we called on one of the Polizei who took us round to find the man Joe had come down to see – a certain Herr Vogel, who worked for the Reichstelle and had information which we needed. After a pleasant chat with him we started for home . . . We finally reached Northerin, which is controlled by the Poles – on the way we saw a slave labour camp and factories where slave labour had been used and surrounded by wire fences. When liberated, they smashed the windows . . . and then had to go back and live in the buildings as there was no other accommodation for them.

The intense suffering of so many displaced peoples was a strange backdrop for romance. I also had to remind myself that communication between Anne and Joe, let alone meeting physically, was often very difficult, but perhaps this intensified their relationship. In a letter of 15 July 1945, Joe writes:

Anne my most sweet . . . To get me by phone you have to ask for Hanover exchange, and then Brunswick, and then Kassel, and then the Ministerial Collecting Center and then my number which happens to be 251. Since we have a limited number of lines to Kassel, it may take an hour or two to get through . . . Golly, I feel much closer now than I have for weeks. Two and three weeks for mail is simply atrocious.

The day of Joe's letter, 15 July, TAF ceased to exist and became BAFOG – British Forces Occupation of Germany. On 26 July, Churchill lost for the Conservatives and there was a Labour Party victory in England. My mother, shocked, wondered about other countries' reaction; surely the British public would appear to them to be ungrateful?

We have chucked Churchill out almost without so much as a thank you and it must be v bitter to him and v mystifying to the rest of the world at this stage, before the end of the Japanese war. Some have a theory that it is the women's vote that has done it, because of the food situation, others think it is because of the muddle over housing. The service vote was undoubtedly overwhelmingly Labour, because the troops considered themselves – with some justice I believe – to have been badly treated by the present government, with which I entirely agree.

Perhaps she had not fully understood the desire for social change felt by so many of her countrymen.

I wonder how America will view this throwing out on his backside of the man who saved England and for whom they have so much admiration! The Belgians I spoke to could not understand it and viewed it with grave suspicion. Hamilton [her cousin, a Conservative MP who was later Parliamentary Private Secretary to Harold Macmillan and MP for Cambridge] *has lost his seat which will break his heart I am afraid. If Labour speed up the demobilisation scheme, at least that will be something in their favour.*

Despite all the obstacles to meeting, on 5 August, just before the first atomic bomb was dropped by the Americans on the Japanese at Hiroshima, my mother was again travelling in the weapon carrier with Joe and Barnes driving, this time to Hamburg. One of Joe's tasks, he explained to her, was to get the names of 'clean Germans' to put into the government when it was reconstituted. Thus, in Hamburg, he took Anne into her first German house.

I felt awkward and didn't like it much. A boy aged about 21, called Peter, and his sister. They are half-Austrian. I talked with the sister. Joe told them that I had worked in the bombing raids and she said: 'Well, you made a good job, I sat in the cellar and trembled,' to which I replied: 'Well, so did I in London.' They all ask whether London was much damaged, to which I replied most definitely, 'No.' She also told me about Russian atrocities and I felt like saying 'What about Belsen and Buchenwald?' but did not though I think we should really. I finally said to her: 'Well, if you had overrun the whole world, do you think it wd. have been a success?' to which she replied: 'Personally, no, but there are others who do think so.' It is fantastic talking to them, it is like talking to no other nationality, almost as though 1 half of their brain does not exist. It never seems to occur to them that one might not want to speak to them, or that Germany is in any way guilty over the war.

By mid-August, America had dropped another atomic bomb, on Nagasaki, and Japan had surrendered. Joe managed to attend the VJ dance in my mother's 'mess', at which, to her delight, they were allowed to wear civilian clothes. She wore green crêpe de chine – presumably bought in Brussels – and *felt marvellous*. She danced the waltz with a Norwegian wing commander – my mother had a penchant for blonds – and next day wrote, showing disloyalty to Joe: *I wish to God I had met this Norwegian before.*

Later that day, however, she went to Hamburg with Joe and a friend of his from the US Army. *Passed beside Belsen camp on the way but couldn't see much except the barbed wire . . . the remaining internees are now living in the S.S. barracks nearby and we saw 1 or 2 of them walking up the road. You are not allowed in without special permission, most of it has been burnt . . . but the ovens where they burnt people are still there.*

These macabre details jar with Anne's burgeoning romance, but undoubtedly it was during that period, from mid-August until October 1945, that she was most in love with Joe Darling, if she ever was truly in love with him. He certainly was with her. Apart from having a wife and three children back in America, none of whom he mentions in his love letters from Germany – though my mother does, sporadically, in her diary – he appears in those letters as a high-minded man with a conscience. In one letter, explaining his duties regarding the subjugated Germans, he writes: *To so regulate fundamentally a person's life, in such numbers, rather sobers one.* He must have been of Quaker origin, as he sometimes addresses Anne as 'thee' in the letters. He certainly idolised her.

For someone with her temperament, who was so intensely curious, and hated dull routine, it also helped that he was able to open doors to her in post-war Germany. He held her interest. Finally Joe pulled off the 'coup' of taking her to Berlin, which she longed to see.

Was getting more and more thrilled as we approached Russian territory . . . was slightly nervous that my 'papers' which were bogus as hell, wd. not get me through, but there was no trouble at all and we sailed in and then saw the Russian frontier post with red flags flying over a photo of Stalin and of 2 Russian generals. The sentries saluted us and we were in the Russian zone! . . . most of them seemed to have quite a sense of humour and were not in the least forbidding or fierce.

My mother would not of course have had this attitude to the Russians had she been German, Polish or Czech; thousands of women, young and old, had been raped by Russian soldiers as they advanced on their victorious march west. But she was always fascinated by Russia and Russians.

In Berlin, Joe had to work, and the rest of that day Anne went out again with Barnes.

As we passed through Schoneberg I saw an elderly woman carrying a heavy basket leaning on the wall in such an attitude of abject despair that it struck me all of a heap – it is these older people that affects me more than the others; they seem more sympathetic somehow . . . as we drove through the Russian zone I saw women sitting in the rubble and grubbing amongst it for sticks and anything they could find. One German woman who spoke to me to try and buy some cigarettes told me that v. small children were dying of hunger and that the Russians had bought up everything.

In Unter den Linden, Barnes got out of the truck to see how much he could get for two American watches. He ended up getting the equivalent of $300 dollars apiece in German marks: *The Russians pulled out wads of 1,000 mark notes, which the Russian Government seems to have printed ad lib and so legalised the looting, the British and Americans have printed nothing above a 100 mark note . . . A red flag was flying on top of what remained of the Reichstag although it appeared to be in what I believe was the British zone.*

Two weeks later, my mother and Joe Darling were in a very different setting. On 1 September, having gone through endless complications to synchronise their 'leaves', they managed to go to Cannes, where they spent six days together.

4th, 5th, 6th, 7th, 8th, 9th, September.
As I write these days in retrospect, it all seems part of one glorious dream . . . we had everything we could possibly want, wine, figs, grapes, melons, in plenty . . . there was a mimosa tree in the garden . . . we stole figs from a tree leaning over the wall of an empty villa where Joe lifted me up on his shoulders so that we could get the best ones. It was fun doing the shopping too in the little shops . . . bread is still rationed . . . Joe and I would walk back feeling very domestic and carrying melons, long sticks of bread and bottles of wine. The front at Cannes is v. little changed.

This was the only time I had glimpsed my mother in a purely domestic setting and enjoying it. Ordinarily she loathed anything to do with food or cooking, always managing to get others to take care of it. Could she have been happy married to Joe Darling, or to someone like him?

On 26 September, for perhaps the only time in her life (except for, briefly, with Alan the pilot) she admits to being in love with a man: ***Don't know why I'm in love with him.***

On 17 October, she went to Frankfurt to see Joe. One of his army colleagues found her in Joe's bed in his flat in Höchst, and laughingly called Joe a 'wolf'. She and Joe tried to visit Berchtesgarten, Hitler's mountain hideaway, but it was too misty. ***No wonder Hitler felt like God***, my mother wrote, impressed by the grandeur of the scenery.

She had decided, with some doubts, to get 'demobbed' at the end of October, since she had by now spent over six years in the WAAF. Joe spent her last evening in Germany with her,

drinking wine and talking. He loves me to such an extent that it frightens me sometimes and seems to need me in a way that nobody ever has before. It is a strange combination of friend, lover and wd. be husband. He is v. sweet with me nowadays and deals with me in a way which is v. tender and makes me feel happy and contented. Joe has been such a part of my life that I don't know quite how I'm going to do without him.

Part 4

Post-war Life

Chapter 20

M y mother's war work was now over. Despite frequent complaints about her various jobs, she had had a good war, clocking up six posts in Intelligence and receiving three medals. In those six years, she had changed from a pleasure-seeking ingénue to a woman of thirty-one who had experienced things that she never would again – the expectations and rewards of a high-pressure job, obligations and duties towards others, and, importantly, bonding with colleagues in a way that she had not done at her various schools, since her mother had removed her from them too quickly.

I thought of my mother as I now knew her – a confused and helpless old woman. And, for at least three-quarters of my life with her, she had often been drunk, self-indulgent and a burden to me. Yet in 1945 Anne Veronica Hamilton-Grace, as a result of the war, was very different. I wondered, as I opened the next diary, whether, in these crucial months after demobilisation, she would go back to her old life.

There was another factor to consider. At thirty-one, she had lost her virginity and fallen in love with a man from another country who was married with three children. Would she remain as Joe Darling's mistress, or consider becoming his wife – he had offered to get a 'clean' divorce – or would she now want to look for a man who was single, whom she could marry respectably and start a family? Most of her close women friends were now wed and naturally my grandmother was hoping that her only daughter would, at last, find a loving husband. *My mother really can't understand why I can't marry someone suitable and settle down to a nice English country life. But that is just*

253

the one thing I can't do at present, if ever. It seems to me that that way of life is dead and I don't want to be tied down to something that is past. One must fit into the new world, Anne wrote on 24 November 1945.

I read how Anne returned to England from Germany in early November 1945, sailing from Ostend to Tilbury on a Landing Ship Tank, which took nine hours. Here, as the only senior WAAF officer on board, she performed her last task in the forces, *in charge of WAAFs, ATS, and other bods, including some immigrant Hungarians* – all she had to do was to supervise their lunch. She went on to Birmingham to complete the paperwork necessary for her final demobilisation.

Back at home, she did not really settle. Having been very patriotic when her country was under attack, Anne now suddenly wrote in her diary that she *hated every stone of London.* (In April 1940, she had written *I love every stone!*) Joe continued writing her love letters, sent her an orchid and, in a letter of 5 December, urged her to rejoin him: *There are various things you could do in a conquered Germany . . .* He arranged to visit her at Knowle for Christmas: *I pray that you will wear a band of gold for me. Maybe Xmas tide will be the time.* (He was not even divorced!)

Not only did Joe revere Anne's womanliness – he praised her for being *so understanding* – but he also wanted her to fulfil herself intellectually, something I don't think my father ever cared about. And I noted that Joe, instead of starting his love letters *Dear Anne*, began each simply *Anne Veronica.* I do not know of anyone else who called my mother by her two Christian names, and the fact that *Ann Veronica* was the title of H.G. Wells's novel about an emancipated woman – although I cannot prove that Joe Darling knew the book – influenced me towards his view of Anne as intelligent and independent-minded. He wrote: *I would never try to cage your independent spirit,* and praised Anne for being *so capable,* a quality I had never associated with her. She, however, only mentions Joe once in her diaries before and during that Christmas period of 1945, when he did spend two weeks in England, in a flat she had found for him in London, and at Knowle.

Although on 12 December Anne had written that she was looking forward *terribly* to seeing Joe, by late November her diary is full of a Russian, whom I shall call Olga, who had been found as a teacher by Aunt K. She was Anne's age, and even had the same birthday. '*That's perfect! Now I understand a lot of things!*' said the Russian, on learning this. The diary recounts Olga's praise of Anne's *real gift for languages* and Olga's affirmation that she would therefore go on teaching her *even if I wasn't v good some days.* Anne, who never could see when she was being buttered up, wrote: *This is the biggest compliment I could have possibly have had, as she doesn't pay them idly, in fact just the opposite.*

Olga's various remarks to Anne in late 1945 – '*As usual, I can't tear myself away from you!*', '*I have never been jealous of a man in my life*', '*My relations with men are governed by my head and not my heart*' – made me wonder if she was even testing the ground for a physical love affair. Olga certainly confided a great deal to Anne about her own unsatisfactory relationship with her English husband, whom, she implied, she had married to get a British passport. Then, in mid-February 1946, Olga sprang on Anne the news that she had just had an abortion, of a baby that was not her husband's, adding dramatically: '*I've left the door on the latch for you to come in, in case I can't get up to open it.*' Nursing was not my mother's strong point and, on going to Olga's north London flat, she was *scared to death* when she found her *lying on the bed and suffering agonies, white as a sheet . . . and rolling from side to side. It was like a nightmare and . . . I cursed myself for my lack of medical knowledge.* Eventually Anne had the sense to telephone both a doctor and her younger cousin Meg, who had nursed during the war. Anne then took Olga down to Knowle for four days, where she recovered, after *terrible pains* and a *haemorrhage.*

In late February 1946, Anne travelled to Brussels with Olga, who had a friend there. The three of them gorged in a tea shop, Chez Buol, on *mille feuilles, eclairs etc and hot chocolate. We made pigs of ourselves.*

Anne's friend Yseult de Jonghe told her that in Belgium *everyone has as much food as they want here now.*

England was still in the throes of severe rationing and would be for several more years. On 2 March, Joe arrived in Brussels, in deep snow, from Germany. However, his meeting with Anne's Belgian friends – Lettice had also come from Germany, with a friend of hers and of Anne's – was not a success. Joe, Anne wrote, quibbled about the price of drinks, although he had more money with him than the others, and Anne was *ashamed and furious with him.*

She decided at first not to accompany him to Switzerland, where Joe had booked himself on a short skiing holiday with a group of other Americans – Yseult had told her that she would be 'making herself cheap' if she went as his mistress. In the diary, Anne lamented that she was so easily influenced and still so unsure of herself. Olga, though, was clever enough not to criticise Joe. Anne wrote that Olga was *the most sympathetic friend I have and it seems we always have great fun together.* However, Olga's husband was back in England from Japan, so she would have to return. Anne decided to join Joe in Switzerland after all; her last night in Brussels was spent in a Russian nightclub. The Soviet Ambassador was there with his wife and Anne wrote snobbishly that she looked *like a cook*, adding that these two Russians behaved in an undignified way by chatting to *a completely drunken couple*. Meanwhile a party of White Russians sat separately, *as usual drinking bottles of champagne and looking very sad.*

On the train to Basel, a Belgian man living in Holland told her that there, if you did not have money to buy black market goods, you could almost starve. Anne wrote: *It is natural that one feels bitter about having to go without those things oneself when one sees a country like Belgium with everything, especially when we put our all into the war and ruined ourselves in doing so.* She was echoing the understandable sentiments of many back in Britain, from where, the following year, as recorded in David Kynaston's book *Austerity Britain*, 42 per cent of people wanted to emigrate.

Switzerland was even more lavish than Belgium. In Davos, she felt compromised by appearing publicly as the mistress of a married man – she and Joe attended a gala night with the group of Americans he was with – and was conflicted about their relationship. However, the morning that he left for Germany she was *in the depths of depression . . . I don't know whether I am in love with him or not, sometimes I can't bear him at all, at others I lean on him a great deal, as he is so crazy about me.* She added that he felt almost like a husband now but *it is queer that it is he and not I that wants to legalise this liaison.*

Back in Brussels, Anne received a cable from Aunt Dita asking her to come to America. In England she saw Millie; the first time since November 1944, when Millie had left for Egypt, though they had exchanged letters. On 26 March 1946, they met again:

Met Millie at Piccadilly Circus, she is just the same except she looks thinner and is rather nervy. Apparently her mother said immediately when she heard I was back 'Well thank God Anne is back, she is the only person who has any influence over you,' she even spoke to me over the phone and said 'Make her go to America with you.' Mrs S. so M. tells me thinks I am the only person who has a sane and sober influence over Millie! I love her dearly and was delighted to see her again. We spent the whole day together.

But her thoughts and feelings now were given over to Olga and, without admitting it, she seems to have been almost in love with the Russian woman, writing, very much as she had done two years earlier about Millie:

no vice could possibly be attached to such a friendship . . . it is just a v. beautiful thing, more of the soul than anything else. It is the nearest thing I know to being one person, instead of always being alone and it is so delicate a thing that one is almost afraid to touch it. When that person is away from you, you feel as though you were only half there. That feeling must be the ideal marriage but it is only given to a few to

*find it perhaps and I am surely not one of them and yet I feel I could
love someone a great deal if only I could find the man.*

Anne did not write her diary at all in April, which she must have
spent in England. In May, Olga went to the English countryside with
her husband, to try to make her marriage a success. She wrote to Anne:
'You'll never know how much I'll miss you', and confessed that she
was *miserable* at the idea of sleeping with her husband, who, Anne
wrote, was *rather common and bourgeois*, whereas Olga was *highly
sensitive and refined.* (I began to feel sorry for the poor husband,
whom I later got to know slightly. Olga never struck me as particularly
sensitive or refined.)

My mother and Olga's strong feelings for each other naturally made
me wonder again if Anne was really only able to fall for someone of her
own sex. But they both wanted to be married and have children and, to
make things even more complicated, Olga had confessed to Anne that
she was really in love with a man in Yugoslavia. Anyway, I am sure
that my mother would not have pushed her love for a woman to its
obvious conclusion, which would have been to settle down as part of
a lesbian couple. She was not strong enough to defy convention in this
way; perhaps few women then were. Certainly, such a decision would
have horrified my grandmother, as well as most of Anne's friends, and
I suppose I cannot blame her for weakness in that area.

On 20 May, Anne set off by plane to visit her American relations. Her
mother, her cousin Meg, Meg's brother Patrick, *Joe* – presumably Joe
Darling, over from Germany – and Olga came to 40 Belgrave Square
to see her off. Olga, dramatic as usual, was *so upset at my leaving that
she had to take 'drops' and wear dark glasses.*

Joe Darling was also going to the US, to visit his wife and children.
He was still mad about Anne, and wanted her to regard his country
as hers, which to some extent she did. *Here in America is my mother's
family and the memories of my grandfather and it is here that I feel I
belong in part.*

Anne was now back with her relations in Long Island after ten years' absence, chatting happily to Peggie, whose own marriage to the *youth* whose photograph Anne had seen on Peggie's hotel dressing table in 1930 was foundering. Anne noted how beautifully dressed her relations were compared to everyone in England, and had to stop herself stacking plates, as she was now used to doing, and allow her aunt's maid or butler to do it. She quickly got used to the luxury of en suite bathrooms at Aunt Dita's and noted that, in that milieu, the women had got *doing nothing down to a fine art . . . making oneself attractive seems to be almost a career here.* This was an incredible contrast to Anne's life for the previous six years.

On 11 June, Joe Darling turned up in New York and she spent the evening with him. *He says he thinks I love him more as a friend and less as a woman than he had hoped. I'm not in love with him physically now as I was with Alan – wish to God I were!*

The next few months in America were full of friends and relations – she saw Leith and Leith's brother, Fife, whose wife, Anne wrote triumphantly, seemed jealous of her – and confusion over her relationship with Joe. She could not help making comparisons between America and England, both during the war and after. She went fishing with Uncle Jay in Canada, where, to her surprise, she was glad to see *the old Union Jack flying in Montreal airport. I feel strangely proud of being English since the war, a feeling that I had never had before, now I feel I really belong.* At the fishing camp in Quebec, near the St Lawrence River, Anne washed her own hair for the first time in her life. She was nearly thirty-two. She had not done so even during the war, probably relying on a weekly hairdresser, as many women did then.

Joe Darling's wife was in debt. He told Anne that he would marry her at once if she wanted, but would rather wait six months till things got sorted out. He then, to her amazement, asked her to visit him – and his wife – in Washington! *He got me worked up to a fine state and I can't think now.*

She did not go. On 6 July, she set off by train with Peggie and Clippy (wife of Peggie's brother Ben) for a long summer holiday. Anne listed all the states they passed through, ending up at the Valley Ranch in

Wyoming. Forty-five miles from the nearest town – Cody, home of Buffalo Bill – it was *a series of wooden huts in amongst the cottonwood . . . we sit in a large building all together at long tables and there are 2 bells . . . at mealtime, you rush in, in case all the food's eaten up! This makes me feel at home.* Anne, again, was half-nostalgic for her life during the war.

In late July, Joe Darling travelled 4,000 miles to see her at the ranch, just for one night. He declared that he could not imagine life without her and begged her to follow him east and be with him again in the US before he left once more for Germany.

Anne in the end decided not to go. Meanwhile my grandmother, by now extremely worried about her daughter's liaison, had written to her older sister, Anne's Aunt Dita, begging her to get *her* daughter Peggie to have *a straight talk* with Anne. Peggie, nine years older, obligingly gave her younger first cousin the following advice, which Anne noted in her diary:

'unless you are absolutely crazy about him and admire him v. much, don't marry him, but carry on an affair to give you confidence as that is always a good thing, & he is obviously crazy about you'. 'If you admire Joe then marry him.' I told Peggie that I was now down to 2nd best in a marriage choice [Anne had not yet met my father] *and she said 'well then, that leaves you with a great no. of choices, marry someone who you admire, even if you are not madly in love with them and you should be v. happy.'*

My mother stayed on in America six more months. She was sometimes homesick for England and tired of *talking trivialities*; she wrote, perhaps with prescience, that *to hear the conversation of Uncle Jay and Cousin Joe, on worldwide subjects, is like listening to children and it is terrifying to think they have such a terrific control of finance and hence, such power.* But on the whole, she enjoyed her time in the USA, shopping, playing tennis at the exclusive Long Island Piping Rock Club, throwing a cocktail party with Peggie in

New York, and having a fling with Sam Winslow, whose family were friends of her American cousins. Occasionally, Anne encountered friends from 'the old country' engaged in more serious tasks. One, Harold Zink, sent her his book

'Government & Politics in the United States' with the following inscription: 'Dear Anne, I should be v. pleased if the presentation copy in some measure dedicated my appreciation of your friendship, espe-cially during the somewhat trying days in London in 1944–1945. Your companionship & remarkably fine conversation were greatly valued then & will not soon be forgotten. With best regards – Harold.'

Another intellectual friend from Britain, Charles Brackenbury,

got me a seat to hear the Security Council and it couldn't have been more fascinating. The debate was a continuation of an adjourned debate on an accusation brought by the Ukrainian Union of Socialist Soviet Republics against the 'Greek monarchists for violating the Greek/Albanian frontier' . . . Sir Alexander Cadogan made a very pleasant and dignified speech, in the true tradition of the British Foreign Office, subtle and funny too. I felt rather proud of the whole thing as he had more poise than the rest put together and the manner I knew so well at home. Charles half offered me a job at the U.N.

Not many women, or men either, would have found such a debate *fascinating*, and it showed Anne's predilection for this type of work, in diplomacy, perhaps. If she had been of my generation or, better still, my daughter's, and intent on a career, she might have seriously considered Charles's offer. Aunt Carrie, an older woman at the Valley Ranch, had asked Anne what she would do when she got back home and when Anne replied that she would work either in a bookshop or in the UN, Aunt Carrie said: *'You must do something intelligent, otherwise you will be miserable.'*

*

In her last few months in America, Anne hardly mentions Joe in her diary; by September 1946, he was back in Germany.

Torn about whether to return home, Anne then waited for my grandmother to come to America for Christmas and in the end stayed on there until February 1947. On 6 February, with the words, *hangover and trying to pack everything, which is agony*, the last immediate postwar diary, written in America, ends, with Anne still indecisive about whom to marry, despite having had more proposals, from Joe, Sam Winslow, Bartie Bouverie (widowed husband of Aunt Lin's daughter, who was run over and killed in the London blackout) and Harold Zink.

Chapter 21

I had now finished reading my mother's wartime and immediate post-war diaries. It quickly became clear that, back in England in early 1947 after America, Anne stopped writing a diary and, as she had in her late teens, seemed to think it worth writing one only when abroad.

My own diaries were different; I recorded my daily life and, just days after my daughter's birth in London in August 1981, had typed details of my new baby on another of my cheap, brightly coloured portable typewriters, observing that her plaintive cry reminded me of a little bird's.

I knew that I had been taken to Spain aged six weeks, so even if my mother had not written about my early babyhood in England (I assumed that, after my birth in King's College Hospital, London, my first weeks were then spent at Knowle), she would surely have written about me once she and I had moved to Madrid. I felt upset that those first five 'Spain' diaries were still missing and I started rummaging again in the various boxes that had come from her old house.

In my studio, where I had put all the photograph albums from her old house, I now found notebooks about her four pregnancies. One, before the birth of one of my brothers, began: *Awful stitch in my right side.*

I found details relating to my own birth, including advice on contraception – a cap. There was no mention of the actual baby, me, although my Baby Book (handed to me by my mother a couple of years before she got Alzheimer's) was conscientiously filled in by both my parents, including the day that I found a four-leaf clover on the common outside North Heath House. The clover was still there, a faded brown-green, stuck to the page with Sellotape, my mother's proud words in capital letters beside it: *FOUND BY ELISA, ENTIRELY BY HERSELF AT NORTH HEATH, CHIEVELEY, NEWBURY, BERKS IN OCTOBER 1953 WHEN SHE WAS 3 YEARS AND 10 MONTHS OLD. AVS.*

I also came across a small brown envelope, on which my mother had written: *Remnants of the Grand Duchess Olga.* Inside were tiny scraps of white material, nothing to prove that they had ever belonged to the Grand Duchess, the Tsar's sister. It was a bit creepy.

In one album was a set of photos of my younger brother's twins, my mother's second lot of grandchildren. She had scribbled in pencil on one page the page's measurements, presumably to make sure that her grandsons' photos would fit. In this respect, at least, she was serious about being a grandmother, although I could not help recalling an unpleasant occasion when she refused to have the little boys to lunch, making all sorts of excuses.

Beside her twin grandsons was a photo of my mother alone, holding in her arms a clutch of toy dogs. This bizarre apparition, of a woman in her seventies with her hair awry, looking already a bit mad, who could have been enjoying herself getting to know her grandsons but preferred a set of toy dogs, was horrible to me.

My search in this studio for the Spain diaries proved fruitless. I moved to a room above the toolshed, a room now full of my mother's old books, many about Russia. Here at last, after some hours searching, I found in a box an exercise book, with *Students MSS Book* printed on its hard grey cover. Inside, surrounded by stickers from Air France and Eastern Airlines ('The Great Silver Fleet'), was my mother's handwriting in pencil: **August 22nd 1947. Anne Hamilton Grace. France, Switzerland, Italy, Luxemburg & Belgium.** In biro she had then added: **'& Spain'.**

I turned the pages and to my excitement found the following entry: **January 15th 1950. Up v. early and off to Northolt with Chow and Mum, Elisa (my child) and Nanny Benny. The a/c took off at 7 a.m.**

just after a brilliantly red sunrise. I felt sad at leaving Nah and Gig and my mother. Elisa was asleep in her Karri-cot . . . This was the start of our lives in Spain.

Further back, I found an entry that was almost equally exciting: *June 1st 1948. This was or is my wedding day – I have dreaded it all my life, but when it came, it wasn't nearly as bad as I thought and I wasn't really very nervous . . .*

I now began reading through the whole of this very thick diary, hoping to find at least a few details of my parents' courtship. My mother did not seem to have been madly in love with my father, I noted with disappointment, though I was not surprised. But it soon became clear again that Anne had recorded only separate chunks of her life – when out of England. I did, however, find that on 23 September 1947 Anne had written: *Who am I to marry? Micky, John Guest, Mike Lloyd, Sam or Willy Segrave? All I know is that I must marry someone soon, as I'm lost at present and rather lonely.*

Instead of accepting any of them, Anne went on a motoring trip, with her Belgian friend Yseult de Jonghe, into mountain villages in Italy; in one remote place, San Felice Curceo, *a little fairytale village*, there was still a notice up in German stating that looting was punishable by death – *it was a rude shock to imagine the Germans in such a place . . . I hid my nails in shame, the scarlet incongruous and superficial in such a setting. From one house came the sound of a man singing, savouring the queer despair of the East. How Oriental still is Southern Italy.*

She describes she and Yseult at Lago de Bolsena among ox carts laden with barrels of grapes, the oxen *with long horns, gentle beasts, fat and well fed looking and as white as snow.* She and I would see these, though not as well fed, pulling carts near Comillas, only a few years later. *We passed a funeral in one place, just a small hearse with a flock of children carrying flowers following behind.* Naturally, I could not help thinking of Raymond's small hearse – which I never saw. What bad luck awaited my mother.

She and Yseult motored on to visit Princess Borghese in her *palagio* near Burgo San Lorenzo during the grape harvest, seeing peasants, tall with blue eyes, bare feet and *kind of white berets*, who shared 50 per cent of the profits of the wine with the Principesa, despite its being *all very feudal.*

Back in Rome, Anne saw Madame Boni of the finishing school – *she lives in the past and is very depressed* – and attended diplomatic parties, writing that she loved the Embassy life. And: *I was told by everyone at the Walmsleys that I was 'the type Slav' as usual!* My mother always loved being thought Russian.

Anne's last entry, on the day of her return across the Channel back to Knowle, records the drowning of Aunt Dita's little granddaughter in America. The child died in a family swimming pool, as Raymond would. Aunt Dita, like my grandmother, had lived at Battle Abbey; perhaps it really was cursed. Frustratingly, Anne's diaries now stopped for a while, in keeping with her routine of only writing them when abroad.

Then, on 1 June 1948, in the same book, came that entry. I read it again: *This was or is my wedding day – I have dreaded it all my life, but when it came, it wasn't nearly as bad as I thought.*

My mother was on a train to Paris with my father on the first night of her honeymoon. Otherwise, I realised, even her wedding day would not have been recorded. As it was, I would probably still never know exactly why, out of those five suitors listed on 23 September 1947, she had finally chosen my father, the last name on that list.

Anne and Willy were married at St James's Spanish Place Catholic Church on 1 June 1948. I read how Peggie's daughter Dita came from America to be chief bridesmaid and was very helpful. There was a reception at 40 Belgrave Square, followed by a small cocktail party at Claridge's, given by Bartie, that previous suitor of Anne's.

My mother's only comment about my father on the day, then night, of their wedding was: *Love in a sleeper is not as bad as one might think!* She must have written this the following morning, still in the sleeper, or in the Hotel Continentale in Paris, where they stayed two nights before flying to Nice. I imagine that she wrote the diary in secret, concealing it from my father. My parents' honeymoon lasted three weeks and Anne stayed close to her new husband's side, even when he gambled in the casino at Cannes, something she found boring.

Six months later, though – there was a gap in the diaries after their honeymoon – I saw that, after taking my father to America for Christmas that year to introduce him to those American relations who had not attended their wedding, Anne was back to her independent ways. Instead of returning with her new husband on 28 December, when he had to go back to his work in the navy – I guess this was when he was stationed at Plymouth and my parents had rented a house on Dartmoor – Anne lingered in America for almost another month, despite my father sending two telegrams urging her to return.

As a result of the second telegram, she did not give in to Aunt Dita's pleas to go down to Palm Beach, and I concluded that this was the turning point (or so he thought) that my father had boasted to me about: 'I told Aunt Dita, "Anne is *not* going to Palm Beach, she is coming home with *me*!"' adding, 'I wanted to go on doing spermia with your mother.' ('Doing spermia' was the phrase that I had invented after trying to puzzle out a leaflet that my mother had given me, aged nine, about the facts of life. I had had to ask my father for a further explanation, knowing that my mother would be too inhibited. He had obliged, at the dining-room table, when she was absent.)

There was another reason why my father wanted to go on 'doing spermia' with Anne, apart from sexual desire, I saw from Anne's diary; they were trying to have a baby and she had had a miscarriage only three months before this trip to America. She writes of her sadness in her diary of 5 January 1949 from Peggie's flat in New York, where she stayed after a visit to Leith's in Maryland, during which she **disgraced** herself by getting drunk at a large dinner party – *Leith and everyone couldn't have been sweeter about last night's business – she really understands the reason.* (Leith, who had married eight years before Anne, already had three children.) On getting her period the following day, Anne wrote plaintively, referring to her recent miscarriage: *Everything I see seems to remind me of it all over again and* *everyone I meet seems about to produce a child . . . I am so depressed I don't know where to turn.* I felt sorry for my mother's sadness and her fears – after all, she was already thirty-four, old in those days to have one's first baby – but I couldn't help noticing the alarming reference to her having got blind drunk at Leith's and, in the manner of most alcoholics, blaming her lack of self-control on something else – the miscarriage.

I also could not help being critical of her treatment of my father, to whom she had now been married for eight months, although she did write in her diary after his first telegram of 4 January 1949, begging her to return on the 17th: *I miss him terribly as a matter of fact and did not realise how much I depend on his love and companionship.*

I could not help feeling angry with my mother over what I saw as her abandonment of my father in these weeks. After all, he must also have been upset by the miscarriage of his first child; he even used to claim to have been ill in sympathy when my mother gave birth to me, and he had had to stay working in Spain. But perhaps my father wasn't a good listener. He had a kind heart, but was indefatigably masculine, charging about like a bull with his head down, shouting and swearing. Also, Anne had always found it easier to confide in women – and in her diary.

My parents, I knew, had been introduced to each other by Alice, the widowed cousin who had taken her teenage children to America in the war. Alice's daughter Maureen told me years later that my grandmother, still worrying about her daughter's liaison with Joe Darling, had begged her and Alice to find Anne a suitable husband. Actually, Anne's diaries reveal that, although Joe was still pursuing her as late as autumn 1947, after she met my father, she had lost interest; she recorded *a wire from Joe, to ask me to call a hotel in Luxemburg, which I did. He is staying there till tomorrow afternoon, if I had known, we were almost next door to each other, still, I don't care much.*

The introduction of my future parents was a success; after the dinner, Willy took Anne out dancing. My father's version to me was: 'I took her out to a nightclub and bit her on the ear.'

My father was a sensual man and perhaps this had attracted my mother initially; she was physically undemonstrative. She certainly admired his war record; he was decisive, while my mother was often tortured by indecision. Perhaps it was a relief for her to at last relinquish control to someone who knew what he wanted – in this instance, to marry her. He was original but not bohemian, good fun and entirely without duplicity; my parents' friend Rosemary Blake-Tyler, who was based in Madrid with her husband when my parents and I were there, told me that my father had been 'a breath of fresh air' in the Embassy. My mother would have appreciated this. Also, she must have known that very soon it would be too late for her to have children.

William Francis Roderick Segrave was born on 22 November 1907, in his parents' house at 40 Onslow Gardens, London SW7. He had a caul – an extra membrane of skin that envelops the head of a few newborn babies – which was considered lucky, particularly for a sailor; the superstition was that you could never be drowned. Willy was the son of Vice-Admiral John Roderick Segrave, and as a boy was sent to Dartmouth Naval College, to take up his father's profession. The Admiral was descended from a Norman family dating back to Nicholas de Segrave, who had fought at the Battle of Lewes for Simon de Montfort. They remained Catholic during the Reformation. My grandfather had a distinguished naval career; he was attached to the peace conference in The Hague in 1907, was naval attaché in Vienna in 1914 and was then in command of the armed liner *Drama*, which in March 1915 took part in the sinking off San Fernandez of the *Dresden*. In 1920 he was for three years chief of staff of our naval representation at the League of Nations. He was given the Légion d'Honneur for his services to the Allied cause.

His wife, Mary Stephanie Ricardo, was from a Sephardic Jewish family which must at one time have converted to Catholicism. According to my father, his mother was such an observant Catholic that she would ring him when he was a young midshipman to remind him of various holy days of obligation – he referred to these as 'holidays of obligaggers'. He also, in an infuriated tone of voice, would tell us children how his mother would use 'one sponge for her bottom, another for her face'. I do not know how he knew this, nor why he found it so disturbing; a Jewish friend of mine told me that her mother had done the same and that it was a Jewish custom. However, my father and his sister Rosemary had been told that their mother, unlike her two older sisters, could not possibly be Jewish, because when she was born her father had syphilis, was in a wheelchair and was too old to sire a child. Charlie Chaplin was seventy-three when he fathered a child and the oldest father I have found on record is Nanu Ram Jogi, aged ninety – so I regard this story about my grandmother's non-Jewishness as a possible unconscious display of anti-Semitism.

My father was a handsome man who certainly did not look English. A boyfriend of mine, seeing a photograph of him taken in Madrid in 1952, said that he looked like a South American general. With his dark eyes, dark hair and swarthy looks, my father could also have been Greek, or from anywhere around the Mediterranean – or, indeed, Jewish. He was tallish and well built, with broad shoulders, and would charge about the house shouting commands as though still on the deck of a ship, making personal remarks.

'You're like a ruddy little prima donna!' he would declare, when, aged thirteen, I changed my outfit several times a day. He was referred to as 'The Commander' and 'Bang Bang Bugger Man' because, while shooting, he would often miss the pheasant and yell, 'Bugger!' Other expressions he used at home and out of it were 'Shit and Derision' and the even worse 'Christ on Crutches'. He also frequently said 'fuck', a word not commonly used then in mixed company; indeed, my mother commented that, despite having worked six years in the WAAF, she had never heard such language used in front of women and children until she met my father.

Anne's diary entries ceased temporarily after that return from America in January 1949. I must have been conceived in the rented house on Dartmoor shortly after that. Then, luckily for me – or I would have had no written records of my early childhood – there was that entry on 15 January 1950 when she, I and Nanny Benny flew from Northolt airport to Madrid's Barajas airport: *Arrived at Madrid airport at 1.10 English time, (2.10 Spanish). As I stepped out of the plane, following Elisa who was being carried by the air hostess, I heard Willy's voice saying: 'I don't know if that's my child, how the hell can I tell?'*

Chapter 22

My father had been made naval attaché in Madrid in October 1949 and started working there several weeks before I was born. Now I read in my mother's diary that, after she arrived, she and my father – and presumably me and my nanny – went to stay in the Hotel Velasquez, very near what would soon be our new home. *Willy had brought me some lovely flowers, carnations and camellias.* Next day she saw the house where I would spend my infancy and pronounced it *heavenly far nicer than I expected, with an enormous patio and a palm tree and flowers and v. light & big rooms, more like a country house.*

Despite her various wartime jobs, some in admin, my mother did not have a clue how to run a household and my grandmother, all too pleased to let Chow run Knowle, certainly had not taught her. It was Natasha, the Russian wife of Charles Johnson, First Secretary to the British Embassy, who, when our new house was vacant a week later, rushed to my mother's aid, lending her pillows, helping her unpack and going with her to buy kitchen utensils. Without Natasha, who quickly became a close friend, Anne confessed she would have been at a loss.

At first, she was homesick, missing her mother, Nah (*my crone*) and her collie, Roy, which her friend Cynthia had given her as a wedding present. She wrote nothing about me, her first baby, I saw with chagrin, until, at last, on 28 January 1950, when I was two months old: *My little bird is so sweet and hardly ever cries. She has the most enchanting, sudden and crooked smile and is so good-natured. She sits out in the patio in her pram most of the day.* I was gratified, and struck by how, in the diary I kept just after my own first baby was born, I had also likened her to a bird.

Like most infants in that social milieu, I was looked after by my nanny; Nanny Benny was a Scot with jet-black hair who, my father insisted, was really a witch who flew over Madrid on a broomstick on her days off, when my mother had her first experience of looking after me alone. *February 22nd 1950. Nanny's day off. Cute Things screams like anything when I change her nappy, it isn't half as easy as one thinks . . . Willy and I pushed her down the Castellana for a walk.*

I was pleasantly surprised to read that my mother *had* occasionally changed her children's nappies, or, at least, mine. My Aunt Rosemary had been sure that her sister-in-law had never done such a thing, and, indeed, I had not been able to visualise my mother performing such a task, assuming that, when Nanny was not there, she had got Julia the maid to do it. But it was true that I had retained that very early memory of my mother trying to master the buttons on my blue 'cherry' dress and laughing happily, so perhaps that was also when she had fumbled with her first nappy.

Her diary extracts – my father would often push me down the Castellana so fast that my mother couldn't keep up – are the only documented glimpses I have of my parents as a normal married couple with their first baby. My father was the more outwardly affectionate. I remember how he would swing me up on to his shoulders, where I would play with the medals on his white naval jacket. He often embraced his wife too, though later, after Raymond died, I recall her always pushing him away. In Madrid, the diary shows that my physically undemonstrative mother did nickname her husband 'Bulldog', which, given her love of dogs, must have been a compliment, and I still have an almost life-size bulldog that barks throatily when you pull his chain, from that time in Madrid.

Despite her initial homesickness, Anne, I read, threw herself whole-heartedly into her new life. She admitted in the diary to feeling *an awful ass* not knowing Spanish, and started taking lessons. She could not get into any of her clothes worn *before Elisa* and Norman Hartnell, the royal dress designer, sent two outfits. I suppose that, as the wife of the British naval attaché, Anne was expected to be well dressed.

My mother loved the diplomatic life and told many anecdotes about its personalities in later years. There was the femme fatale, *an old girlfriend of Willy's* and *a very pretty woman,* rumoured to be having an affair with another Brit in Madrid. There were the Oswalds – Adolf Oswald, the American military attaché, and his wife Dorothy became lifelong friends of my parents, as did the Blake-Tylers; Harry Blake-Tyler worked for Shell. My mother enjoyed all these characters and encounters – the home movie show of a British couple which went on into the small hours sent her, retrospectively, into fits of giggles:

they are very Anglo-Indian and the shots were interspersed with subtitles such as 'The Queen of the Valley' followed by an enormous lotus flower on the screen and a picture of Tory Murray wearing some shoes made of grass for fishing entitled 'Not Quite Bond Street but –!' . . . We progressed onto the Norfolk Broads and tobogganing at Egham! The Marquesa de Civia was yawning openly and I was exhausted.

A major part of my father's job involved this constant socialising, at Embassy parties and dinners, and at functions outside Madrid specifically to do with the navy.

My mother, in this respect, must have been an ideal wife. She was charming, a good listener and eager to reach out to all manner of people. She had joie de vivre – indeed, my memories of her in Spain are of her always smiling. She must have complemented my father, who could be uncouth and frighten people with his loud voice; after all, he had spent much of his life on a ship. She accompanied him to the many parties, getting on particularly well with the Spaniards, and they soon became a popular couple.

Although, in the diary, she does not express towards my father the passionate feelings she had had for some of her earlier loves, she seems to have depended on him and respected him. Despite her private income, at this early stage in their marriage he was the dominant one;

his job took precedence. And I remember a very domestic, cosy atmosphere in their shared bedroom in that house in Madrid – my mother suggesting one morning: 'Go and ask Dad if he wants to go to the mountains today!' I had rushed into the bathroom to find my father sitting on the lavatory. 'Get out! Get out!' he'd yelled, and I'd run back to my mother, hiding my face in my parents' sheets. Our Sunday trips to the mountains – I recall the car breaking down, leaving us waiting in the parched landscape – were family outings almost certainly instigated by my mother who soon, I saw, did *not* perceive it her duty to be always at her husband's side. She took advantage of being situated in the centre of Spain to go to wilder, more remote parts, and was often away, just with the chauffeur, for several days, simply exploring.

In early March 1950, she visited Avila, *surrounded by a mediaeval wall*, and fell in love with it: *Spain seems at its most beautiful at sunset when the hills are blue and the old walls are golden against the sky*. Paco (Don Francisco Maroto y Pérez del Pulgar, Marques of Santo Domingo), whom she had met first in Madrid, had a house there, and it was to Avila that she would take me, a year and a half after Raymond's death, to visit him and Miss Ettie, his English governess, who had allegedly saved his life in the Civil War. Paco, my mother found to her delight, was descended from a sister of the renowned mystic Santa Teresa of Avila, whom she admired.

These entries about our first months in Madrid ended on 1 April 1950, the day of Franco's annual victory parade to celebrate his winning the Civil War; my parents had to attend, my mother taking her place with my father in the diplomatic stand. That was the end of that thick diary, which had contained her post-war travels, her wedding day and her honeymoon.

It was time now for me to hunt again for the sequels, the 'Spain' diaries leading up to Diary 6, which started in mid-sentence: . . . *flowers that smelled exactly like heather honey*. I was almost beginning to despair of ever finding these missing four, and even wondered if my mother had destroyed them – reading about Raymond later might have been too painful.

I searched again among the clutter from her old house. At last, under a pile of old photograph frames, I found the missing 'Spain' diaries, all together in a box. On the cover of each my mother had written 'SPAIN', then the number in Roman numerals. At last! I felt joy, relief and gratitude to my mother for having not only written them but kept them for all those years. Now, unknowingly, she was giving back to me my very early childhood, the time when she loved me; when she, my father, I and then Raymond were happy.

10th April 1950: Cute Things looking too sweet for words and with a wide smile. She is 'so good' and is quite enchanting and growing prettier.

Yes, my mother loved me, but her love for travel had also taken hold. She was becoming entranced by Spain's unspoiled, often dramatic, landscape. In the new 'Spain' diary, Diary 1, I read that, on her way from Madrid to Seville in early April, she had passed *the reddest earth I have ever seen* and *the half-eclipse of the moon, with the moon reflected in the sky and looking like a cross*. On that journey she and my father lunched in Cordoba with new Spanish friends, the Viernas, in their *palacio* with fourteen patios – the family had owned it since 1430. Fausto Vierna's sister, the Duchesse de Rochefoucauld, had left her husband to live with a gypsy woman in the caves below the Alhambra; the gypsy's husband lived with them and the duchess was said to wait on them both like a servant. Anne was fascinated; I recalled her pictures of that gypsy and of his wife, and how in Spain she would talk excitedly of *los gitanos*, encouraging me and Raymond to clap hands with her and chant:

My mother <u>said</u>
That I never <u>should</u>
Play with the gypsies
In the <u>wood.</u>
If I did

She would say
Naughty little girl
To disobey!

Although the implicit lesson was to warn a child off disobedience, the message that I took from the chant, and that I am sure my mother intended us to take, was the opposite: she wanted us to be bold and daring, and when Raymond and I got overexcited, shrieking and dancing about, she would call us admiringly: 'Wild Things!'

My mother was seduced yet repelled by Spain's old-fashioned, often grim Catholicism; she was shocked to discover that a Spanish wife could not cross a border without her husband's permission and that a man had the right to go in front of a woman in the queue for Confession. The Catholic Church, she wrote, encouraged this submission.

My father, though, may have found it easier being in a Catholic country, since in England Catholics were still considered outsiders. There were references in these new diaries to his determinedly going to Mass even when he was travelling round Spain for naval duties and it was inconvenient.

My mother, however, was disgusted, after being taken to the birth-place of St Ignatius of Loyola, founder of the Jesuits, by her Basque chauffeur Julian, by the Church's *worship of outward form, forgetting entirely the humility which Christ taught . . . and all these awful relics (bones blood etc) which to my mind would be better on a rubbish heap and the almost idolatrous worship of which shocks me terribly, as does the utter worldliness of this, the seat of the Jesuits.*

Julian, who also showed my mother the plaza where his father and 108 others were killed by a bomb during the Civil War, told her that the Jesuits were *the real rulers of Spain* and had money in all the best business enterprises. He added, though, that he admired *the hardness of their training.*

I was struck by my mother's criticism of the inimical aspects of Catholicism. She had a religious nature and used to pray on her knees by her bed every night. As a child in Sussex, I had envied her Protestant hymns and what appeared to be the softer, less disciplined nature of her religion – we Catholics had to fast then before taking Holy Communion. I occasionally went with her to St Margaret's, the little church across the fields from our house. In Franco's Spain, Protestant Bibles were not allowed, and the British consul was put in jail for four days after being found in possession of one.

However, my mother, I saw, in her travels around that still-poor country, could not help but fall in love with its very primitiveness, and with many of its Catholic practices. On 8 June, she took my grandmother and Gig to a Corpus Christi parade in Toledo – *in the streets thyme had been strewn . . . it smelt divine and from all the balconies were hung Spanish silk shawls with colours of every kind and beautifully embroidered. Girls in mantillas (small ones) stood waiting on these balconies to watch the procession pass.*

Indeed, some of the beautiful aspects of Spain were inextricably bound up with its bigoted and savage history; she admired the glamorous pro-Franco Moorish Guard, known for their ruthlessness and fierce fighting. But in keeping with Franco's intransigence towards 'Reds' and other 'heretics', a Spanish Protestant soldier was put on trial for not kneeling at the correct moment during Mass; my mother was gratified that the British Embassy was asked to intercede.

She also detested the Spanish Catholic attitude to women. Visiting San Pedro el Viejo, one of the oldest churches in Spain, originally a Cistercian monastery, she saw *a hideous statue of the Virgin recumbent, looking like a demented corpse – hideous colours, a monstrosity . . . around which were devout peasant women.* She added: *I only hope that the Catholic cult of the Virgin helps the women to bear the burden which they undoubtedly have and which is forced upon them by the relentlessness and rigidity of the Roman Church, controlled of course entirely by men who have no conception of women's minds and feelings.* I was impressed here by my mother's forcefully expressed feminism.

One of my early memories is of hearing the name 'Franco' often on my parents' lips, and assuming that he was one of their friends. (I even mixed him up in my mind with Frank, the Knowle chauffeur, whom my grandmother would sometimes address affectionately as 'Franko'.) Of course I did not have a clue who this Spanish Franco really was but had picked up that he was important to my parents – and, indeed, to everyone in Spain.

My mother, with her habitual curiosity, at once took an interest in Spanish national politics and tried to glean what she could of the current state of affairs. She wrote that the monarchists (many of the Spaniards she met socially) owed their position to Franco *despite abusing him continually. None of them though want the king back as he would be forced to be more liberal than Franco.*

At the time of my father's arrival in Madrid in October 1949, Spain was ostracised by Britain and the other countries who were members of NATO – established in Washington that April. Franco was running a brutal, nationalist regime, fuelled by his hatred and mistrust of Communists and other dissidents. Democrat President Truman was anti-Franco but was also conscious of the threat of communism, both from Soviet Russia – which had blockaded Berlin between June 1948 and May 1949 – and from China, where, on 1 October 1949, Mao had founded the People's Republic. A third world war was feared and, as a military ally on Europe's southern flank, Franco could be useful. But the British Prime Minister, Labour's Clement Attlee, sided with the other NATO countries rather than with the US, arguing that it was better to support a post-fascist, newly constructed Germany than a currently fascist Spain.

Naturally, because of my father's job, my parents often had to attend functions involving Franco. In March 1950, my parents had gone to a procession in honour of the Brazilian Ambassador, who was presenting his credentials to Franco; an old lady with tears in her eyes spoke to her of the days of the King, when such an occasion *had really meant something.*

In July 1950 my parents went to the royal palace at La Granja, to celebrate Franco's victory and the end of the Civil War; this was considered *muy especial*, wrote my mother:

The gardens all lit up . . . the road was lined by young Falange in blue shirts and red caps. Inside the palace gardens the Moorish guard was lined up with their lances, they wore white turbans and magenta and white uniforms and had on white kummerbunds. They are very dignified and impressive and are always tall men . . . The music started to play and Franco and his wife came out and shook hands with all the Diplomats lined up – the men bowing over his hand, which, apparently is done by the service people here because of his army rank. After this, Franco mixed among the crowd, followed by Artajo (the minister of foreign affairs) and he shook hands with all of us. Franco is v. young looking for his age and a tiny little man – I never realised how small, until I stood beside him.

My mother's justified excitement at meeting Franco reminded me of her triumph of getting so close to Mussolini at the Excelsior Hotel in Rome in April 1932, when she was seventeen – she was always fascinated to glimpse these political figures in the flesh. I also noted that she enjoyed my father's status as a 'Diplomat', giving the word a capital letter.

Another important aspect of life in Spain was the close friends that she and also my father made there. Natasha's father, like hers, had been killed in 1915, *fighting the Austrians.* Natasha had also sensitively asked Anne if she missed America. It must have been Natasha who introduced my parents to the Infantes, a couple closely related to both the Spanish and the English royal families. Natasha's cousin – Alfonso – was, my mother wrote, *an Orleans Bourbon and a first cousin of Alfonso XIII* (the former King of Spain). She was particularly impressed that the Infante *took out the 1st Spanish pilot's license in 1910 and still flies today.* His wife Beatrice was one of the last grandchildren of Queen Victoria, and sister to Queen Marie of Romania. Better still, the Infanta had spent a great deal of time in Russia! (I recall her, from when I was seven, as very thin, wearing black, and rather stiff compared to her warm, informal husband, who took me with him into the garden to see his aviary and brushed off my attempts to call him 'Sir', as my mother had instructed me to do.)

On 21 April 1950, my parents made the first of several visits to the Infantes' *palacio* at San Lucar de Barrameda in the south. My mother loved the Infantes' historic and royal connections and would often tell me the Infanta's tale of a tea party she had attended as a child, given by her grandmother Queen Victoria for all her grandchildren, ending in a lesson to the oldest about not being greedy.

My mother kept in close touch with home, making the occasional visit to London and Knowle. In May 1950, Aunt K came, and she and my mother drove via Avila to Alba de Torres, where *Aunt K was really thrilled to bits at seeing it and read out about my great-grandfather, Sir John Hamilton, defending it against the French during the Peninsular War.*

My mother sometimes travelled with my father for his naval duties. They went frequently to Gibraltar, once in July 1950, when in the harbour she saw four American destroyers and an aircraft carrier. *22nd July 1950. Watched the carrier and the destroyers leave this morning from my balcony. Thank God for the strength of America which is the only thing in the world today that gives one any feeling of security.* My mother expresses here her views unequivocally. My father, who hated the way America was so business-driven, would probably not have taken this attitude.

In Gibraltar, my parents met the new British admiral, Lord Ashbourne, and saw the Barbary apes on the Rock. After meeting the consul, Mr Russo, they flew back to Madrid via Tangier, where my mother bought an American movie projector – *(Bell and Howell) which I have wanted for ages.*

This must have been the projector on which she later showed her films of me and Raymond, in Spain, and among the poppies at North Heath.

Chapter 23

Earlier that July, I read, I had been sent with Nanny Benny to Knowle. I was now shocked to see that I then had not seen my mother for two months. No wonder I loved Knowle, though; I was there so often. My mother was able to feel completely secure in placing me there with my nanny, grandmother, Nah, Gig, Katherine, Mr Tash and Frank – Frank, who, four years later, would teach me and Raymond the two times table in the garage, with a chart he had made specially. He would deliberately say the table wrong, so that we would then shout out the correct answers.

My mother saw me again, two months later, in England, on 11 September 1950: *Elisa is awfully sweet and crawls all over the place and manages to stand up holding onto things. She understands quite a few things you tell her to do and loves animals and flowers.*

Nine days later, she learned she was pregnant. She wrote that she hoped for a son. Anne does not record any marital arguments; the only thing that she baulked at was the idea of being obliged to have her next child baptised Catholic as I had been – like most non-Catholics in those days who had married 'Papists' (my father's flippant term), she had had to agree before marriage that the children would be brought up in the Catholic faith. In the diary, she writes angrily that she does not think it right for children to be brought up with a different religion from their mother and even declares: *It may end in divorce from Willy.*

In this early period of their marriage, however, Anne appears close to Willy and often in the diary admits to missing him when he had to go on naval duties – did she ever tell him so, I wondered, or was she too reserved?

My mother wrote lyrically about many of the sights she saw, but, each time she returned to Madrid, seemed overjoyed at seeing me again:

8th October: Elisa is sweeter than ever, she still does not walk at all though she occasionally stands.

18th October: 'Cute Things' thrilled at seeing a horse, made clicking noises in her mouth and jumped up and down as though she was riding.

My father too was involved with me: *22nd November 1950. Bulldog's birthday. He pushed Elisa for an hour and she went to sleep.* It was unusual then for a man to be seen pushing a baby. My father didn't care what people thought and obviously loved me.

Two days later, I had my first birthday party; my grandmother and Gig came out for it: *'Cute Things' behaved admirably and smiled all the time and was very amiable with her guests.* I have my mother's photograph, in which Eleanor Brewer, future wife of Kim Philby, stands behind her daughter Annie's chair at my birthday tea. Eleanor was then married to Sam Brewer, a *New York Times* correspondent. When Philby was unmasked as a Soviet spy in 1963 and fled to Russia, she would be abandoned by him in Beirut.

Anne sounds happy in the run-up to our first Christmas in Spain – it had snowed earlier that month and she wrote of cold bright weather, shops full of Nativity figures for cribs and carts of holly pulled by donkeys. She even gave up a social lunch to look after me all day on Nanny's day off, as she didn't want me to catch Julia's cold. She bought me a little Christmas tree, but she left me on Christmas Day itself for Paco's, where Miss Ettie let off a whoopee cushion and a two-day-old, very white, lamb sat in Paco's hall. On 27 December, though, she was back with *Cute Things. Elisa is sweeter than ever.*

I had been used all my life to my mother's many departures and returns. Now I saw that this pattern had been set from when I was a baby. Because of these frequent absences, followed by our joyful reunions – each time I must have been relieved, as well as happy, to see her again – I must, from very early on, have perceived my mother almost as a magic lady with whom I must not misbehave or else she might go for good. I must not displease her. I was, by her accounts, a good-natured baby and toddler, but I also wondered if I had perhaps been *so good* out of fear that one day my mother really would not come back. Perhaps this was the reason why, as an adult, I had tended to reject men who offered me love and stability and instead was drawn to those who were emotionally withdrawn, married, unstable or, as in the case of foreign correspondents, often away working. Like my mother, these men were always dancing away, out of reach.

But, despite all her absences, Anne, I saw in these 'Spain' diaries, came into her own as a mother when Raymond and I began to show imagination, verbal ability, and physical boldness. As I grew older, she noted down details of my development, as mothers tend to do. At fourteen months, I took eight steps, *the first time I have seen her really walk . . .*

January 19th 1951. Cute Things sweeter than ever calling Mama and Dada and 'Poor Bow-Wow'. She walked quite a bit in the garden . . .

January 21st 1951. My father's birthday. I hope Cute Things will grow up with some of his traits . . . Cute Things a shameless flirt, she loves men and boys! . . . Elisa ignored Willy after he spoke to her in a loud voice and was determined not to give him a nut, smiling to herself all the time.

My mother was taking me out more, to the zoo, to the country road beyond the Escorial and to the Casa de Campo for picnics. We were often together.

March 21st 1951. Wonderful sun again. All our trees in the patio are out and the apricot tree is in full bloom. Spent the day with Elisa.

April 25th. Baby could be born any day. Had Elisa all day. She was v. sweet and good and full of fun – smiling and playing happily all day.

May 1st 1951 [a week before Raymond was born]. *Took Elisa to the Casa de Campo – she stood and refused to move, holding up her skirts and saying: 'Prickies!'. She loves going in the car and talks like anything, picking up new words all the time.*

I read all these extracts about myself as though my mother was passing me a bowl of cherries. I hoped that they would never end. I was overjoyed to have these records of that time when I – then Raymond – had been loved, when my mother and my father had been happy. I spent several weeks reading and re-reading them; I wanted to never leave them. They showed my mother at her most pleasant; after Raymond's birth she became even more maternal, upset that she could not breastfeed him, calling him 'my Spanish love' and changing my own pet name from 'Cute Things' to 'my old love', and relating how I had shouted for 'Yaymond', my new brother.

Unfortunately, I could not help noticing references to my parents' drinking; apart from falling and tearing some ligaments after a reception to welcome the new British Ambassador and his wife, my father also slept in his clothes after a Burns Night dinner. He broke his arm on a visit to Gibraltar, although Anne does not say whether or not that was caused by a drunken fall. As for her, she was sick after too much Spanish gin in Barcelona; my father guessed that the British consul there had swapped it for the superior English gin allocated for entertaining, which he was probably flogging on the black market.

Anne spent twelve days in hospital after Raymond's birth and, as I did after my first baby was born, wrote her diary about the baby: *an amusing little face and nuzzles like a puppy. Elisa saw him and seemed thrilled with him. I love the little chap already.* She recounts how my father brought her gold and ruby earrings *to match the brooch/ clips he gave me when Elisa was born* and notes that Raymond was born on a Tuesday, Tuesday's child being 'full of grace'. (She christened him 'Raymond Roderick Grace', perhaps for this reason, and because it was her maiden name.) She described hearing the *burritos* from her hospital bed each morning at 7 a.m. and how this would be one of the things she would remember about Spain – perhaps this was why she had bought those two donkeys when we moved to Sussex. In the same hospital was the celebrated English bullfighter Vincent Charles – 'Vicente' – who visited Anne in her hospital bed. Women were mad about him with his *gypsyish looks*. She found him modest and childishly endearing.

Doreen now arrived from England to look after me while Nanny Benny dealt with the new baby. *Elisa likes her and calls her DingDong.* Anne had to give up breastfeeding and agonised over this. She was behaving almost like a 'normal' mother.

In early July 1951, my mother took us on a seaside holiday to Zarauz. She described delightedly my chatter on the train: *Elisa thrilled with everything, 'Moo-cow fight', 'Bull-fight', and 'Trainy-puffer'. She really is a joy to take around.*

In San Sebastian, she witnessed a child's funeral; other children held white ribbons attached to the little coffin. Reading this, I could not help thinking that I should have been given a role like that at Raymond's – in certain aspects, the Spanish Catholic Church got it right.

At the seaside that summer, Minervina, the girl from the riding school outside Rome in 1930, visited us at Zarauz. She was now the Duquesa de Diario Sforza and, after attending the smart *Montellano ball* in Madrid, was on her way to Lisbon to see the King of Italy. The other visitor was Millie, almost certainly Anne's great love from Bomber Command. There was no inkling in the diary of Anne's former feelings for her; instead she complained that Millie, now married to a Freddy Scott, had turned anti-American.

Now, gratifyingly, my mother was focused on me, worried that I had been ill, then relating how she had taken me to see the boats in the harbour in my pushchair – *I was proud to be seen with her . . . she is a joy to take about and is so interested in everything and so funny and sweet.*

The whole tone of my mother's diaries now is more confident – dubbing characters she met at Madrid parties that autumn *a tough baby, a tart, a soaker* and *vain as a peacock*, and she seems, apart from intermittent health problems, to be enjoying every aspect of her life, which included arranging a portrait of me by a French artist which I have inherited. I am in a white dress and scarlet shoes and hold 'Grandma', the toy panda my grandmother gave me.

On New Year's Eve, my parents attended a glamorous ball given by an aristocratic Spanish couple, Pepito and Millie Elda, Anne cock-a-hoop that they and one other couple were the only members of the British Embassy there. She danced the Lancers, and she and my father went to bed at 5.30 a.m.

On 15 January 1952 my mother noted that two years had passed since she had arrived in Spain with me. Churchill had been voted in again as Prime Minister in October 1951; in October 1950 the American government had resumed relations with Franco and now Churchill wanted to follow suit, taking up his country's special relationship with Truman. My mother wrote that *the Ambassador*, Lord Balfour, wanted my father to stay on in Madrid; he had just heard that he would be relieved as naval attaché that October. There is no mention of how that decision was reached; it seems most likely that his superiors in the navy had decided it, and this would overrule any request by the ambassador.

Meanwhile Natasha and Charlie Johnson had left Madrid for good, for him to take up the position of a counsellor in the Foreign Office. Natasha had asked Anne if my father wanted to stay on in the navy because, if so, she would 'have a word' with Prince Philip.

I do not know if my parents took up Natasha's offer and frankly it does not seem likely that Prince Philip would have wanted to use his influence to help a naval officer he did not know personally. In any case, my father would not have liked using such influence. Either it was my parents' joint decision for my father to retire or, more probably, the Admiralty had ultimately decided it; after all, despite his 'good war' my father had not been promoted beyond commander.

The Admiralty no doubt decided to let another officer have a turn at being naval attaché.

It meant that we would definitely have to leave Spain that October of 1952.

On 6 February 1952, my father rang from work to say that George VI had died. Anne's **legs shook** and she was **almost in tears.** Referring to his having had to take over on his brother's abdication, she wrote: **the king had sacrificed his health for his country and for all of us.**

The American Embassy flew its flag at half-mast and my parents' Spanish cook observed: **'queria mucho al pueblo'.** She said she had seen the King on newsreels, visiting the wounded, the sick and the poor. The aftermath went on for days; the English community were **suddenly all told to wear mourning – Lady Balfour has had to order 18 veils to be made up in 24 hrs.**

My mother was proud that over 4,000 signed the condolence book at the British Embassy, a number of them Spanish Communists who had been rescued by the Royal Navy during the Civil War.

She now seems settled happily into domestic life with me and Raymond, recording, on 4 March 1952, **Elisa came down and was very nice with the Infanta, who kissed her. The children are sweet together and love each other.**

Perhaps I *had* loved Raymond. My mother certainly thought so, or wanted to think so, although I had also declared: **'I will skin you, I will kill you!'** However, **the next moment, she was kissing him all over his face and on his hands.**

Now she described him, at three months, as **a dear smiling little thing.**

On 9 March, she and Doreen took me to the mountains, where there was still snow on top. The car broke down – a frequent occurrence – and **Elisa was sweet and v good all day talking ten to the dozen. She threw snowballs and ran all over the place, chattering all the time and pretending to be different people.**

In April, my grandmother came and she and my mother took me to the Casa de Campo – **heavenly day, warm.** Anne was gay and happy during this time; writing of the shepherds watching their flocks – boys of about fourteen, or old men with criss-cross sandals, a blanket round their shoulders like a cloak, of the sheep and goat bells sounding an Arabic mournful note:

Spain, as I will always see it, consists of the silent shepherds, the sheep and the cowbells, the swaying cloaks of the Civil Guard, the storks in their nests on the church towers, a procession of loaded donkeys silhouetted against the sky as they cross over an arched bridge and these great big gentle oxen as they draw the overloaded carts guided by the stick which they have been taught to follow blindly. I must also not forget these great black plodding oxen as they draw the wooden ploughs slowly and methodically across the great Spanish acres.

That summer of 1952, my mother arranged the first of two holidays to Comillas, a fishing village in the north of Spain, near Santander. We two children were sent ahead with Doreen and Nanny Benny, then, after an absence of nearly three weeks, our parents arrived. At first my mother was overjoyed to see me – I had run to meet her and my father on their arrival – and pleased that I had learned the Spanish for 'butterfly' and 'flowers'.

However, a couple of days later she was in a rage, writing: *the children are the most awful water funks*, and then, after a Madame du Pavillon had brought her four well-brought-up French children to tea:

Elisa was most unattractive, wouldn't play, yelled and says 'No' to everything she is asked. I was very ashamed. She is v spoilt now and has no manners at all. She is a little 'softie' too. This always seems to happen when we leave the nurses for some time. Raymond is better, but a Nanny's darling too. Nanny is really impossible, a bigoted old fool, hates all foreigners and spoils the children, besides being terribly possessive with them, which makes Elisa terrible with everyone else.

It did not seem to occur to my mother, who, after all, had been enjoying herself without us in the preceding three weeks on yet another motor trip round Spain, that Madame de Pavillon was probably 'hands-on' with her children, disciplining them and monitoring their behaviour on a daily basis.

I had now almost reached Diary 6, the first 'Spain' diary I had discovered on its own long before the others turned up. The broken sentence that began Diary 6 – . . . *flowers that smelled exactly like heather honey* – was, I now saw, the continuation of a description of yet another excursion my mother had made, on the afternoon of 26 August, the day she had enjoyed taking me alone to the beach. She and the chauffeur had driven to a village called Barcena Mayor,

situated amongst chestnut trees and green meadows, with maize fields . . . a village out of this world in antiquity, with muddy lanes for streets and 12th century houses, still lived in. A dear old man took us round. The village was full of bees and they keep them in hollowed tree trunks, with a slab of wood over the top and a small round hole for a 'door' near the bottom. There was a young priest (the Padre of the village) who we talked to. Mass is said in the church there once a day. This, of all the villages that I've seen round here was a real look back to the past. In the fields nearby were growing some lovely pink mallow flowers . . .

Here, in Diary 6, was the continuation: . . . *that smelled exactly like heather honey.* Inside the light purple cover I read: *Anne Segrave. Prado de San Jose, Comillas, Prov. Santander.*

September 1st. This afternoon, Willy and I took Elisa blackberrying. She was thrilled and kept saying: 'Elisa didn't prick Elisa's self this time' . . . In the evening, we all went down to the plaza in the village and watched some travelling singers.

My mother then went to buy a leaving present for Nanny Benny. After escorting us back to England, Nanny Benny would end her stint with us, and Doreen, who was having a break at home with her parents, would be in charge.

On the morning of 9 September, my mother took me, Raymond and Nanny Benny to Santander, where our ship turned out not to be sailing till 6.30 p.m.

However we went on board in a launch, to find that people were still in the children's cabin. Elisa was crying and was nervous but Raymond was delighted with everything. I got them organised and Elisa thought she was 'At England' when she arrived on the boat and said: 'Where's Mr Tash?' I said goodbye to Nanny and left them and felt very sad . . .

We would not see our mother again for two months.

The next two weeks of the diary describe the winding down of my father's job in Madrid and yet more road trips of my mother's, one ending in Barcelona to join my father. My parents stayed at the Barcelona Ritz and, on the morning of 15 September,

the fleet arrived . . . the 'Glory' (an a/c carrier), the Eddy Beach and Destroyers – Chequers, Chieftain and Chevron. It is the second visit to Barcelona in 22 years! The Consul gave a cocktail party in the Ritz tonight. Not v. exciting as there were not nearly enough women. The admiral Cerverea came with one of his daughters (Paquita). I got given Spanish gin and got rather tight. (Terribly ashamed.) I didn't drink much [my mother as usual made excuses] *but didn't realise that it was Spanish gin . . .*

The following day, my mother, feeling very ill, lunched with Captain Charles Keyes on board the *Chequers*: *Keyes very amusing.*

There was more sightseeing, more parties on board ships and a tour of the aircraft carrier, *The Glory*. My mother was fascinated by its flight deck and by the way it could carry thirty aircraft. She noted each type of plane, how many bombs it could carry, and at what speed it could land on the carrier – she was back briefly to her old days in the WAAF. On 20 September, she and my father went with the consul and his wife to see the fleet sail away.

On her return to the Ritz after sightseeing with the consul's wife, my mother found my father and the consul *in an awful state*. A young sailor, supposedly recovering from having his appendix out, had developed peritonitis and

wouldn't live through the day. Willy rushed off to see him and I met Don Lorenzo Correa who was taking us out to lunch. Willy came back practically in tears and we lunched with Don Lorenzo in a great hurry, then I suddenly thought that we must get hold of the best specialist in Barcelona on that 'disease' to see the boy, so we telephoned all over the place and eventually got the consul to get permission from the head of the hospital for a civilian doctor to see the sailor. We then left in a terrible rush to catch the plane, throwing the clothes in the suitcases but knowing at least that the doctor had been got hold of . . .

Two days later, they heard that the young sailor had died. The specialist had seen him, but could do nothing.

Although very sad, this, for me, was an inspiring incident, as it showed my parents united over something important, my father's protectiveness for those under his care in the navy and my mother displaying maturity, presence of mind and helpfulness.

Anne spent the next days emptying our rented house in Madrid. She was back to her 'spoilt child' mode and made an awful fuss about it. On 28 September, she moved to the Madrid Ritz alone and my father went to Gibraltar on naval duties. On 6 October, she and my father met my father's replacement, the new naval attaché. My mother took a dim view of the successors, writing heartlessly that they had a dog and *a child with a broken thumb*, that no hotel would take their dog, and that he looks *like a co-respondent* – did she mean journalist or a co-respondent in a divorce case? Then, when my mother asked the wife if she wanted to go and meet 'the wives' at a knitting party – which I wouldn't have thought was my mother's cup of tea either – the wife *flatly refused!* My mother dubbed her *second rate and affected and 'antipatica'*.

She and my father stayed on in Madrid until 1 November, receiving many presents and good wishes from their Spanish friends, whereupon they flew, not home to see me and Raymond, but to Paris, where they met the British naval attaché there and his assistant, who had wanted to be posted to Madrid. My mother wrote that he would have been a much better choice! She was pregnant and wrote she hoped that she would not have another miscarriage.

She enjoyed meeting my father's French cousin, Robert de Nexon, but noted that she found Paris depressing, with a *kind of heavy sad atmosphere that it never had before the war.* She does not mention her visit there in 1945, when she first spent the night with Joe Darling. She finally flew home to England with Julia the maid, while my father returned in the car.

My mother reached Knowle in time to see us go to bed. *Elisa has grown and Raymond is enormous. Was thrilled to see them and no miscarriage so far!* Unfortunately, she must have then had one, as Nicky was not born for another fourteen months.

Chapter 24

Now, in 1953, with my father's naval career over, there was a big change in my parents' lives. However, as my mother kept to her habit of only writing diaries when abroad, there is nothing regarding our life in North Heath, about which I have so many fond memories.

From the next diary entry five months later, it appears that my father was now being assimilated into a leisured existence. On 2 March 1953, she writes of them flying to the US, where, in New York, they attended a business meeting at the family company. They saw Peggie and her new second husband, Etienne, then flew to Palm Beach to stay with Aunt Dita and Uncle Jay. *How beautiful it all is, I had almost forgotten.*

Anne very much enjoyed this Palm Beach holiday, swimming, playing tennis, shopping and going to cocktail parties. What my father thought about all this my mother does not say, though in one entry she comments: *How dull this café society really is!* They returned to England on 22 March and arrived at Knowle to find me with a temperature.

I have a vivid memory of the three of them, my mother, father and grandmother, all coming down the small landing staircase at Knowle. I still have a bright postcard my mother had sent me from Florida, of orange trees and a steam train.

The following day, my mother heard some exciting news. An article by her on Spain, commissioned by the *International Women's News*, was considered *most excellent* and *is to be published in the April or May issue.*

I understood her pleasure over this (thinking of my own first published article, in the *Guardian*, when I was twenty-three, and how pleased my mother had been, though my father had teased me) and felt sorry again that she did not become a professional writer or journalist.

Her diary restarts in Comillas, four months later, and this holiday lasted two whole months. There is no reference now to my father's doing a job of any kind – he drove the car out to Comillas from England while we all flew, my mother noting that she missed him. She was now pregnant with Nicky. At Comillas, she quickly met friends made the previous summer: Viviana, a redhead who had shown her the best prawning, now taught my mother to surf properly, something she later passed on to me.

My mother's diary is full of details about me and Raymond. He fell down in the sea, then kept asking: *'The sea won't hurt me?'* But soon he started sailing his boat in the rock pools.

August 12th 1953.
Great excitement on the beach, as three very Moorish children (I remember them from last year) stole Elisa's 'boatie.' Juan [the new chauffeur] *very cleverly persuaded them to give it back by appealing to their sentimental side and saying that it belonged to children like themselves who were crying like anything because it was lost . . . Elisa had been very philosophical about the loss of her 'boatie,' saying 'I don't suppose we shall get it back, as boaties are lovely things to play with.'!*

How tender and sweet my mother was then! The childlike side of her – the way she used our baby word 'boatie' in her own private diary, meant that in those days she identified with us, her small children.

On 14 August, the large picture of the son of *the Duquesa* (presumably the owner of our house) fell from the wall and smashed a coffee cup and saucer, the glass of a table and the picture's own glass. *I hope it is not unlucky, but only because the cord has not been looked at for years and years. Luckily it fell whilst no one was in the room, as it hangs just above where my mother usually sits on the sofa.*

A picture falling off a wall is often said to presage bad luck. My mother would later see the occurrence as having been a warning of Raymond's drowning. She noted that if the picture had fallen in the daytime or early evening, my grandmother would have been injured as she always sat in that chair – strange, I thought, when it was she who, through carelessness, would later be responsible for the death of her grandson.

It was only now, reaching the end of Anne's diaries, that I began to appreciate how awful my grandmother's role had been, and awful for her too.

During the long holiday my father was bored, and furious that no English newspapers had arrived, due to strikes in France. Had my mother yet realised it was bad for him not to be working? After all, she, for much of her life, had been used to leisure, whereas he had experienced only a disciplined and structured existence.

Despite my mother's enjoying herself again at Comillas with me and Raymond, it seems to me now that my parents were already slightly adrift. Did they expect to be on permanent holiday, even back in England?

My grandmother had told me that my father, after Madrid, had confessed to her that he was lazy, and had begged her to make him work. She said he had thought of trying to be an MP, but that my mother had dissuaded him, saying that he saw things too much in black and white. I do not think that he was ever actually employed properly again (though I recall a rumour of a brief office job in London), but, from 1957, he ran our small farm in Sussex and busied himself with my mother's financial affairs.

Of course, as a three-year-old I knew nothing of all this, and, because of the tragedies that would later befall my family, my mother's diary entries about that last Comillas holiday for me have an elegiac quality.

August 31st 1953. Spain.
Almost the hottest day since we've been here. No wind. On the beach

this morning. This afternoon, my mother, Gig and I took the children to Colveces beach . . . Elisa and Raymond played alone for hours on the beach in and out of a pool, splashing and shouting with laughter. Elisa bathed, but only on the edge as the waves were enormous and there was a lot of 'resaca'. I bathed Elisa this evening and she said 'That was the nicest day in the whole world!' Dear little love. Raymond was cute too and full of mischief. Juan loves the children and they him. This evening, it was so warm that I sat out after dinner listening to the waves breaking and the noise of the cicadas, which I find very soothing. There was a glow worm with a very bright green light outside the front door tonight and the lights from the fishing boats were bright across the sea.

Soon after this came a passage that confirmed my own powerful early memory:

September 2nd 1953. Lovely day . . . In the afternoon I took Elisa to San Vicente beach . . . I went in bathing, leaving Elisa playing on the edge of the waves. It was v. shallow and I had to walk out for miles. She was <u>so</u> good, played around by herself and waved to me every now and again. When I started to come in she walked out in the sea to meet me right above her waist! I was so proud of her and she is such a pleasure to take out.

My mother, I saw, had had no inkling of my terror that she would never come back out of the sea. I had known, though only three, that she had thought me brave to have waded so far out to meet her.

My most intense memories of Comillas are of my mother happy, always smiling, her eyes very blue. I remember what must have been that last summer there: big white oxen pulling wagons, wild foaming waves, Raymond and I running down the garden to the hydrangeas to see the Big White Ship on the horizon sail to Santander. *Sept 12th 1953: Raymond saw it from the garden and ran to tell Doreen and Elisa that he had seen 'a big white boatie'.*

I can recall even now the smell of cooking blackberries. I read how my mother and my father took us blackberry-picking and on our way home, I told her of my night fears:

Elisa tells me that she doesn't dream about the lost Train anymore, but that when the wind howls round the house at night sometimes she wakes up crying because she is afraid that her crab (that she has in a pail) out on the balcony will be blown away. Now that it is back in the sea (she took it to the beach today) she won't cry any more. Dear little love.

One of her last entries, before we left Comillas forever, is this:

September 21st. The sea is making a tremendous roaring tonight and as I look out of my window (it is a clear night) the bay is long lines of white horses as the sea thunders onto the beach.

Our privileged and happy childhood went on. In January 1955, my mother took us all to America on the *Queen Mary* – my father, Raymond, Nicky, my grandmother, Gig, Doreen, and our cheerful black-haired nursery maid Margaret, whom Raymond and I called M'Paul. We drank Bovril on deck for elevenses, going up in the elevator and asking for 'Promenade deck please!' There was a children's party where a conjuror magicked chocolate milk into a cone. I recall looking through the ship's porthole at night from my bunk and hearing the boom of other ships in the dark ocean.

Aunt Dita had lent us her guest house in Palm Beach, the Dream House, and indeed, the visit was like a dream, particularly for children from England, used to rationing, porridge every morning, meat with fat and gristle, 'sitting comfortably' for *Listen with Mother* on the wireless and a compulsory long walk with Doreen and M'Paul every afternoon.

Aunt Dita had a black gardener in a leopard-skin hat. Raymond and I loved to chat with him. In the garden of the Dream House were grapefruits and oranges, hot from the sun, and coconuts we shook to hear the milk inside. Each morning we walked with Doreen and M'Paul to the beach by Aunt Dita's house. We would pass an enormous tortoise, taller than Nicky, and watch him chewing lettuce, his mouth moving sideways. We played on the sand and in the sea. There was no one on the beach except David, a boy of my age with red hair. My mother arranged swimming lessons for me and Raymond in Aunt Dita's pool. At the end, we would say to our teacher: 'Thank you, Mr Holmes!' 'You're very welcome,' Mr Holmes would reply. I learned to dog-paddle more quickly than Raymond and I even learned to dive.

Now, among my mother's diaries, I find her entries about the holiday and am pleased how my memories tally with these:

February 22nd 1955. Palm Beach. Drove to the Dream House, where Aunt Dita met us. They have provided us with everything possible here, including a car and a television. It is kind and it really is a Dream House! This evening the pelicans flew low along past the house and over the lake, with the sunset sky behind them back to their nesting places farther up the lake. The children are thrilled with everything, especially the oranges, coloured people and coconuts.

My American godmother Leith and daughter Taffy, a little older than me, came to stay. Taffy's fair skin was sunburnt and then covered with calamine lotion. There were little mixed packets of American cereals. The raisins in the bran flakes seemed an unimaginable luxury, like the pink ice cream Aunt Dita gave us, which contained real strawberries.

Though I was only five I was aware that we were lucky to have gone to America. When we returned home, Miss Booth, my teacher, questioned me about Florida and the habits of the Americans. I was aware that my mother had a kind of glamour, because of her connections there.

Our years in Spain, and in England until Raymond's death, now seem to me a special time, surrounded with a kind of halo, and North Heath a place of enchantment. I recall, in spring, outside our house, sweet-smelling polyanthus of all colours, and inside our front door a little trough of primroses in fresh earth. I had two guinea pigs, Syrup and Treacle, for whom I made daily bran pies and fed crab apples, and I often played with Raymond under the big copper beech tree, and on the lawn with Nicky, a cheerful toddler. I recall the loud explosions of planes overhead – 'breaking the sound barrier', the adults told us – and Raymond and I on ponies, Betty and Ginger, at a local riding school. There was nursery school, which I started at four – the first day transcribing the letter 'A' over and over again by a picture of an apple – run by Miss Booth, who always made me feel clever and special; I never again had a teacher I loved so much. And often my mother was there, playing with us in the garden, walking with us on the common, her own delight in our home making the place a 'merry meadow' like the one in the book she would read to me at night, the meadow where there was always sunshine.

Then, within a few hours of us leaving North Heath, everything changed.

In that bag full of Raymond's things is a small exercise book of my mother's that, when I had first found it, I hadn't felt like reading; it was too private, too anguished. However, I did read a few sentences: ***My son, without whom I find it almost impossible to live . . . After Roddy was born, I had everything and more than I had ever wanted, my husband and four children, a happy house and garden. I asked for nothing more in life than this.***

My mother was only forty-two when I, my father and my two remaining brothers lost her – to grief.

During our new life in Sussex, my father did his best. His adherence to the Catholic Church and its rigorous rules in the 1950s may have helped him during this difficult time. He took us three children each Sunday to Mass at the newly built Catholic church next to the convent where I did my weekly catechism class with the nuns. He always strode to the front and would give us orders throughout Mass in a loud voice: 'Strike your breast, damn you!', 'Bow your head, you little fool!'

Various parishioners were given nicknames, such as 'Half-wit' (our doctor, who later diagnosed a broken rib when my mother had pneumonia, always at Mass with his five daughters) and 'The Bespectacled Cod', a woman always first up to Communion, my father pointed out, as though this was a crime. After Mass he would drive us into the town to buy the Sunday papers; I would get a box of Maltesers with my pocket money and eat the lot.

I loved Buzzy, my brown and black terrier, given to me by my mother's new friend Audrey, whose only son had died and who must have realised that I would be lonely. I played with Buzzy, walked him and took responsibility for his food and water. He slept in my room in a basket. When I finally went to boarding school in late 1961 – my brother Nicky had been sent already, at seven – I was upset about leaving my dog. I told my mother this and she replied that she had preferred Raymond to any of us. Was this a childish – and brutal – reaction to my implication that I would not miss *her*?

My human playmate was Nicky. Being four years younger, he was tractable. I induced him to join in my invented games – one about cavemen, another about a Scottish family – and each Christmas I wrote a play and made him take part. Nicky looked up to me and I was protective towards him. My mother had more or less abandoned him during the period after Raymond's death, and our Irish nanny preferred the baby.

Nicky, having been robust and happy as a toddler under Doreen's care, was now, as a boy, not tough enough for my father, and I recall picking up a knife in the dining room when he attempted to hit Nicky. When Nicky was recommended to try for a scholarship to Eton, the only boy in his prep school ever to do so then, he declared: 'I hope he's not going to turn into a ruddy little intellectual!' He wanted him to learn boxing, something that Nicky and my mother disliked, and I remember my parents arguing about it. My father had been toughened up early, first being sent to a Catholic prep school, then to Dartmouth naval college, where, he told us, boys jeered if they saw a schoolmate being kissed by his mother or sister.

My mother must have found my father's prejudices trying. He was anti-intellectual, anti-American and anti-Scot, calling the celebrated Scottish poet 'Rebbie Bairns!' and jeering at my mother's favourite children's book, *Little Lord Fauntleroy*, the first part of which was set in America.

My mother's love for America and her times spent there – the only real family life she knew, with Aunt Dita and her four cousins – affected my own early life. I remember the book of exotic American birds – 'Golden Oriole', 'Hoopoe' – that I was given to colour in and also our Little Golden Books. One, *The Saggy-Baggy Elephant*, was about a little elephant who tried to fit in with the other animals in the jungle and ended up being happier with his own kind; another described a little girl being taken to a supermarket by her mother and asked to choose between three toys. I was intrigued by the illustration of the supermarket trolley.

Then there was my mother's American songbook. Neither my mother nor I was musical (unlike my father), but, aged nine or ten, I learned to sight-read music and on our upright piano banged out the old songs – 'Poor Old Joe', 'Swanee River' and other more cheerful American tunes such as 'Camptown Races', 'John Brown's Body' and 'Marching through Georgia', though my mother explained that this was a Yankee battle-song and advised me not to sing it loudly all over the house when Leith, a Southerner, came to stay.

One day I was playing 'Swanee River' on the piano and my father strode in, telling me to 'Stop that bloody row!' My mother defended me, saying that I must be allowed to express myself. She had understood that, like her, my imagination had been caught by those sad, often sentimental songs of the American South. This is one of the few occasions that I remember my mother being really on my side; perhaps she would have spoken out more often if she had been surer of herself. Despite my father's loud voice, he wasn't that sure of himself either. Colin, a writer older than me who knew both my parents, says that he remembers as a young man my father charging into a room with his head down; the overwhelming impression he gave to Colin was of shyness. Surely, with his own disappointment about his truncated career, my father therefore wasn't the best person to help my mother with her inferiority complex or with her literary aspirations? I remember him saying to me: 'Your mother thinks she's a writer manqué.' He gave the impression that there was nothing to be done about it; this was just another of her whims.

Chapter 25

I did not always dislike my mother, as I came to do in later life. I often longed to please her. I remember a shell box I made for her of cowries, and her approval when, each year, I was second or third out of my whole school in running and high jump. Like her, I was athletic.

I remember afternoon trips to the seaside with my mother in Sussex, usually with my brothers and one or two dogs. We would cross a small railway line on foot and end up on the shingle, the port of Newhaven on our right. Sometimes we would drive straight to Newhaven beach and swim from there – the only sandy beach in the area. I also recall my mother taking me to tennis lessons – I was in my school tennis team – and riding lessons for me and Nicky in Ashdown Forest. But I wanted more from her. Too often she would seem distracted, or preoccupied with her next trip abroad.

When I had bronchitis, aged eleven, for the second time and was confined indoors, I wove two scarves for my parents from a weaving kit I had been given. For my father I chose dark red and for my mother I chose kingfisher blue, which, because of her vivid, almost turquoise eyes, seemed to be then the colour that was as magical and rare as she was.

I had an autograph book and asked both my parents to write in it. My father, who, during my incarceration with bronchitis, would read aloud from Enid Blyton's *The Castle of Adventure*, putting on a girlie voice to imitate a 'wet' character, Lucy-Ann, and screaming 'Kee-Kee!' whenever the parrot, Kiki, appeared in the story, jotted down the following:

304

Life is mostly froth and bubble.
Two things stand alone.
Kindness in another's trouble.
Courage in your own.

My mother also read aloud to me, but would unnervingly stop every few seconds and glance at me unconfidently, to see if I was listening. Beside her autograph, she wrote down part of Juliet's speech from Shakespeare's *Romeo and Juliet*:

Give me my Romeo and when he shall die, take him and cut him out in little stars, and he shall make the face of Heaven so fine, that all the world will fall in love with Night, and pay no worship to the garish sun.

I do not think that, despite her romantic, and perhaps inappropriate, choice of quote here – after all, I was still a child – she ever loved a man in the way that Juliet had loved Romeo. My father, however, did love my mother, I am certain, although my parents, both being so highly strung, would probably each have fared better with a more placid partner.

But my father tried to protect my mother. Even when he was terminally ill in hospital, he was preoccupied with her welfare. 'I don't want her to get anxious about getting nurses for me. I don't want to worry her,' he told me, before being brought home to die. Her women friends – I have to remind myself again that she was popular with other women – rallied round her at that time and found nurses.

My father protected his wife but also patronised her. He called her Tubby Fat Lump; when I was small she would regularly embark on regimes which I called 'Going On Diet', and he teased her about her girlish enthusiasms. 'Mum shouted: "There's a camel!"' he told me on their return from a holiday in Egypt.

My father used me as an accomplice. When my mother got drunk at the dining-room table and started making her extravagant hand gestures, he would turn to me and raise his eyebrows. He needed a companion to help him deal with his wife's instability.

I adored my father, although, being so explosive, he was difficult to live with. I sometimes fought with him and he could be physically aggressive. He did not conceal his lust for other women and would make inappropriate remarks in front of his wife and daughter: 'Wouldn't mind doing spermia with her!' he said of one of my fifteen-year-old schoolfriends.

My mother may have felt undermined by my father's lustful remarks about other women. Fifteen years after he died, she suddenly showed me some photographs from their early married life in Madrid. My attention was caught by a tall woman with dark hair and a sensual face. I asked who she was and, when I heard her name, I remembered overhearing that it was she who had had a long affair with a married friend of my parents. My mother said: 'Dad had a walk-out with her.'

Direct communication from my mother was so unusual that I did not question her further. Privately, I was shocked. I worked out that my father could easily have had his affair – if 'walk-out' meant that – with this woman in Madrid while my mother was in England having me. My parents had been married then for less than two years. If that was so, for the first time I was on my mother's side against my father, and that felt strange to me. My mother admired my father's 'guts', a word she liked. She was proud of his having been awarded the DSC with two bars for his courage in the North Atlantic, and was sympathetic that his favourite ship, *The Kite*, was torpedoed and most of the sailors whom he had known were drowned. My mother said that he was devastated, and had written to the sailors' wives and mothers, who wrote back, some stating that if he had still been in command of the ship she would not have gone down. 'How could I expect him to work after he'd had such a hard war?' she said.

If she had had a living father, even one brother, and a more down-to-earth upbringing, she would surely not have taken this view. My father should have gone on working.

However, despite his daily intake of whisky and wine, he did try to pull his weight, running our small farm – I remember his anxiously practising telephone calls, half under his breath, rehearsing instructions about something to be done. He became a local magistrate and would tell us colourful stories at the dining-room table. One lurid case concerned two kitchen porters called Tony at a local hotel. One Tony had murdered the other with a carving knife, then buried him down the road in bits in the grounds of my former school, the one I had left at eleven. Remains of one of the Tonys were found months later by Boy Scouts camping. My father told us how a finger was held up in court and how Tony the murderer had announced in the dock that the other Tony's ghost had come to him and forgiven him.

My father's behaviour, I now realise, was uninhibited. He would frequently come down to breakfast in pyjamas and dressing gown; his pyjama cord would be undone and my brothers and I would often see his penis (which he referred to by a nickname), as he helped himself to scrambled eggs. I have already described his freewheeling comments about other women and his frequent use of the phrase 'doing spermia'. In contrast, my mother's attitude to sex seemed to be associated with secrecy, even shame. She always gave me the impression that she had been a virgin until marriage and had once muttered, in answer to one of my questions when adolescent, that the important thing about sex was that you both had to be 'in harmony'.

But I had a physical and an emotional connection with my father that I did not have with my withdrawn mother, always dancing away out of reach.

My mother's situation was unusual. She could not cook, so did not look after my father in the manner of most wives of that period. I remember her sometimes waiting on him at table, taking plates from the sideboard, instead of asking me or my brothers to do it, although Nicky, when she complained about him leaving dirty dishes in the sink in London, remarked to me: 'She's never washed up a cup for me in her whole life.'

It was her money that gave my father his post-war lifestyle – a country house with servants that he could not have afforded on his naval pension. But, as my aunt had pointed out, it was my father who interviewed cooks, nannies and other household staff – duties that normally belonged to a wife. My mother did not have to cook, wash clothes, clean, or even take us to school. If she had, perhaps she would have been able to distract herself a little from the pain of Raymond's death. It was clear after she was widowed and the extent of her helplessness was revealed that my father had taken charge of her financial affairs.

Did he resent, deep down, his reliance on her money? It made him physically comfortable, but certainly did not make him happy. Indeed, after his gallant war and his – and her – popularity in Madrid, his life also quickly became a sad contrast of wasted potential.

Soon after we moved to Sussex, my mother joined the WVS, perhaps to take her mind off Raymond. By her own admission, she was hopeless at arithmetic, but the local WVS for some reason asked her to do their accounts. She was intrigued by three women who worked there, Miss Gaites, Miss Whiteleg and Mrs Pinecoffin. One was sacked, then, my mother told us excitedly, she met this lady in our town. My mother did not know where to look, but quickly realised from the other's friendliness that she wasn't in the least embarrassed.

My mother was entertained by these day-to-day encounters, and willingly threw herself into many aspects of local life and derived pleasure from life in the country. She was president of the village's Forget-Me-Not club for pensioners and even shortly before getting Alzheimer's was still making friends. I remember her delight when a newcomer sent out invitations for 'Open House': *Please nod in!* My mother pictured herself and the other locals entering the house one by one, nodding. This was her good side.

When I was thirteen, long before I got my first period, she decided to give me a 'talk'. We were in London, the year before my great-grandparents' hundred-year lease on the Belgrave Square house ran out.

My mother sat on my bed, underneath that tinted photograph of the Florida cormorant and semi-tropical trees reflected in water. After a few words on menstruation, she wanted me to know that men were 'fundamentally jealous' of women's ability to give birth. Although I did not argue, I did not agree with this and I concluded privately that her view was somewhat unbalanced. Nevertheless, I found what she had said disturbing. Was it she who was jealous of men, rather than the other way round?

Soon after this, I discovered that my mother's bedside-table drawer was full of forbidden books – *The Perfumed Garden*, *Lady Chatterley's Lover*, *Fanny Hill*, *The Kama Sutra*, *The L-Shaped Room* and Simone de Beauvoir's *The Second Sex*. I removed them one by one, reading the first four quickly in my own room at night, then returning them when she was out. I filched *The L-Shaped Room* for longer, taking it to my convent, where my three closest friends and I read it under the cover of *The Young Traveller in Belgium*. In the holidays, I put it back in my mother's drawer. I never put *The Second Sex* back. I still have it. Maybe that book was a necessary substitute for the dialogue I should have been having with my mother about being female. She never asked me if I had taken *The Second Sex*, nor did she ever mention that secret drawer. She was indeed so unlike my outspoken father, who would nowadays be described as having 'no boundaries'. (Aged thirteen, I had tried to get my hands on *The Third Sex*, a book he was reading on holiday in Greece, but he threw it overboard, off our ferry to Mykonos. He did, however, let me read *Lolita* on that same holiday. It remains one of my favourite books.)

Despite hating to leave my dog when I went to my convent boarding school at nearly twelve, I ended up liking it. I made many friends and enjoyed breaking the rules. After I had been there just over a year, my father wrote a letter to our head nun.

November 6th 1962.
Dear Mother Shanley,
I am disturbed at my daughter's bad conduct. I have no doubt that you are justified in stopping her going out, but it does not seem to have much effect. You write that she is to be fined five pounds for climbing

on a roof. I really don't see the point of this punishment; it means that I will have to pay, and in my view it is the responsibility of the school to devise a suitable punishment to deter the child from breaking the rules . . . My wife is on a cruise in Cretan waters at the moment. She writes that she is much impressed with Rhodes and the old auberges of the Knights of Malta.
Yours sincerely,
Willy Segrave.

My father's letter resulted in the fine being waived. Instead, I was not allowed to go home for the weekend.

Susan S – my mother's friend in Sussex – remembered that on my sports days and school concerts, my mother did not always attend (being often abroad), but my father always did, sometimes with my grandmother.

Nicky also broke the rules – in a different way. He had not won a scholarship to Eton as predicted, but had still gone there almost a year early, as he was clever. In his last year of prep school he had started a satirical magazine (modelled on *Private Eye*, which first came out in 1961), but subsequently seemed to find his adolescent and teenage years very difficult. He ran away from Eton, then was expelled from his next boarding school, the Catholic Worth Abbey, as he was friends there with a group of boys who smoked cannabis – they also had to leave. Nicky then went to a progressive day school in Hampstead which he liked, but I seem to remember that in the end that placement foundered as well.

My father proved inadequate in dealing with all this and on one occasion, when I was seventeen or eighteen, and smoking hash regularly, he rang me and asked agitatedly, several times, about Nicky: 'Did you give him pot?'

It seems to me that in the late 1960s, or even before, my father abdicated his responsibilities as a father to Nicky. Like our parents, Nicky drank, from his mid-teens or even earlier. After I left my convent at sixteen, Nicky and I wore velvet trousers, paisley shirts and smoked hash together – he went on to take many more drugs, unfortunately. I then went to Edinburgh University, but dropped out after a year. I had missed my brother during my first term and had had severe psychosomatic stomach pains, then bronchitis. Back in London in autumn 1969, I found a job in a hospital linen room and in the afternoons did a Sight and Sound typing course, hoping to go to America. My mother found the job for me in New York in the family company in public relations and communications – and after that I travelled round America on Greyhound buses with a writer from London who was collecting underground newspapers.

I can't help now contrasting my own situation, the $5-a-night hotels, sleeping often all night on the Greyhounds as we crossed the American desert, and my worries about Nicky back in England, with my mother's position at the same age – being cosseted in Long Island and Palm Beach by Aunt Dita and Leith and Fife's parents, and receiving Fife's adoring love letters.

My life as a young woman seemed so different from my mother's, so unprotected. I thought of a letter I had found from Peggie to my grandmother: *Anne seems to think it is all right for Elisa to travel alone all over America on the Greyhound Bus.*

My mother did not know that I was going to travel with a male companion. I suppose she was wrapped up in her own future travel plans and she too must have been worried about Nicky. Or maybe she was thinking of her own travels through Eastern Europe with Jean in *her* early twenties and knew that she would not be able to stop me.

In 1973, I decided to live in Paris. My grandmother, who would miss me, did not want me to go but my father wrote me a letter: *Your grandmother is very lazy and very spoilt. It was her fault Raymond died. Of course you should go to Paris.* My grandmother had told me that she admired my father for never having accused her of causing Raymond's death. Her daughter, however, had. One evening while I was at Knowle, my mother had driven over from her own house while Katherine and

Violet were out looking for my grandmother's and Katherine's West Highlands, both hunting in the Knowle woods. My mother declared: 'You're more interested in finding those damned dogs than you were in finding my son!' After she had left, my grandmother said nothing about Raymond but only that she was worried about her daughter driving while drunk.

In Paris, after an attempt to work as an au pair, and to learn how to teach English as a foreign language, I wrote a novel. I returned to London with this in autumn 1974 and was in England for my father's last weeks. He died of cirrhosis just after Christmas.

Nicky was away in India with his girlfriend and could not be reached. So it was I, my mother and my youngest brother who went in the funeral car to Mass at the Uckfield Catholic church my father had taken us to so often as children.

The young priest, like her, was obsessed with Russia and knew all about the Russian imperial family. He even knew the names of their dogs and had been to a fancy dress ball dressed as the Tsar. He sometimes came to tea with my mother and they talked about their common interest.

During the funeral Mass he read out a prayer for ships at sea, a tribute to my father's naval career. At the wake at Knowle – my father was buried in Frant churchyard almost on top of Aunt K, whom he'd found irritating – Frank, now suffering from a bad heart, said to me: 'Your father was a brave man. I couldn't have gone in those convoys!'

A few months after my father's death, my mother and I were walking near the little church beside the river where, over a hundred years ago, the boy and the two oxen had drowned on St Margaret's Day. We found Nicky lying on the ground outside the church door. He was sobbing. 'Even the church is locked!' he cried.

That autumn Nicky, twenty-one, accompanied me to Peru. I had embarked on my next book – about my great-grandfather's work in South America. Soon after Nicky and I arrived in Peru, I was shocked to see that he could not walk up a mountain path without panting heavily and that he drank a whole bottle of Pisco, cheap Peruvian liquor, every day. When I returned to England, I confronted my mother.

'Don't you realise, Nicky is an alcoholic? *He is an alcoholic!*'

My mother looked uncomfortable. Unfortunately, I didn't tell her that she was one as well. Maybe I didn't fully realise it then. But *she* must have known. Was that what she meant when she'd said to me, about Nicky: 'I'm afraid he's inherited my weakness'?

I have a photograph of Nicky, sitting on the sea wall in Callao, the port of Lima. Over a century earlier, our great-grandfather Michael, younger than my brother was then, worked there in a ship chandler's. He had sailed from Ireland to join his older brother William, both starting on the path that would make their fortune. The brothers would get their employer to better the other ship chandlers by anchoring a supply boat at the Chincha Islands, where guano – seabirds' droppings – was scraped off the cliffs by unfortunate Chinese coolies, brought from their own country on overcrowded ships. The guano was then transported round the Horn by clipper ships, to be sold as fertiliser. How tragic that my brother, just as talented, in his own way, as our great-grandfather Michael, never fulfilled *his* promise. When I look at my photograph of my tall, handsome brother with his dark eyes and dark hair in a widow's peak (so different from his great-grandfather Michael, a determined, short man with light blue eyes and a blond-grey moustache), and I see how despondent he looks at twenty-one, when he should have been carving out a future for himself, I feel very sad.

In April 1977, I visited Nicky on a smallholding in Cornwall. He was living there with his girlfriend and another boy I shall call Mac. They had two cows with calves, a tractor, a Land Rover and three mongrel dogs. The floor of their little pink farmhouse, near a railway line, was covered with mud and the building was in disrepair. Mac took me aside and said that my brother must get hold of some more money, to run the farm. I didn't like Mac, but I had to admit that, of the three of them, he appeared to be the person with his head screwed on. Nicky's girlfriend, a pretty girl who went to art school in London and whose parents were divorced, seemed to be in Mac's thrall. Because my brother was drinking, it seemed that Mac had taken charge. Since the house was not properly furnished and there was nowhere for me to sleep, I went to the local B&B for the night, very close by. The couple running it were worried about the situation up at the farm – they were concerned for my brother. The next morning I said to Mac that I knew nothing about getting more money and that he must speak to my mother about it. As I drove back to London I fell into a terrible depression and that night I dreamed I watched a little bird die.

Three months later, just after I had published a comic article in the *Guardian* about a feminist writing group, Mac telephoned from Cornwall: Nicky was in hospital, following a drinking bout. I told him to telephone my mother, who later reported to me that she'd asked Mac why he hadn't told her immediately about my brother's collapse. He said: 'I'm running this place and I haven't any funds', to which she replied: 'What have funds got to do with it?'

It must have been then that my mother became suspicious. Family funds had been originally advanced to Nicky on her say-so. I am sure she thought that, after a history of expulsions from schools, drugs, drink, depression and no work, now that my brother had settled on the idea of running a very small farm, he should be encouraged to do so, as it was something positive. However, she now realised that Mac was taking advantage. A very decent farmer who worked for my parents and grandmother went down to Cornwall at my mother's request to find out what was going on and reported to my mother that Mac had asked him: 'And what do you get out of this family?'

Nicky, like my mother, lacked some sort of protective skin. It was easy for anyone predatory to exploit him. He was kind-hearted and had often given friends or acquaintances cash. I'm sure he felt guilty that, at his age, he had more of it than they did.

What was my mother's attitude during all this trouble with her second son? I suppose that, in her own way – by putting a stop to 'funds', for example – she thought that she was doing her best, even as she watched Nicky go downhill. Her husband had died three years earlier of cirrhosis and she was an alcoholic herself. It is only now, over twenty years later, that I can begin to understand my mother's situation then. At the time I loathed her drinking and I was terrified that everything would crash down on me, that I too would lose my bearings. Like many of my age then, I had experimented with cannabis and LSD but I did not crave these – or drink – in the way that some other members of my family seemed to do. Indeed, cannabis made me feel introverted, even a bit paranoid, so I gave it up. I wonder now, after reading of recent studies suggesting that it can sometimes induce psychosis or schizophrenia, if regular smoking of it since his early teens – to say nothing of his consumption of alcohol – could have contributed to my brother's almost permanent depression. I had warned my mother that Nicky was an alcoholic, but she had not done anything about it, probably because that would have meant her dealing with her own drinking. I had even invited an older man who had just given up drink to come round and talk to my brother, which he did, to no avail. He explained to me afterwards, 'You see, drink is his friend.' Nicky's drinking continued.

On 4 August 1977, my mother and I were in London when the telephone rang at 9 a.m. It was the police from Cornwall. I thought, as I passed the telephone to her, that Nicky might have committed suicide, but it was not that. The police had arrested Mac the night before – they would not say why – then let him go. Later Nicky rang. He had left the hospital that afternoon.

The next day my mother, having returned to Sussex, rang me in London. Nicky had now been arrested by the Cornwall police and they were sending him home. My mother was coming up to meet him.

My diary describes Nicky arriving like the Prodigal Son. We went to a Greek restaurant, where he ordered a bottle of retsina. The next morning, he went to Sussex with our mother, after first slipping off to a local off-licence, only to find it shut. My mother was plainly incapable of restraining him.

*

I was sick of the whole thing, I wrote, sounding callous, though actually I was terrified. At that stage in my life I did not know anything about addiction. I had never been to Alcoholics Anonymous, and had barely heard of it, and I had certainly not fully understood that all the members of my immediate family, including my deceased father, were alcoholics.

As I look back now, I can see that I was desperately trying to stop myself going under. I had tried to help my brother but now I did not know what to do. ('He's weak, and you can't do anything about that!' my grandmother said brutally.) That year I suffered from stomach problems and glandular fever, the latter triggered by a failed affair in London. My escape to the States – I was no doubt taking my cue from my mother, who had once sat me down and told me seriously that her solution for dealing with 'troubles' was to go abroad – was a bid for my own survival. That October, safe in the mountains of Vermont with my friends, I wrote of what I had just escaped:

London was becoming more and more excretal. Nicky and my mother were both in the house, drinking. The situation was impossible. The order that I had tried to impose on my life had disappeared. I had become prey to all my mother's fears of calamities and 'troubles' as she sometimes calls them. I was drawn tighter into the net with the two of them – I couldn't get out.

I can feel sorry for my mother now as I recall her trying to deal with her son. However, I do not think that she was a very good mother to him. Perhaps she did not know how. My grandmother, after all, had let her five-year-old grandson wander off alone, knowing that he could climb over her swimming-pool wire. And my father had not helped Nicky in later life either.

I recall that image of my grandmother's mother – Grandmoods – assisting the little girl, Anne, the only bridesmaid at her mother's second wedding, with that huge bunch of delphiniums, taller than she was. Yet, despite her difficult early childhood with its double bereavement, then her first son's death, I also cannot help blaming my mother for what I perceive as her weakness and self-indulgence, and for the way that she ultimately failed my brother Nicky. On Nicky's first day at public school, instead of accompanying him, my mother had yet again gone abroad, leaving my father and grandmother to take the petrified twelve-year-old and leave him there. My grandmother reported that he was 'shaking like a leaf'. And I remember also my mother's peevish complaint to my grandmother when my brothers were in their early teens: 'Why can't Elisa look after the boys?'

The farm was sold and I never saw Nicky's girlfriend or Mac again. My mother was very bitter about the way Mac had treated her son. He had written her a threatening letter and she was afraid that he might come to her at night when she was alone in Sussex, demanding money. She even said that if he did come, she might try to kill him.

On Christmas Eve 1977, I flew back from America, where I had been since September. I went straight to Knowle, to spend Christmas with my grandmother. There, I was told that Nicky had decided to stay alone in London for Christmas.

The telephone rang and Violet came in. I was saying how selfish it was of Nicky to stay in London for Christmas.

Violet burst into tears: 'Poor Nicky's dead, Elisa!'

My grandmother went behind the sofa to the big partners' desk still full of Chow's possessions since his death in 1953 and picked up the telephone.

'Darling, I'm so sorry about what's happened. How awful it must be for you . . .'

Later, my mother would remark on how strong her mother's voice sounded, as though she was young again.

Nicky had died over an overdose of Valium, prescribed by a London doctor for his depression. I drove over to my mother's, to be with her. Her old friend Cynthia was staying, and my other brother. The whole thing was unreal to me and I didn't want to talk about Nicky. My mother declared: 'I admired him tremendously, more than anyone else I know!'

She was referring to Nicky's moral courage, for demonstrating in Grosvenor Square against the war in Vietnam while only fourteen and for being a pacifist. Nicky, in some ways timid and fragile – which infuriated my father – also had nobility and gentleness. He was buried in early January 1978 in the churchyard near Knowle. My brother Raymond and my mother's infant brother Raymond lay there; so did my father and Aunt K, and my mother's paternal grandparents and great-grandparents.

Soon after Nicky's death, three gypsy women called at my mother's London house. I bought a strip of lace from one, who then warned me: 'Your mother has a terrible pain in her leg!' I expressed surprise and decided that she must be referring to my mother's rheumatism. She added: 'Your mother will get a boyfriend you won't like!'

Perhaps the gypsy did have second sight, in which case the 'terrible pain in her leg' alluded to my mother's breaking her hip – for the first time – the following summer. The 'boyfriend' would turn out to be someone whom I certainly didn't like.

Chapter 26

Most of my life, I did not see many expressions of intimacy between my mother and grandmother – I never even heard my mother call her 'Mum' or 'Mummy'– though I had the impression that before Raymond's accident they were closer. My grandmother and mother, separately, told me of their holidays at Loch Choire – they both loved fishing – of dressing-up parties at Knowle, of sports days in the Knowle garden, in which they and Aunt K and all the Knowle staff took part. There were visits to America and Ireland, to see each of my grandmother's surviving sisters, Dita and Lin, their string of dogs – Zost, Jerry, my mother's Scottish collie Nicky and all the many West Highland terriers owned in succession by my grandmother – those little white dogs that my brother Nicky had nicknamed, to me, 'the Sugar Lumps'.

Nevertheless, I was aware that my mother and grandmother were very different. My grandmother, despite her own tragedies – in particular, the early death of my grandfather, with whom she was deeply in love – was tougher and worldlier than my mother. And, unlike her daughter, she seemed at peace with herself.

When I was in my early twenties, my grandmother came to lunch with me and my father – my mother was away travelling again. On the hall table was a sealed letter to my grandmother from my mother. My grandmother opened it and started reading out loud. My mother gave the date of her return, then suddenly the letter became personal – my mother was thanking my grandmother for all she'd done for her and saying how much she loved her. My grandmother's voice faltered when she came to this bit and she stopped reading out loud.

My mother would never have been able to say this directly, she had to write it. She found it difficult to communicate, except at one remove. And of course my grandmother must have been surprised to suddenly find herself reading out something so personal.

In June 1978, when the Knowle garden was scented with golden and coral-coloured azaleas, my grandmother died. She was cremated – her wish – but there was also a service at the church where our other relations were buried. I didn't put on black, as my grandmother, who always wore bright colours, wouldn't have liked it. I wore a pale yellow dress with mauve patterns and an orange straw hat.

My mother and I waited in the hall at Knowle for the undertakers. My mother suddenly tried to dart into the garden, to avoid seeing her mother's coffin being carried downstairs.

Katherine said: 'Mrs Segrave's wreath is the yellow roses!' Then she added: 'Mrs Segrave insisted that our wreaths [hers and Violet's] should go on the coffin.'

However, there was room for only three wreaths and one was mine. My mother kept saying: 'I don't mind if mine doesn't go on the coffin.'

'For God's sake, have yours on the coffin!' I cried out.

Why was my mother being so self-effacing? At other times she was self-centred. It was confusing. Anyway, it was *her* mother who was dead. My mother should definitely have had *her* wreath on the coffin. It was inconceivable that my mother would weep at a funeral. She didn't approve of that sort of thing. She once praised a local widow for showing 'great dignity' at her husband's grave.

Perhaps my mother did not want to see her mother's coffin being carried downstairs because it reminded her of Nicky being taken to that churchyard only five months earlier. She wasn't going to tell me. Was she similarly cut off from *her* mother?'

*

Neither my mother nor I kept my grandmother's ashes. Katherine put the urn on her mantelpiece in the cottage my grandmother had bought for her, a few minutes' walk from the churchyard.

She told me some weeks later: 'The Rector asked me what he should do. I said Gran'd wanted her ashes scattered over the dogs' graves at Knowle by the azaleas. He wouldn't do it himself, but one of the undertakers came down and did it. Your grandfather's horse is buried there as well.'

Two months after my grandmother died, I went to America and was with Peggie in Long Island when my mother rang with the shocking news that Violet had drowned herself in the Knowle swimming pool. Soon after that my mother fell, again, and broke her hip.

It was I, not my mother, who had to deal with the subsequent sorting out, then the sale, of her childhood home; Knowle and many of its contents were finally sold in 1980, two years after my grandmother's death. It would have been too expensive to keep on. One of many unpleasant tasks I had – I was staying with my mother that weekend – was to inform the son of an old farm worker that he and his young wife would have to leave the flat above my grandmother's garage. The wife had tears in her eyes, but at no time did it occur to *me* to cry over the sale of Knowle. I hardly ever cried; I had not done so over the deaths of Raymond, of Nicky, of my father or even of my grandmother.

That afternoon, after leaving the garage flat, I lingered for a few moments alone by the garage. This was where Frank had taught me and Raymond the two times table. Frank's future wife, Elsie, had as a girl helped Nah look after Anne and Anne's little brother, and Frank had fallen in love with Elsie then. The night he proposed, he had threatened to shoot himself if Elsie turned him down. My mother had told me that.

As I turned my car out of the Knowle gates, to drive back to my mother's, I suddenly saw Katherine, getting off the local bus. She confided that she had felt lonely in the cottage that my grandmother had bought her in the village and had come to see the Knowle daffodils. Although I had known Katherine since I was a baby, I had never warmed to her, as I knew that she had been jealous of my closeness to my grandmother. (The morning after my grandmother's death, I had watched her rip off the wall a sheep stitched on to card with yellow wool that I had made for my grandmother when I was four.) But now, both missing my grandmother, we walked round the garden together and I saw again how beautiful the place was.

When I returned to my mother's at teatime, she said nothing about the impending sale of Knowle, her childhood home.

The gypsy who had predicted my mother's pain in her leg – perhaps a reference to her fall and breakage after Violet's drowning – had also said she would get a boyfriend I wouldn't like.

I was already accustomed to a procession of women through my mother's life. One of my earliest memories is of her and a friend sitting close together on a step in a garden in Spain, both showing their long, flesh-coloured undergarments. Since these were the same colour as skin, I half-believed that the two women were wearing nothing under their skirts and announced to my father: 'Mum had no knickers on!' With the instinct of a very small child, or small animal, who wants to be close to its mother, I must have sensed that there was something exclusive in the two women's friendship and felt left out.

My father's way of dealing with these women who appeared throughout his married life was to belittle them, sometimes giving them nicknames. When I was seven, soon after Raymond's death, there was Audrey, who had given me Buzzy – a wonderful gift. Her only son had been killed falling from a train and she and my mother's mutual bereavement must have made them closer. Audrey was *soignée*, with red hair in a chignon, and bossy. My father, no doubt jealous of Audrey's intimacy with his wife, called her 'The Little Bitch' – not very subtle of him. Then there was Olga, who, I now knew from the diaries, had been introduced to Anne as early as 1945. Olga often stayed with us in Sussex with her two little daughters, and they came several summers with us to Hope Cove, which my father found boring, perhaps because he was tired of the sea, on which he had spent so much of his life. Olga had a deep throaty voice and green eyes, like the eyes of Lady Ann Cole in 1930, I now realised. Olga seemed to love my mother and my mother, in her turn, expressed irritation to me when, on one holiday, Olga rang her husband in London every evening.

Then, when I was an adolescent, my mother met an older married woman on a group trip to the Middle East. She, like my mother, I read in a very short travel diary I had found, had a *very masculine* husband. My father furiously made up a song which he would sing round our house, rhyming one line – 'She never gets my ire!' – with this new lady's surname. Another line was: 'She is so calm, she's full of balm.'

In January 1979, my mother and I were at a hotel in Tobago with four other women. One, Betty, was a divorced woman in her seventies, tall, with grey hair and greenish eyes with a fleck of brown in them. She put her head on one side like a slim tall bird, a cormorant. My mother was immediately interested in Betty, whose former husband was a diplomat.

In our group also was Knotty – whom my mother met in the WAAF in 1944 – and Dodo, widow of Aunt Elisa's son Michael; he married Dodo after his first wife died. Dodo, who lived in Ireland, had brought Betty with her. My mother was in a wheelchair, due to a broken hip incurred from her fall the previous summer, soon after Violet drowned. Mary, our cousin who lived very near Knowle, a little older than my mother, was also with us.

Time passed with endless meals and endless drinking of rum punches. Knotty and I swam in the sea and chatted to some English medical students. More than once, Knotty and I were deliberately left out of rounds of drinks.

My mother and Betty became extremely rude to Knotty, frequently poking fun at her behind her back. They made it clear that they thought her inferior, and no doubt Betty was jealous of Knotty's thirty-five-year friendship with my mother. Betty kept flattering my mother, who seemed to love it, and Betty, I noted, brought out a complaining side of her, encouraging her to moan about not being able to get a taxi after a

West End play and so on. Actually my mother had never cared much about physical comfort. Now, however, she kept agreeing with Betty. Was this the same woman who, each time she went to Russia, left the group and walked round the back streets on her own and, only a few years ago, tried out a canoe in rough waves at Hope Cove?

I was disgusted by my mother's attitude to Knotty, who had been such a good friend, and who, unlike my mother and Betty, worked, as a secretary, in a nine-to-five job. My mother seemed to have no loyalty, no understanding of friendship. She was capricious and often played her women friends off against each other, like a little girl at school. 'Now you're my best friend! Now you're not!' She ditched people, seemingly without guilt, when she got tired of them.

Did my mother fall in love with Betty that first day they met in Tobago? Her disloyalty towards Knotty, which began almost from the moment she met Betty, must have been a result of that sudden bonding, but did not justify her behaviour – Knotty, after all, was doing her best to help, attending to my mother in her bedroom, for example, something which I did not want to do myself because I feared her drunkenness.

The evening that my mother first got talking properly to Betty, there was a steel band playing. My mother and Dodo complained of the noise, and everyone in our group, except me and Knotty, went to bed. We went and sat near the band. At a table near us were a mother and daughter, also staying at our hotel. The girl kept being asked by West Indian men to dance, and her mother looked furious and worried – Knotty pointed out that she was anxiously puffing on her cigarette. At one moment the older woman looked at me and closed her eyes as if in horror.

At first the daughter seemed pleased by the attention. She half-smiled and wiggled her body to the music. She didn't dance, however, and after a while the two of them left. The next morning my mother said how naïve Knotty was. They were not mother and daughter, but a lesbian couple.

*

CHAPTER 26

I became pregnant with my daughter at thirty-one, a few weeks before I got married to Andrew. Although my mother proudly announced our engagement at a Christmas drinks party she had in Sussex, which Andrew and I attended, I did not tell her about the expected baby. Anyway, she was wrapped up in her romance with Betty at that time.

It was to a stranger I turned for advice, an Irishwoman who worked in the White Knight Laundry at Notting Hill Gate. A cheerful lady, her hair newly dyed red, she'd been spending Christmas with one of her daughters, who'd just had *her* first baby. My Irish friend told me that she herself had had six children, including one little daughter who'd died. Her husband had then died at only forty-seven, leaving her with her remaining five children, so she'd had to go out to work. She'd worked in a shop and was able to live in the flat above, so that after her children came home from school they could come down to her if they needed anything. (How unlike *my* mother – it was *she* who was the needy child.)

I asked my Irish friend for a few tips.

'When I had my first baby,' she said, 'I didn't know how to hold him when he was slippery with soap. I was terrified I'd drop him. But now my daughter has a plastic bath in which she can soap the baby without having to hold him at the same time.'

Soon after that conversation, I married Andrew in a Catholic church in Kingsway. It was a tiny wedding, with only our immediate families and one friend attending. Andrew's maiden aunt Jean, from Cumbria, was there and so was my Aunt Rosemary and her second husband, Harry, her first, my cousin Elizabeth's father, having been killed in the war.

My mother, I wrote on 27 January 1981, just after my wedding, came to meet me wearing a fur jacket of Betty's. It was snow leopard. I wrote: *Why she couldn't have worn her own fur I can't imagine.*

My first pregnancy was overshadowed by my mother's troubling relationship with Betty. Betty gave me and Andrew several gifts – spring bulbs, a casserole dish and even an exquisite baby's matinee jacket that she'd made. However, I knew that she was jealous of me and wanted all of my mother's attention.

My daughter was born in late August 1981. The week before, my mother went to Majorca for a whole month with Betty, who, when I had said goodbye, had remarked to my mother: 'I hope the damn baby doesn't arrive while we're in Majorca and spoil my holiday!'

The day of my daughter's birth, 23 August, was one of the happiest days of my life. There was a storm in Majorca and the telephone lines were down. My husband tried to send his mother-in-law a telegram. Was she, an older woman, envious of my ability to give birth? Or had she gone away because 'I can't face it' – her favourite phrase? Was *any* strong emotion, even something as positive and joyful as the birth of her first grandchild, something that my mother could not handle? Or was she simply being subservient to Betty?

Years later, in one of her photo albums, I found her telegram to us, congratulating me and Andrew on the birth of our baby. Why did my mother stick that telegram in *her* album? Was she trying to prove – to herself, or to posterity – that she was a good grandmother after all? Or was she simply scared of sharing?

My mother never changed the nappies of either of my children but on one bizarre occasion, just after we arrived to stay with her for Christmas in 1983, fourteen weeks after my son Nicholas's birth, my mother, laughing in a slightly embarrassed way, scooped some of Betty's excrement off her sitting-room floor on to a small coal shovel and carried it out of the room. No one said anything but I assume now that Betty – almost certainly my mother's girlfriend – must have become slightly infirm.

We had hired a temporary nanny in an emergency; my lower back had collapsed and I couldn't lift Nicholas or his carrycot. My son woke continually in the night, and was often sick just after I had breastfed him, while I had developed something that the doctor called a rotavirus, so was on antibiotics. My daughter, aged two, no doubt jealous of the baby, was being very demanding, shouting and giving me and Andrew orders during the night, and wanting a bottle.

Only now, over thirty years later, does it occur to me that it would have been normal for a woman with a two-year-old and a new baby to ask her own mother for help. But it never entered my head to do so, and I did not even find it odd that my mother was more involved with her girlfriend and her new dog – another basset, Mr Plod – than with me and my children.

My grandmother had had an over-maternal mother and three loving older sisters, but I did not have one sister to help me; it was usually non-relations who did so. Mrs Dixon, who moved into the bungalow next door in Sussex when my children were small and worked for me part-time, became my son's surrogate grandmother and in some ways a mother to me, helping me with Nicholas and knitting us all jumpers for Christmas – she had even knitted outfits for my daughter's toy animals. I cannot help contrasting my mother's emotional poverty in this respect. She too had not been able to consult a sister, or share experiences on how to bring up children, and her own mother, I was beginning to realise now I had children of my own, had betrayed her by her failure to look after Raymond that day. In the light of that failure, I wonder at my mother subsequently allowing me, when still so little, to be so often alone with my grandmother. Was it generosity to entrust her with another of her young children, her only daughter? And was it later hurtful to my mother that, certainly from my teenage years, I preferred being with my grandmother at Knowle, where I felt safe, to being with her?

After Knowle was sold, Andrew and I moved into the Sussex house that my mother had bought at the instigation of Susan S, also recently widowed, who lived at the end of the garden. However, my mother had never moved in – she 'couldn't face' clearing out her other house and selling it – and, shamefully, the house that we, and our daughter, quickly grew to love was left empty by her for nearly two years. Betty, meanwhile, spent a great deal of time at my mother's larger house, my mother even installing a chair-lift for her, and once, in an uncharacteristic fit of extravagance, flying Betty, after she had been ill, in a helicopter from Battersea heliport to my mother's Big Lawn.

Meanwhile Betty was so rude to Molly, and so interfering, that Molly left my mother's employ. There had also been an incident with a female gardener – who had renamed Okie the terrapin 'Amy', and who developed a crush on Molly. My mother, indecisive, would not get rid of the gardener or tell Betty off for meddling and it was Molly who left – she was later very kind to the gardener when she became terminally ill.

My mother's relationship with Betty went on. Once, when Andrew and I visited, we found them both standing together to greet us wearing exactly the same suits and shoes. No comment was made by any one of us and I wonder now whether, by their identical outfits, they were trying to convey the closeness of their relationship, as my mother certainly would never have been able to state it directly. Due to various comments made by close friends such as Susan S, and because of my own instinct, it seemed pretty clear that my mother and Betty were in a physical as well as an emotional relationship.

Years later, an elderly writer friend of mine recalled socialising with my mother and Betty, with a male friend of his. Both men were homosexual and my elderly friend told me that they had naturally assumed that my mother and Betty were a couple. Perhaps my mother felt at home in these two men's company and was relieved that there was no need, as there was among her other, more conventional friends, for her to pretend. Certainly, her leanings were never spelt out, but always had to be guessed at, by her husband, children, friends such as Susan S and those who worked for her. The full extent of her intimacy with Betty was never admitted by her – certainly not to me – or, I suspect, to anybody.

If Betty had been pleasant, perhaps I could have got used to the idea of her and my mother as a couple. But Betty was ill-mannered – to me, to my mother's friends and to those who worked for my mother. She liked to make out that others were doing my mother down. But actually it was Betty who, well off herself, and with no children, accepted all sorts of gifts, including the helicopter ride and several holidays in Majorca. Once, Betty told me off for ringing Peggie from my mother's Sussex house, saying rudely that no one rang long-distance from *her* house. My mother did not defend me, although I had rung so that my mother could talk to Peggie. Betty seemed cold and uninterested in anyone except my mother. I saw her as an interloper and was shocked when I realised that she was sleeping in my father's old bedroom; an adjoining bathroom led to my mother's room.

It was in the mid-1980s that Betty became ill with what must have been osteoporosis; I recall hearing that her neck was crumbling. I cannot be sure how loyal my mother was to her during this period, which ended in Betty's death in 1992, and by this time, my mother didn't seem to have very much to do with her. As usual, my mother did not divulge to me what was going on, though I do remember Susan S explaining: 'Your mother's relationship with Betty was a love affair rather than a friendship, so when it was over, it was over.'

I had one confrontation with Betty, on holiday in Majorca in the early 1980s. She had seemed frightened and I realised that she was a bully, and that you had to bully her back. (I was surprised recently to read in my diary that, about a year after, Betty unexpectedly alluded to 'your sweet children'. And my grandsons recently both wore the exquisite matinee jacket she made for my first baby.)

I suppose that she was a stabilising influence in my mother's life, in that she stopped her drinking so much. My mother, I believe, had had no inkling, until she died, of how much she depended on my father. She turned out to be hopeless on her own at home, unable to summon any inner resources. Instead of spending solitary evenings on her hobbies – photography, her old movies of Eastern Europe, her books about Russia, or learning Russian on tape, something she had started to do years earlier – she spent the time drinking.

By the mid-1980s, with Betty ill and mostly out of the picture, my mother again became more difficult. One new friend was a librarian from San Francisco she had met on a trip, who came to Hope Cove with us when my children were small, in the summer of 1988, when we all attended the Defeat of the Armada celebrations. My mother had broken her hip at least twice by then and could not climb up to the field where the giant bonfire was to be lit. The American, I noted in my diary, was a slightly mysterious woman, enormously tall with a hat with a brim pulled over her dark eyes. Andrew could not see what my mother had in common with her. She accepted everything that she was offered, mostly by my mother – the taxi from Totnes station there and back, drinks, meals at our house and dinner in the Lobster Pot Hotel, for which she did not thank Andrew.

On our last evening at Hope Cove that summer, we invited some neighbours in for a drink and this caused frightful drunkenness in my mother. Andrew mixed her a weak vodka and tonic but when the guests left, she rushed into the dining room saying she must have another, and sloshed an enormous amount of vodka into her glass. She then became almost incoherent, but luckily had the sense to go to bed early.

Another woman friend after Betty was a lady who had first come as a temporary cook, then returned several times as a guest. In 1986, she and my mother ganged up on a pleasant professional companion whom Andrew and I had engaged, out of desperation, through the London agency Solve Your Problems, for which Knotty then worked. (My mother, as a Problem, should have been permanently on their books; though perhaps, as Unsolvable, she would have put the agency out of business.) Only a week earlier, my mother had been so drunk after the death of Mr Plod that it had been unsafe to leave her alone in case she fell again or even set the house on fire with a dropped cigarette. My last brother's ex-girlfriend had gone and looked after her. Andrew and I, with Knotty's help, had then employed Mrs Peru. Mrs Peru told us that when she had been with my mother only two days, the former cook had arrived to stay. She and my mother then confronted Mrs Peru, who was told 'Your services are no longer required!' and sent packing.

My mother, then in her seventies, was living her life like an irresponsible naughty child, changing her 'best friend' whenever it suited her, and leaving a trail of hurt or angry female hearts in her wake. (Susan S, during the regime of the former cook, pronounced bitterly to me and Andrew: 'I'm right in the background again as a friend. Anne has completely dropped me.') It is difficult for me, as a daughter, to see why, despite her bad behaviour, her friends found her so engaging. Certainly, she had a lively and original mind and an enormous capacity for enjoyment, despite her past tragedies and her depressions, which she hid from most people and which she must have tried to alleviate by drink. Her helplessness ensured that others would undertake practical tasks which she could, and should, have done herself. Indeed, the qualities that made her unsatisfactory as a mother, her whimsicality, childishness and unpredictability, were perhaps what charmed others.

Part 5

Steadily She Walks towards Me

No one knows me . . . no one will ever know me . . . <u>very</u> few people know what I am like inside.
Diary of Anne aged sixteen, 23 October 1930, Rome.

Chapter 27

My son had observed: 'Granny is hidden!' and it was true that for much of her life, and mine, my mother had hidden herself – in alcohol, compulsive travel, childlike helplessness and her secret love for women. Her diaries were therefore a catalyst for me. In the years after I found them, I learned more and more about her. Besides reading and typing them on to the computer, I gave myself the task of going through her photograph albums and putting them in order. I ended up feeling grateful that she had produced this catalogue of our family life – and of *my* life, some of which after all had been happy. Here were our two holidays at Comillas; in one snap me and Raymond are with Nanny Benny, me touching her hair as though secure with her, despite my father having told us that she was a witch. On the second Comillas holiday, me and Raymond play together, on the beach on all fours like little dogs, pretending to lap the water in the shallow pools.

Then, North Heath House, 1953, our first spring there, me and Raymond, always together. Me and Raymond with Roger – an older local boy – and a Jersey calf, then me and Raymond on the lawn with Captain, our brown horse on wheels; I still have him. My children played with him.

Me and Raymond in Trafalgar Square with Father Christmas on 21 December 1953. My mother has captioned it: *THE NIGHT BEFORE NICKY WAS BORN.* Then our first summer holiday in England, at Hope Cove, in August 1954: me and Raymond, always together, on the beach, Doreen paddling, bending to hold Nicky upright on the edge of the sea, just months before he learns to walk; Kevin, my grandmother's new West Highland puppy, sniffs Nicky's hand, which he holds out to the little dog.

I suddenly realise, as I leaf again through these albums, that I am often looking at people who will die sudden or early deaths. I see Raymond riding Captain on the lawn and know that a few months later he will be dead. The same applies to that photo of Gig holding Raymond's hand as they step off the *Queen Mary* in New York Harbour in 1955, Raymond wearing the brown velvet pixie hood that Gig made for him. She died soon after, of cancer. And what about Nicky, here on the lawn at North Heath, a happy two-year-old in a duffel coat, his feet on the pedals of our third toy horse, a little dapple-grey Dobbin, made of tin?

My mother once labelled all these photographs so painstakingly.

I return to that much later album with those macabre snaps of her holding a clutch of toy dogs. I had thought it grotesque that the twins, her grandchildren, were placed beside these. However, now I perceive that in her arms my mother holds *four* dogs – like the four children she once had, who should all still be alive.

I visited Chow's niece Honor at her cottage near where Aunt Lin had lived in Sussex. Honor and Anne had liked each other. I complained to Honor that my mother had not helped me clear up Knowle after my grandmother's death and she replied: 'Your mother had no fight left in her!'

Honor introduced me to Frank and Elsie's granddaughter, of my age, who had loved walking with her grandparents in the bluebell woods at Knowle as a little girl. She gave me Frank's idiosyncratic and observant memoir of his life in Sussex. Frank wrote of my grandmother: 'The tragic loss of . . . the boy in the pool before a coming Christmas was a Knock out for us all, the Blow to last long . . . But this Lady Having taken Knock out blows all her life Rode the tide again . . .'

My mother's old friend Angela showed me snaps of her and my mother at Loch Choire. Angela admitted that the teenage Anne was indulged by Nah and sometimes by Gig, and that when Angela caught more fish, Anne wouldn't speak to her for several days. Angela even went to my grandmother and asked: 'Shall I go south?' My grandmother then made her daughter apologise.

Angela said that my parents were 'two very unhappy people' and that she had often felt sorry for me and my two remaining brothers. She had had one to stay, after my father refused to have his own teenage son in the house. She said that my grandmother, shortly before she died, had begged Angela: 'Look after Anne.'

The day after that visit, I took my daughter back to school after the long summer holidays. We called on my mother at Camelot first. She had now had Alzheimer's for nearly ten years and once my poor daughter had burst out to me that she didn't want a grandmother who only read 'Gummy Bears' books.

Although my daughter didn't want to go, as she found it upsetting to see a grandmother with whom she had once had a good relationship so deteriorated, she was, as usual, kind to her grandmother. She sat close to her, holding her hand, and when my mother talked animatedly, although the words came out as gibberish, my daughter said to me: 'I think she's going over and over scenes from the past in her mind, trying to make sense of them.'

I realised that this was what I was trying to do with the diaries, photographs and letters, and my visits, make sense of my mother's life – and my own.

I wrote a newspaper article about finding Raymond's things, and in response received three letters from strangers, one of which went:

I am your age and my mother has Alzheimer's and now lives in a nursing home. These things we have in common. I did not lose a sibling however, I lost a daughter. My two daughters were born 20 months apart, and, like you and your brother, were great friends and inseparable. When my daughters were 10 and 8, the younger one died, not abruptly, but after 2 years of illness. When she died our baby son was almost 3.

I read your reaction and your family's reaction to your brother's death with great sympathy. I have often wondered how our daughter, now 20, feels about the loss of her sister. I do not know – it is still too painful to talk about.

I have a bedding box in my bedroom full of my dead child's belongings, school books, favourite cuddly toys, Mother's Day cards – just as you discovered in your mother's house. I have a couple of small photos of my daughter displayed at home – not blown-up portraits – there's no shrine – but I need them there.

You have made me wonder what my children think. Do they resent my continued love for my daughter? Is my surviving daughter 'jealous'? My daughter's death 'knocked our family sideways, so that it never recovered.' I think we have learned to live with what happened, but the scars are deep.

When I had finished your article, I imagined my daughter cleaning my house and delving into the chest of mementoes. I wonder if she will feel as you do. Please do not be too hard on your mother. I feel for her. With any luck her Alzheimer's will have dulled or removed the pain.

I love my two children, but the child I lost still shapes the way I am and influences me. If my house caught fire and I could save only one thing it would be her photo. I can't help myself for feeling this way.

That last sentence stuck in my mind.

I felt great sympathy for this woman, this mother, whom I had never met. However, I was still not quite able to extend that sympathy towards *my* mother over the death of *her* child, Raymond. I was still a child myself, who resented my mother's lack of attention.

Doreen also wrote me a kind letter. As a result of my article, I had appeared on *The Esther Show*, presented by Esther Rantzen, talking about Raymond – by chance the day after his birthday, 8 May. Doreen's Aunt Eva had seen me on TV and had rung Doreen.

Doreen wrote:

It has always been, and always will be a great heart ache to me, feel-
ing if I hadn't got crippled up with my back and landed up in hospital
all this would never have happened . . . If ever there was a black hole
in one's life it was mine . . . I always felt a tragedy such as happened,
could not possibly pass without leaving its scar, and my heart has been
with you especially ever since, I do think of you so often and wonder
how you are, when I go to see your mother I come away feeling simply
devastated . . . I hope you won't mind me sending this to you, but felt
I wanted you to know how I feel. One day it would be nice to see you
again. How I loved you all. My love and best wishes. Doreen.

Unfortunately I did not feel as warm as I should have done to Doreen.
I had always felt that she had sided with my mother over thinking that
Raymond was more important than the rest of us.

It was Jean, my mother's friend who had been on those trips to
Eastern Europe with her in 1937 and 1938, who helped me most in
taking a more forgiving attitude towards my mother. Jean came to my
flat and I showed my mother's old films of them as young women in the
Balkans. Jean had taken the good black-and-white photographs in my
mother's albums of those trips, and she and I talked about their friends
from Novi Knezevac who had come to unfortunate ends. Jean tried to
piece together what had happened to each of them.

On my mother's eighty-fourth birthday, Jean wrote me a letter:

You confirm what I have always feared since Raymond's death, that
the surviving members of the family would be left feeling they were
perpetually in the shadow of the deceased. Life so often follows a
pattern doesn't it? When people are unable to compete with a family
tragedy this is what happens. In the same way alcoholics follow a pat-
tern. I know they are impossible, exasperating and appalling to those
who have to cope with them – this too is a tragedy from the alcohol-
ics' point of view. They are not entirely to blame I think. They inherit
genes which give them a craving for alcohol – some rise above it but
this must call for help and enormous strength of mind. I think for Anne

her tragedy and alcohol were more than she could survive. I always imagine that when Raymond died she had what used to be known as a 'nervous breakdown'. Alcohol was her only consolation. Poor Anne . . . Yet it was unforgivable to take it out on all of you. I think she never understood what she was doing.

There were other positives. I found in a wooden box Aunt K's hand-written notes about her own life: *Happy childhood. No hatred, full of excitements & adventures. Parents never quarrelled . . . School in Light Cart . . . death of Mother at 18 . . . Travel with father . . . Marriage 1909. Ten years a widow.* Her cheerful tone made me realise that early or unexpected death might not be the end of everything. Aunt K had also made enthusiastic notes of her travels with her widowed father – to Russia before the Revolution, to Egypt, Greece, Norway and Sweden. They had even visited the Empress Eugénie.

In a letter to her daughter at Madame Boni's, my grandmother had praised K's '*naturalness and kindliness*'. (She had also referred to K's '*strange friends*' and commented that K wasn't very well dressed.)

Aunt K had often visited us and always used to stay for Christmas. She had bad rheumatism and I recalled her horribly swollen ankles. Despite this and despite being a widow with no children, Aunt K had seemed to enjoy life. But my father, as he could be with those close to my mother, was impatient with Aunt K, and my mother even sometimes implied that her aunt was a burden.

Nicky and I had enjoyed visiting Aunt K in her house off Haverstock Hill, where she had an old Irish cook who would send me karrogeen (seaweed) from Connemara for my bronchitis. Aunt K's life was full of friends and cousins; she and her brother had obviously benefited from those loving parents who never quarrelled – and, unlike Anne, they found it easy to show affection. I was struck by the sweet letter my grandfather wrote to his new mother-in-law from his honeymoon hotel in Paris in 1912, assuring her that he would take the utmost care of her youngest daughter and that he regarded 'Moods' as his second mother. And there were the love letters to him from my grandmother that I had inherited from Knowle, still in the army chest that he had sent back to her in late 1915, for safekeeping, just before he was killed.

Now, in Aunt K's papers, I found his letters back. Their letters spanned the twelve months from August 1914, when he was sent to fight, until July 1915, shortly before his death. My grandmother wrote on 15 January 1915:

Sweetheart,

I was having such a lovely dream this morning. You remember how we said the other day that one saw very few places that one was seized with a desire to live in? Well I dreamed the most lovely place. A big grey stone house, a bit bigger than this with most lovely gardens and grounds falling away from it. Stone terraces and steps and a huge lake with a sandy bottom so that the water was quite clear. It was summer and I was having breakfast out on the terrace and the flowers everywhere and the sun. Oh Ninny I nearly cried when I woke up to a bleak winter morning and a snuffly head and the war. However, I found your letter by my bed and that made things worthwhile again. Our happiness is something worth waiting for isn't it?

I wondered if she was dreaming of Knowle after the wing was added, the garden landscaped and a lake, part of the water gardens, created in the woods, long after my grandfather was dead?

In early spring 1915, my grandmother sometimes stayed with her mother at Battle Abbey, and then my grandfather wrote to her there:

Feb 4th 1915.

My own darling Glad,

The post has just come in bringing a letter from Poods but nothing else. I am disappointed darling I do want a letter from you so badly. The postman tells me that they threw some aeroplane bombs on HAZEBROUKE as he came through he didn't seem to mind and yesterday they threw some on BAILLEUL, some unfortunate civilian children were killed . . .

Bronco is going so well and looking so fit I do hope I shall be able to keep him after the war. Tell me all about what is happening at Knole and also all your doings – it really looks as if the spring was coming dear, doesn't it? I love darling G. more than ever and I should like to be with you and enjoy the spring together . . .

How is your birthday punt getting on? I hope you will be very very happy. R loves you so much.
Yr R.

My grandfather had just inherited Knole, his father having died that January. Aunt K, the daughter of the house, despite having been married for six years, was running it. My grandmother had not yet moved in.

My grandmother was pregnant – the baby, if a boy, to be christened Raymond after his father – *Little R*. That April of 1915, my grandfather was granted a few days' leave but then summoned back to France after only twenty-four hours. My grandmother, after seeing him off at Folkestone, expresses her distress. She was now living at Knole and was trying to get used to it.

April 24th 1915.
. . . Darling, it was a sickening disappointment for my darling R having to go back . . . I think I love you more than ever, and I just live for the day when it is all over and we can take up our glorious life again, happy beyond dreams in our love . . . I love you so, I'm going to be happy here I think dear, because it's R's and he loves it. I think I shall love it all very soon . . .

Little Anne has been evil all day, but a great duck. She has an awful temper but K says my R was an awful child so there is hope for her. We'll have our work cut out with her I think. She got another tooth today, the 7th. Goodnight dearest in the world. G would have liked to come on that ship yesterday with her loved one.
Your own, G

*

She was right about 'Little Anne', but of course, as regards having their work cut out in bringing her up, there would be no 'we'.

My grandfather's letters back were intimate and loving but also practical. Instructions were given about matters such as the Knole drains and the installation of electric light. He also gave his wife instructions about the care of his horses. His favourite mare, Dundancer, was in foal and he often asked how she was.

My grandmother missed their rented house near Salisbury Plain, where they had lived as newlyweds when my grandfather had been based at the Netheravon Cavalry School. But she wanted to please him.

Knole, Frant, Sussex.
April 25th 1915.
. . . You must teach me the woods darling. I love them because we have been so happy there together. They seem to speak of my R. I went there one day after war began. It must have been soon after you left for I was so weak and I could hardly get along and the others kept shouting for me and calling but I went on and on and never answered. I was so miserable darling, and I seemed to be nearer to you there.
. . . Goodnight, love of my life. I shall exist (quite happily but only half alive) till you come again.
Your own, G.

She busied herself at Knole gardening – *I spent a long time this morning standing on my head in the seed bed.* She waited excitedly for her greenhouse to be delivered and wrote about their little daughter: *She was such fun going to bed. She is in your old room as they are going to paint the greenus outside her nursery windows. She rolled about and tried to climb onto the big bed and talked and laughed, you would have loved her. She uses her head to crawl with and looks too funny . . .*

While she led a domestic life, he described some gruesome scenes from across the Channel.

April 30th 1915.
My darling Gladys,
Letter from you dated 27 and I'm so glad you are feeling better and able to garden. I went through YPRES today and there is little left of the town it is a mass of debris, dead horses and broken vehicles – the cloth hall just exists. On the far side of YPRES shells come from every side and it is distinctly unhealthy.

My grandmother was being won over by his favourite place:

April 28th 1915.
Dear, how beautiful the woods are. I had no idea they were so big and empty and the walks so pretty. I went for miles this morning. Petie and Jill got away hunting and Nah and I went to look for them. We found them very quickly, Petie with a wire snare on his leg which he scarcely noticed . . .
You and I, loved one, will go often thro' the woods together, shall we. G. will adore that.

Knowing that they would hardly ever walk through the woods together again made me sad. However, I found my grandparents' love letters inspiring. At least someone in my family had found true love. My mother was the child of parents who had cared deeply for each other. And my grandfather, despite not seeing his daughter much, wrote tenderly about her: *I am so glad that Poods is well and liked little Anne she really is a dear isn't she?* He also sounds homesick.

May 2nd 1915.
Tell me are the bluebells out in the woods & have you heard a nightingale? Is it really summer there yet? Oh G I do want to spend a lazy summer with you in the sun sometime.
Yr. own R.
Please send me out some CAPSTAN NAVY CUT MILD also tell the Cook to send a cake or something.

I found the boyish postscript about the cake disarming – my grandfather, like many men of that era, had had responsibilities thrust on him early. He had already fought in India and in the Boer War while in his twenties and now in 1915 was only thirty-four. His writing style reminded me of his daughter's diaries – both used dashes instead of full stops; he, like her, wrote as if he was always on the run, full of energy.

May 10th.
I love the woods don't you – they are so pretty & full of flowers – we will buy them some day when we are rich & make lovely big rides in them for G to wander in & we will make a lovely view from the front of the house.

My grandfather had not owned the woods, I realised. It was after my grandmother's marriage to Chow that the woodland was bought; with Chow she fulfilled my grandfather's dream of those *lovely big rides* and *a lovely view from the front of the house* . . .

Soon she too was beginning to love Knole.

Knole
May 10th 1915.
My darling,
Hurrah! Two letters from you, one by the mid-day and one by the evening post. Such darling ones . . . Our life together has been such wonderful & perfect happiness dearest, I think heaven must be like that. It's been nice today dear and R's home is getting so pretty. I don't wonder you love the woods dear. They are more beautiful every day. K and I went into them today . . . We took the dogs . . . We came back by the little pond R wants to make a lake of. The whole wood was a carpet of blue & masses of primroses and violets. It was perfect.
. . . I just worship you my beloved.

May 14th. Knole.
My darling, Yes, G is very happy here, I knew you loved it, dearest and
I used to want to like it awfully. This is just the cream of the year and
the woods are so lovely tho' yesterday rain has knocked the primroses
about a bit. The garden is so pretty with the lilacs out & the Japanese
maple is just perfect. The coal-tit is still sitting.

When I read about *the little pond R wants to make a lake of* . . . I was
excited. I had assumed that it had been Chow's idea to make the water
gardens, because I had seen his designs. But it had been my grandfather
who had wanted to make that lake in the woods, so in a way the water
gardens (despite Chow's big part in their execution) were a memorial
to my grandfather. All those walks that my grandmother had done for
nearly seventy years, into her late eighties, often in bad weather and
over rough ground, she had begun to please him. He had loved those
woods and now I, his granddaughter, nearly a hundred years later, was
still able to walk in them.

Chow had worked hard running Knowle and Katherine had told
me he was popular with those under him, as he was fair. He had been
a good husband to my grandmother. But she had once confided to me
that she hoped he had never realised that it was my grandfather whom
she had loved best.

After reading my grandparents' love letters I went again to the woods
to see if anything could be done about their overgrown state, and
about the now almost wild water garden. An expert on woodlands
accompanied me.

The brambles and bracken were as thick as they'd been on the day
I'd come that first time after a break of many years. As we walked
through the trees – it had started drizzling – I was very conscious now
that Knowle, and the woods, had been loved by my grandfather. By
the lake I saw the remains of a flat little wooden boat, and wondered
if it was the birthday punt of February 1915, his present to my
grandmother. The expert said that most of the older trees had been

planted about 150–200 years earlier and that, long before that, the whole area was forest. As we approached the bigger lake, where, in 1940, an Italian plane had dropped a bomb, below the village where so many of my family were buried, I remembered how one Christmas at Knowle, my brother Nicky and I had walked to that big frozen lake in the snow.

During the next few years I returned to Knowle often, even entering the house itself – I made friends with two of the women who lived there. One, who owned the old part, where I had often sat with my grandmother, made a short film of me talking about Knowle and its past. Despite the tragedies that had taken place there I realised that Knowle had been a source of pleasure and stability for many of those involved with it, such as Frank, Mr Tash, Katherine and even Frank's granddaughter, with her memories of the bluebell woods. I found myself turning back to my mother's diary, to find more of her own memories of Knowle.

June 14th 1944. Knowle.
The more one stays in the country the more fascinating it becomes as one watches flowers and birds. There is a Turtle Dove which I see every day flying about the garden and Piney Walk. He sits cooing that harsh frog-like note all day. There is a Water Wagtail which bathes in the pool each day and feeds 2 young ones and today I watched a Goldfinch hovering about alone in dandelions almost like a humming bird and feeding a young Goldfinch which was chirping and flapping its wings on the path beside it.

This is what one does whilst other people are fighting for their lives (& ours) on the other side of the Channel.

This was seven days after the D-Day landings, the Allied invasion of France. My mother was on leave then from Bomber Command, where she soon would meet Millie. How different was that wartime Knowle from the one I knew. And yet in many aspects it was similar. When I saw the phrase 'Piney Walk', a wave of nostalgia came over me. My grandmother would name parts of her garden, and other loved objects such as 'The Funny Gates' (the kissing gates beyond the ha-ha) and the 'Litter Pigs' (the newborn piglets at the Glebe).

June 16th 1944. Knowle.
Warnings all night. The window in the hall blown out . . . just after lunch, we heard the noise of an a/c, the engine making a rather loud and tinny sound. Terence, Jean and I went out to look and saw the most queer shaped looking a/c approaching v. noisily. It looked about the size of a fighter, but was nothing like one in shape, having a v. long nose (a single engine) it appeared to be flying at a high speed and was quite low. What one particularly noticed was its long thin nose and the tinny rather raucous sound of its engine, also the speed, it passed over between here and Manor Farm in the direction of Tunbridge Wells. I didn't know what it was, except that it was quite unlike any other a/c I have ever seen, but Gig says it was like the pilotless one that went over this morning.

The 'pilotless' plane was the V-1, first used by the Germans in southern England on 13 June 1944. A few days later, Anne and Jean were in the Lost Field when they heard another V-1.

In those accounts, despite the precarious wartime circumstances, I still got that sense of safety and continuity which I had always loved about Knowle. Although she was often away in the WAAF, my mother remained part of that.

Now I wanted it to continue and I realised how important to me were the woods which my grandmother had left me. A Yorkshireman who had helped my son when in his late teens worked with a volunteer group to clear the water gardens and mark the old paths. Later, I managed to get the lake cleaned and the water gardens cut back to show their original design, and I had more rhododendrons and azaleas planted. Many times a year now I walk in the woods, particularly in spring, the season that my grandmother in that love letter to my grandfather had called 'the cream of the year'. And, as my daughter points out, I have unconsciously imitated my grandmother in walking in those woods with a little white dog. I had thought he was a Jack Russell but my dog turns out to be part West Highland, the breed that my grandmother had all her life. I often go around Armistice Day into those woods where my grandmother had so looked forward to walking, until old age, with my grandfather. The smell of the acorns makes me feel I am coming home.

I now have Okie the terrapin, who must be nearly a hundred, in my small greenhouse in Sussex. I take my three-year-old grandson regularly to look at him in his tank, as my grandmother used to take me at the same age at Knowle. My grandson pushes Captain up and down my garden. My mother kept him all that time. I even found photographs of Captain in Madrid, wearing a smart saddle and bridle; now his hair is worn and his mane missing.

I have watched again the family movies that my mother had made in the 1950s, put on to video for her by Mr Mainwaring just before she started losing her mind; she had shown some to me a few months before I got breast cancer. My daughter sat with me the second time I watched these and commented how sweet I was as a little girl. In one, I was on a swing, seated between Gig and my grandmother. I had been a much-loved child.

I saw me and Raymond in thick beds of wallflowers at North Heath – he a little boy making his first steps. Later, myself and Raymond playing in the sandpit at North Heath House, in our Coronation outfits of red jumpers and navy-blue shorts – then we were running across the lawn carrying Union Jacks. Here we two were with Captain, then there was Nicky in a paddling pool, then me leaning over his pram, he in a duffel coat. He looked healthy and confident, so different from the timid, fragile boy and teenager he became later.

Some of the last shots were of me and Raymond in a sea of poppies. This was almost the last film my mother ever took of Raymond, and our last summer in North Heath.

There were two more shots, of me and my grandmother, also at North Heath. Perhaps she had given us a new tricycle, because she was pushing first me, then Raymond, on it. The very last picture of all was my grandmother giving me a push and me sailing off on my own. As I watched this, I felt that my grandmother and I were the survivors, had weathered the storms, my grandmother had shown me how.

And what of North Heath House and its enchanted common? I returned there with my son soon after my first book was published, forty years after my seventh birthday. It was Frank who had collected us children that day and driven us to Knowle; Raymond and I had sucked barley sugars to avoid being carsick. Doreen had already left us; now I sometimes think of her letter to me ending *How I loved you all* and wish I had been able to respond more affectionately.

Nicholas, on our visit to North Heath in 1995, even suggested I become a lodger for a while in a house nearby. He and I walked on the common and down the lane, where I recalled old man's beard in the hedgerows in winter. Raymond and I had wandered together down that lane one day, thinking that we had seen Doreen go that way. She was furious and, probably having been frightened for our safety, smacked our bottoms for not staying on the common.

I have returned a few times to North Heath after that visit of 1995, twice in summer, when I walked again in the Merry Meadow where I had once walked with my mother. I saw again the cornflowers, not quite as blue as my mother's eyes, and the waving scarlet poppies of my childhood. I found myself peering through North Heath House's hedge at the huge copper beech tree in the garden where I used to play with Raymond – and I realised that I was looking for my brother.

On my last visit I went inside the house, invited by the owner, and into what had been my old bedroom, where, rather like Black Beauty among the apple trees in the book I had read often as a child, I had once looked out on to a little orchard with pear trees. I stood inside our old front door and gazed out at the lawn where I had played with my little brothers, and with Captain. I smelt again the scent of the polyanthus in spring; it was as though I was in heaven.

My mother died in August 2003. The death certificate gave two causes, 'congestive cardiac failure' and 'alcohol induced dementia'. She had had to be removed from Camelot due to physical deterioration and had been in a home run by nuns for those with Alzheimer's for one and a half years – it was the same order of nuns that had run the homes I had looked at for her in the mid-1990s. I enjoyed visiting my mother here without interference – the three nuns, and their staff, made it so easy and pleasant – and she seemed content, sitting in the daytime with other women in a large bright room looking over a valley. On one visit, at a nun's suggestion, I even fed my mother her evening meal with a spoon.

By then I had read all her diaries and felt closer to her. On one visit I put my hand on her arm and told her: 'Well done! Well done for writing those diaries.' I hope she understood.

When she first moved in, I took in two photographs for her, one of my father in naval uniform and one of me with her, in Madrid. I am in a little white dress and look serene and happy. My mother is smiling straight at me; her attention entirely on me, as it never was in later years. She seems delighted with me.

Six days after my mother's death, I found on my kitchen table a letter. It was as though a wind had blown it in, directly from her to me. In fact, my daughter had found it in her own files that morning and put it there.

May 3rd 1991.
Dear Elisa,
I am so glad that you enjoyed the film show of Spain and saw yourself as a child, together with darling Raymond on the beach at (I think) Comillas and Dad as a young man with you, looking very handsome and all of us happy as we were. I was particularly happy to hear that darling Nicholas is so interested about Raymond and asks questions about him – I have so often thought that those two were very alike, in their gentleness, intelligence, good looks and charm. Both so delightful in every way and most lovable and loved.

Hope to see you about the twelfth. L. has made such an <u>excellent</u> drawing of the pony's head. Give my love to her and Nicholas.
Love from, <u>Mum</u>

The letter had been written just before my mother started to lose her mind. I had been so angry about her frequent falls and drunkenness I had not taken it in. Now I wondered if her inadequacy in relation to my son was partly because he had reminded her, as a small boy, of Raymond. I see from my diary about a visit to Hope Cove with her in summer 1985, when Nicholas was nearly two, that *my mother seemed to get quite attached to Nicholas on that holiday and once, when he came out of the bath carried in a towel, her eyes filled with tears.* I had even added: *I daresay she relates to Raymond at that age.* Unfortunately I see from another entry that she secretly bought a bottle of whisky while shopping with my husband. *As a result she was completely plastered before supper. I was extremely annoyed.* I had named my son Nicholas after my brother but never addressed him as 'Nicky'; it was too painful. I had not consulted my mother about my son's name and she had not referred to it. Now I wonder if her failure to find the church where Nicholas was christened was something to do with this.

After her death, I started visiting the graves at Frant, as she used to do, and had their headstones cleaned, according to my mother's wishes. I took a photograph one January of the tiny graves of the two Raymonds, her little brother and mine, side by side, covered with snowdrops. (I found an envelope among Aunt K's papers with a lock of his hair in it, and written in the left-hand corner 'Violets'. He had died at his Aunt Lin's, on Nah's birthday, 14 December 1918.) I visit the other graves – my parents', Aunt K's and Nicky's, his in another part of the churchyard, next to a young woman who was born and died at exactly the same age as him. I once met her mother there, bringing flowers. I would like to be buried next to Nicky.

In 2000, I visited Serbia, and found Novi Knezevac, the village, then in the new Yugoslavia, where my mother and Jean had stayed in 1937 and 1938. I went to Germany, twice, and returned to some of their owners the passports my mother took of those former prisoners of war. Just before she died, I heard from the Imperial War Museum that two pages of her Bletchley diaries would be exhibited there in a special temporary exhibition, *Women at War*. How proud she would have been.

Six years after my mother's death, I visited Comillas and the house we had rented those two summers so long ago. In its sloping garden I looked at once for the hydrangeas, where Raymond and I would run down to spot the big white boat on the horizon. As I had at North Heath, I realised I wanted to see him again. At last, I really could feel sorry for my mother and for *her* lost paradise. (She had once shown my daughter, but not me, photographs of *her* little brother.) I knew that if I had not had access to her diaries, I would not have had the means to understand her, or her life. Also, she had opened my eyes to larger aspects of history – I would never be able now to go to certain parts of London without remembering her descriptions of it during the war. Because of her diaries, I had had vivid glimpses into pre-war Rome under Mussolini, post-war Germany with its bombed towns and starving old women running for coal falling off lorries, and Yugoslavia in the 1930s before the Nazis, then the Communists, got there. Most importantly for me, my mother had given me, to reinforce my own early memories, those pictures of Spain. How grateful I am that she wrote about that lost Spain of my childhood, with its shepherds, its white oxen, its storks on their nests, and of Comillas – of how, that afternoon of 2 September 1953, she had gone into the sea leaving me alone on the sand. Then I had waded in to meet her, the water above my waist: *I was so proud of her.* Taking that last 'Spain' diary, I found the long, long beach where huge waves dashed wildly against the shore – the beach where my mother had walked back to me out of the sea.

ACKNOWLEDGEMENTS

I would like to thank my two children, my son for his insights into both my parents, although he never met my father, and my daughter for her wisdom and loyalty.

I would particularly like to thank Matthew Bell for his editing skills and encouragement, and my previous editor James Loader, above all for his sympathetic understanding of my mother's character.

Alex Clark of Union Books has since then done many hours of patient editing, and Rosalind Porter, also of Union Books, besides later editing, has performed other important tasks. I am grateful to them and to David Graham for publishing my book. Clare Alexander, my former agent, kindly read my contract.

I am indebted to my former therapist Maya Parker – who once made an omelette for herself during a session – for her knowledge of alcoholism and for her intelligent and sensitive interpretations of my mother.

Duncan Fallowell continues to give me spot-on advice and wrote me a wonderful letter after my mother's death.

Others who gave me help and encouragement are: Kirsty Gunn, Rachel Calvocoressi, Robert Skidelsky, Rupert Christiansen, Ricardo Mateos, Jimmy Burns, Sheila Yates, Hartmut Pogge von Strandmann, the late John Keegan, the late Ralph Bennett, Andrew Fergusson-Cuninghame, the late Honor Anstruther, Sue Gaisford, Nicholas Gibbs, Alex Gage, Henrietta Foster, Katie Joll, my three cousins Edward Hamilton, Cate Stone and Elizabeth Constantine, and my late Aunt Rosemary – a very good aunt. Thank you to Hilary Greene, Charles Kidd, (editor of Debretts who compiled family trees at short notice), and Margy Kinmonth, who introduced me to Kelsey Griffin, Director of Museum Operations and Museum Relations at the Bletchley Park Trust. Katherine Lynch, Media Manager at Bletchley, arranged for some passages about my mother's work there to be checked. The late Tony Sale read my mother's Bletchley diaries and commented with expertise, as did the late Peter Calvocoressi.

I would like to thank my American cousin Dita for her memories of my grandmother and for being such a friend to me. Similarly my beloved American godmother Leith, my mother's old friend, who is nearly a hundred.

I am grateful to Victoria Blake-Tyler, for sharing our early childhood memories of Spain and for shedding light on some of the political and historical background of that time. Beville Pain was also very knowledgeable about this and about diplomatic life. Hugo Vickers was tireless in referencing characters in Madrid in the early 1950s.

Jenny Sivyer gave me her grandfather Frank Sivyer's memoir of life in the Sussex countryside in the early 1900s which included Knowle, my grandparents' house. Pat Wright of Frant typed this out and supplied some local history.

I am extremely grateful to Lorraine Pinkerton and Heather Sewell, who let me visit Knowle so often after it was sold; Heather's daughter Anna showed a touching curiosity about my mother as a little girl.

Thank you also to those who helped me put onto computer my mother's inscrutable handwritten diaries: Diana Bundy, Helen Stevenson, Alice Yates and Anne Wheeler. And to Susan Hauser who kindly visited the old people's homes with me in Sussex.

I would like to remember my mother's three loyal friends (now deceased) who gave me their time and sympathy: Jean O'Neill, Angela Harding and Diana Tennant.

I thank Pat Woodley and Mrs Wilson for finding the diaries and above all I thank my mother for writing them.